THE ABC'S

of

DISEASE

PHILLIP DAY

Credence Publications

The ABC's of Disease

Copyright © 2003
Phillip Day

The right of Phillip Day to be identified as the Author of the
Work has been asserted by him in accordance with the
Copyright, Designs and Patents Act 1988.

First published in 2003
by Credence Publications

ISBN 1-904015-12-7

Manufactured in Great Britain and Australia by
Credence Publications
PO Box 3
TONBRIDGE
Kent TN12 9ZY UK
www.credence.org

1st ed.

Table of Contents

Introduction

Hello, my name is Phillip Day.

Thank you so much for taking the time to read this book.

I am a health reporter, researcher and international speaker who, for the past twenty years, has been fascinated in research concerning sickness, disease, health and longevity. In fact, the brief of my company, Credence, runs quite a bit wider than just health issues. We report on agendas that are harmful to the public, and our mission is now based in many countries around the world.

We report research, often conducted at the highest levels of the various fields of professional specialisation - research which, for various reasons we discuss in other Credence titles, is deliberately not being covered in the mainstream media, or if it is, is not given the prominence and importance it deserves. All of what we are going to discuss in the pages that follow has been written up in scientific and medical journals, as well as used by physicians around the world to tremendous effect. But, let's face it, who on earth a) has the time to read those inscrutable reports except beleaguered medical and science students and b) has time to travel around the world finding new treatments out? Well... I do.

Most of us have too much going on in our lives to plough through the massive amounts of often highly technical information, both good and bad, that gushes out of our institutions daily. Most, who actually read a newspaper or watch the TV regularly, find themselves relying on the national and international news programs to give them any good news that may be springing out of all that medical research into which billions are invested annually. Sadly, rare it is today to find a newspaper that prints any good news, let alone medical information that people can use directly for the benefit of themselves and their loved ones. And that's where this book comes in.

The ABC's of Disease is a compendium of the leading trouble-spots in health - what they are, what their symptoms are, what

3

causes them, and what we can do about them. Often the solutions to what ails us can be so simple, a change of diet and lifestyle is all that is required. Unfortunately, doctors are not being trained in nutrition and most of them have little knowledge of the effects our environment and lifestyle can often compel upon us. And so we see the unsavoury picture today of billions being spent by our health czars on research for cures for the major diseases, and even minor ailments, such as headaches and the common cold - treatments that often have little or no effect in solving the problem itself, let alone the underlying reason why it all happened in the first place.

Our need for potions

Credence researcher Steven Ransom remarks: *"While it is not entirely fair to say that everybody runs to the doctor with a headache, just about everybody has a selection of the usual headache tablets, painkillers, cough mixtures and general aches and pains ointments in their kitchen cupboard. Every year in the UK, £95,000,000 is spent on conventional cough mixtures alone. However, BMJ* [the British Medical Journal] *has reported a recent trial involving 2,000 participants which found that in most cases, the mixtures were no more effective than placebo.*[1] *These medicines merely fill the gap in the market, created by our in-built need to take something when we are ill. Pharmaceutical and alternative markets alike are falling over themselves to sell us these generally unhelpful tinctures, with no end in sight to their income."*[2]

Steven Ransom's *Great News on Cancer in the 21st Century* examines this phenomenon further and states:

"A huge number of remedies being sold as 'medicine' today contain no sensible methodology, yet perhaps not surprisingly, they are selling as well as ever. In truth, were the general public to be given clear information on the nature of self-limiting illness and the wondrous ability of a properly nourished immune system to overcome and repel almost all ills unaided, the bottom would fall

---

[1] 'Cough Mixtures Under Scrutiny' at
http://news.bbc.co.uk/hi/english/health/newsid_1807000/1807252.stm
[2] **Ransom, Steven**, *Wake up to Health in the 21st Century*, Credence Publications, 2003

out of the minor ailments market tomorrow, conventional medicine included."[3]

A *New England Journal of Medicine* report told us back in 1991 that: *"90% of patients who visit doctors have conditions that will either improve on their own or are out of reach of modern medicine's ability to solve."*[4]

Chronic illnesses however are not self-limiting. They are disorders that will not go away without intervention of some kind. What constitutes a chronic illness and what doesn't is of course the raging controversy, depending on your definition of the word 'intervention'. Over the years, I have seen miraculous recoveries from serious, life-threatening chronic disorders accomplished by many patients themselves, and, as each year passes, another blessed crop of these healings simply confirms what our scientific researchers and courageous doctors, often in the most intimidating of circumstances, have been applying for years – the certain fact that our bodies are incredible machines that are capable of correcting many serious functional errors if given the raw materials and the opportunity to do so.

This philosophy forms the basis of what is known as complementary medicine. Complementary medicine is medicine that isn't free(!), it's an approach to healing that understands, accepts and expects the body to heal itself if the antagonist/trigger/cause of the affliction is removed, and the body is given the correct materials and opportunity to effect the healing.

Two different belief systems

As we will discover, complementary and orthodox medicine have two opposing philosophies. In orthodox medicine, nature is weak. The body and mind are treated separately. The body usually cannot heal itself without intervention by the doctor and his medicines. Symptoms are treated, not the underlying cause. The physician is the unquestioned authority. There are a myriad of different medical specialties, depending on the affected organ of the body.

---

3 **Ransom, Steven,** *Great News on Cancer in the 21st Century,* Credence Publications, 2002
4 *The New England Journal of Medicine,* 7th February 1991

In complementary medicine, nature is strong and the body has a tremendous ability for self-healing. Body and mind are intricately connected and the approach to healing integrates the two. Here, the physician is really a bystander, assisting and advising the patient on how to help themselves get better. Patients have an integral part to play in this exciting process, as they are in charge of their treatment decisions. I have noticed a consistency to the five golden rules these amazing survivors have knowingly or otherwise devotedly followed, which have given them the optimum shot at recovery:

1. They take responsibility for their illness
2. They research their afflictions thoroughly
3. They work, in conjunction with properly trained health practitioners, to apply natural and effective strategies their body can use to heal itself
4. They apply these strategies consistently
5. They have a positive attitude and never give up

Of course some died – their illnesses having made irreparable inroads into their life-systems. Then again, I have seen many others, condemned by a doctor's fateful diagnosis, who, by rights, should not have survived more than a few months more, make complete and amazing recoveries and go on to devote their lives to educating others with what they have learned.

Science has done its job

Science has, of course, made tremendous advances in medicine. Then again, because of the blinkered and money-driven 'drugs, radiation and the knife for all' approach pursued by our medical peers, there are many diseases, which should have been buried years ago, that continue to afflict us. It is my hope, with this book, to encourage the reader to appreciate that they have nothing to lose and everything to gain by adopting properly researched and referenced natural strategies to improve their health and combat the root causes of the illnesses which may afflict them. Eliminate the obvious first, and then work backwards from there.

I am particularly excited about recent reports and research done on the effects of yeasts, fungi and their mycotoxins and am indebted

6

to the researchers, authors and physicians who have contributed their work to the betterment of mankind's health. Today, we have a wealth of data with which to examine in detail the woeful effects western diets are having on the population and what can be done to reverse the extraordinary infestations that have become paramount in our societies today.

And so, *on with gusto*, I say. *The ABC's of Disease* can also be the ABC's of better health, happiness and a peace of mind from the fear that disease conjures in the mind. And in that respect, what better mission do we have to occupy our time at the present hour than one which can play an important role in protecting and extending the lives of those we love?

Good health!

Phillip Day

How to Use this Book

Please read this first ☺

This book is not designed to replace proper, qualified medical advice. Patients suffering ill-health are, of course, advised to consult a physician. This book *does* encourage patients to be discriminatory in what they do with the health advice they receive, and encourages them to take control of their healthcare decisions. Ultimately it is you, the patient, who must decide on the course of action you feel is most appropriate for your condition. In this respect, the doctors are your servants – an arrangement often forgotten.

Please note that this book should not be construed as diagnostic or treatment advice for any individual's particular condition. Information contained herein is provided for educational purposes only.

Most of the following sections deal with a 'dis-ease', a condition where the body is presenting symptoms. Each disease has a **Profile** on what the condition is, along with various manifestations; a **Symptoms** section describing the physical or mental manifestations of the problem follows next; and then a **Commentary** section dealing with information relating to the cause of the condition, its make-up and what research has been done on it. Naturally the following sections are in overview, and so should be regarded as summaries. Finally the **Take action♥** section describes suitable, sensible regimens the patient and their physician may wish to consider. If an ailment you are researching does not have its own section, please search the **Index** to see if it is referenced there, or check under **Other Disorders**.

Set regimens

Throughout the book, you will find three regimens used repeatedly. They are:

- **THE ANTI-*CANDIDA* DIETARY REGIMEN**
- **THE *FOOD FOR THOUGHT* LIFESTYLE REGIMEN**
- **THE BASIC SUPPLEMENT PROGRAM**

These protocols are designed to summarise standardised patterns of action to save repetition and complication. If the **Take action♥** section you are examining contains one or more of these, please examine the appropriate section to learn about the techniques in more detail. For instance, **THE ANTI-*CANDIDA* DIETARY REGIMEN** has some do's and don't's upon which the success of the program relies, so the importance here is *consistency of application*. You will find summaries of these three regimens in their appropriate sections at the end of this book (see **Table of Contents**).

THE BASIC SUPPLEMENT PROGRAM contains a simple, standard regimen of supplements, but the **Take action♥** section of a disease might demand either higher doses of a particular nutrient, or additional nutrients not contained in the basic program. In this case, the **Take action♥** section will describe the total intake for a given nutrient. For instance, where a section states:

- **COMMENCE THE BASIC SUPPLEMENT PROGRAM**, ensuring:
- Vitamin C complex (ascorbates plus bioflavonoids), 3 g, twice per day

... this means the total intake of vitamin C will be 3 g, twice per day, NOT 3 g, twice per day in addition to the vitamin C intake listed in **THE BASIC SUPPLEMENT PROGRAM**!

Other titles

The *ABC's of Disease* is a summary of leading conditions afflicting 21st century humanity and, of course, is not the last word. Credence has other titles which deal more specifically with key conditions and subjects relating to health. These are summarised under **Other Titles by Credence** at the end of this book.

Acne
(See also **Skin Disorders**)

Profile
Blackheads, whiteheads, nodules and cysts. Most of us, especially the fellas, know all the bad news. Ladies too fall prone to this most unsightly of conditions, which usually contrives to show up the morning before a first date with the captain of the football team. There are three types of acne:

Acne vulgaris: a common disease caused by increased testosterone release, usually during puberty, which leads to an over-secretion of oils and waxes (sebum) produced by the sebaceous glands in the skin. Testosterone during puberty also stimulates the production of keratin proteins in the skin which can also block pores. Outbreaks usually occur on the face, but also on the back, shoulders and chest.

Acne conglobata: a more severe form of the above which can result in cysts and scarring from deep pustules which accumulate pus compounds which do not discharge their contents to the surface but infect surrounding tissue.

Acne rosacea: a condition that occurs in middle age (usually between ages 30-50), where the face becomes flushed and covered with pimples, similar to the above acne vulgaris. Thought to be caused variously by menopausal imbalances, fungal/parasite infection, metabolic imbalances, digestive problems and malnutrition, usually a shortage of the B-vitamins.

Commentary
There's nothing much you can do about reaching puberty, except to think dark thoughts, endlessly play those awful Marilyn Manson or Christine Aguilera records and ponder how the CIA is going to do you in. But I've got a better idea about how to combat the main problems surrounding acne. The chief culprit here is malnutrition and an excess of sugars, transfats and fried foods in the diet which depress your immunity, destroy enzymes and cause all sorts of anti-social goo to ooze its way to liberty.

As usual, physicians will throw Roaccutane, tretinoin, benzoyl peroxide and antibiotics at the problem, which can variously cause suicidal tendencies, depression, burnt skin, peeled and crusty skin, a compromised immune system, or an outbreak of our old Jekyll and Hydian horror, *Candida albicans*, a normally beneficial yeast with dark, Napoleonic ambitions for the total control of your organism.

The key to defeating acne in puberty is to understand one basic fact: your body is going through some pivotal changes and it needs the right type of fuel to accomplish these without punishing you with the downside. Teenagers are normally quite rebellious about their diets (rumour has it), and don't often listen to what Mum says about all those tempting veggies. They prefer instead to dine out at Chez Kebab, Tennessee Fried Rat, Murder King and the Golden Starches.

Take action♥

So, if you are a teen, and you have a hot date and a face full of Martian landscape, you have a choice: either continue to be rebellious with your diet and lifestyle, in which case you will be spending most of the evening whispering sweet nothings in her ear through the visor of your crash helmet, or TAKE ACTION (I love those words!) and wade in amongst the following:

- **DIET: COMMENCE THE ANTI-*CANDIDA* DIETARY REGIMEN** for a period of 28 days and then review results. If satisfactory, switch to **THE *FOOD FOR THOUGHT* LIFESTYLE REGIMEN** thereafter
- **DIET:** Avoid processed foods, fried foods, sugars, dairy products, hydrogenated oils (margarine, etc.) and sweets/candy
- **DIET:** Avoid oils and greases as far as possible at work if you are industrially-minded
- **DIET:** Drink 4 pints of clean, non-tap water a day (a still mineral water sold in glass bottles is fine)
- **DETOXIFICATION:** Consider reviewing your continued use of existing medications, over the counter topicals, steroidal or corticosteroidal medications
- **DETOXIFICATION:** Clear your pipework out with a magnesium oxide bowel cleanse

- **DETOXIFICATION:** Use safe personal care products (see **Environmental Toxins)** and wash face and body using a non-irritant formula
- **RESTORE NUTRIENT BALANCE: COMMENCE THE BASIC SUPPLEMENT PROGRAM**

Acquired Immune Deficiency Syndrome (AIDS)

Profile

In the 1970s to early 1980s, a group of otherwise seemingly healthy males were diagnosed with immune deficiency problems. Later, the common denominator found for those suffering from this 'new disease', AIDS, appeared to be that they were variously:

- homosexual
- intravenous drug users
- haemophiliacs

Symptoms

AIDS, actually not one disease but a collection of many different conditions brought under the AIDS umbrella, manifests itself variously with opportunistic infections such as thrush, yeast infections like *Candida, pneumocystis carinii pneumonia* and other, so-called AIDS-defining diseases. Sudden, unexplainable commencement of fevers, sweats, flu-like symptoms, diarrhoea, swelling of lymph glands and rashes on the body. Dark, cancerous skin lesions, such as Karposi's sarcoma, are often found on the body.

Commentary

One of the greatest scandals in medicine today surrounds the classification of AIDS as an infectious disease. The supposed pathogen, human immunodeficiency virus (HIV), despite much fanfare and fear-mongering, has never been isolated according to any recognised and appropriate scientific procedure. And so, from a scientific standpoint, HIV can be deemed not to exist. In the 16 years since Dr Robert Gallo's 'discovery' of HIV (for which he was later indicted for science fraud), no empirical proof of the existence of an HIV virus or retrovirus has ever been furnished to the scientific establishment, much less satisfactorily connected with how AIDS symptoms are supposed to be caused by it.

First world AIDS

All the evidence shows that immune suppression ('AIDS') in the First World is primarily brought on by long-term recreational or pharmaceutical drug toxicity AND IS NOT INFECTIOUS OR SEXUALLY TRANSMITTED. AIDS in the first world *does not behave like a sexually transmitted, infectious disease at all.* AIDS is still within its risk groups after over 25 years supposedly rampaging through a sexually driven public. Only 5% of the homosexual community have a problem with immune suppression. 95% don't. The 5% who do will usually have a history of immuno-suppressant activity, drug-taking, etc. which will adequately explain their current predicament.

If you are going to tell the public that HIV is spread sexually, then where is the AIDS epidemic in Britain today? Did Britain suddenly stop having unprotected sex? And how come HIV is supposed to be spread through the transfer of blood and other body fluids, and yet mosquitoes don't spread it? **You do not need HIV to explain the phenomenon of AIDS either in the western world or in third world countries.**

Third world AIDS

Third world or 'African' 'AIDS' is nothing more than the cynical reclassification of diseases that have always killed Africans and other citizens: dysentery, cholera, diarrhoea, malnutrition, TB, malaria and parasitic infections, brought on by the frequently contaminated water supplies poor citizens in these regions are forced to consume. Africans are almost always classified as 'AIDS carriers' through the arbitrary visual-only Bangui definition.

Bogus testing procedures

Many unwitting victims in the first world are drawn into the AIDS nightmare after being frightened by advertising or newspaper articles into believing that they might 'be at risk'. And so they are talked into taking 'an AIDS test'. The ELISA (Enzyme-Linked Immuno-Absorbent Assay) and Western Blot tests are designed to highlight the presence of the supposed HIV, not by identifying any virus itself, but by tracing the presence of antibodies in the blood, allegedly unique to, and said to be stimulated by a virus or retrovirus no-one can seem to find.

The only real difference between the two tests is that the ELISA is supposed to measure antibody activity as a whole, whereas the Western Blot measures reactions to separate proteins supposedly making up the virus. As a result of this claim, the Western Blot method is deemed by most in the AIDS industry to be more specific than the ELISA test, and will often be used to confirm a positive ELISA test. [5] The problem is, all the diagnostic methods employed by the recognised laboratories are far from specific. Author Christine Maggiore, herself a victim of these fraudulent tests, states the major problem as follows:

"Both tests are non-specific to HIV antibodies and are highly inaccurate. Non-specific means that these tests respond to a great number of non-HIV antibodies, microbes, bacteria and other conditions that are often found in the blood of normal, healthy people. A reaction to any one of these other antibodies and conditions will result in an HIV-positive diagnosis. A simple illness like a cold or the flu can cause a positive reading on an HIV test. A flu shot or other vaccine can also create positive results. Having or having had herpes or hepatitis may produce a positive test, as can a vaccination for hepatitis B. Exposure to diseases such as tuberculosis and malaria commonly cause false positive results, as do the presence of tape worms and other parasites. Conditions such as alcoholism, liver disease and blood that is highly oxidated through drug use may be interpreted as the presence of HIV antibodies. Pregnancy and prior pregnancy can also cause a positive result."[6]

The triggering of an HIV positive result will lead invariably to prescriptions for the deadly cell toxins AZT, ddI and other 'HIV' drugs (protease inhibitors, etc.), which have an appalling history of causing the very immune deficiencies they were supposedly designed

---

[5] **Lake, Douglas**, *The Biology Project*, University of Arizona School of Medicine
[6] **Maggiore, Christine**, *What if Everything You Thought You Knew About AIDS Was Wrong*, Alive and Well, Studio City, CA 90604, USA

to prevent, but they do rack up the drug profits. South African barrister Anthony Brink remarks:

"In truth, AZT makes you feel like you're dying. That's because on AZT you are. How can a deadly cell toxin conceivably make you feel better as it finishes you, by stopping your cells from dividing, by ending this vital process that distinguishes living things from dead things? Not for nothing does AZT come with a skull and cross-bones label when packaged for laboratory use."[7]

And indeed that is the case. With a skull and cross-bones on the outer label and a reminder to wear *suitable protective clothing when handling,* the inner contents of the AZT packaging include the following side-effects advisory notice:

WHOLE BODY: abdominal pain, back pain, body odour, chest pain, chills, edema of the lip, fever, flu symptoms, hyperalgesia.

CARDIOVASCULAR: syncope, vasodilation.

GASTROINTESTINAL: bleeding gums, constipation, diarrhoea, dysphagia, edema of the tongue, eructation, flatulence, mouth ulcer, rectal haemorrhage.

HAEMIC AND LYMPHATIC: lymphadenopathy.

MUSCULOSKELETAL: arthralgia, muscle spasm, tremor, twitch.

NERVOUS: anxiety, confusion, depression, dizziness, emotional liability, loss of mental acuity, nervousness, paresthesia, somnolence, vertigo.

RESPIRATORY: cough, dyspnea, epistaxis, hoarseness, pharyngitis, rhinitis, sinusitis.

SKIN: rash, sweat, urticaria.

SPECIAL SENSES: amblyopia, hearing loss, photophobia, taste perversion.

UROGENITAL: dysuria, polyuria, urinary frequency, urinary hesitancy.

I spent some years in Los Angeles and San Francisco working among homosexuals deemed HIV positive by the medical

---

7 **Brink, Anthony,** *AZT and Heavenly Remedies,* Rethinking AIDS Homepage: www.rethinkingaids.com

establishment. In all cases, their plight could be laid at the door of malnutrition, parasite/fungal infections, and recreational or pharmaceutical drug abuse. Their sure and ready remedy was to cease the drug abuse and move towards wellness with a properly constructed regimen of sound nutrition and supplementation.

Our full report on AIDS is contained in *World Without AIDS*, the result of 15 years' research into this tragically misunderstood realm of medical error. The further tragedy is that expectant mothers are now required to take an 'HIV' test, resulting in more than a few cases being deemed HIV-positive simply because of the antibody load picked up by these tests. The resultant medication is as catastrophic to the baby as it is to the mother. For this reason, we issue the following advisory to all pregnant mothers around the world:

Health warning to expectant mothers

If you have recently become pregnant, you may be recommended to take an HIV test as part of a standardised ante-natal care package.[8] This test is highly inaccurate and remains scientifically unproven. It should be refused on the following grounds:

1) All manufacturers of these tests include the following or similar disclaimer with their test kits: "At present, there is no recognised standard for establishing the presence or absence of antibodies to HIV-1 and HIV- 2 in human blood."[9]

2) The reason for this disclaimer is because the AIDS test does not measure the presence of a virus.[10] The AIDS test has been designed to detect levels of antibody activity in the blood. Antibody activity in the bloodstream is a normal occurrence in humans, but is being misinterpreted by the AIDS test as indicative of the presence of HIV.

3) As a result of this misinterpretation, healthy individuals are being wrongly diagnosed as HIV positive. Since this information has

---

[8] Refer to "Review of antenatal testing services", NHS Regional Office, London, UK Dept of Health. Recommending the HIV test became UK national policy in July 1999, and is now mandatory in some US states.

[9] The above disclaimer is included in all Abbott 'AXSYM' AIDS tests, the world's leading supplier of AIDS test kits.

[10] Monetary rewards offered to leading organisations within the scientific community by concerned organisations for reasonable evidence that HIV exists remain uncollected.

come to light, in excess of 60 different medical conditions have been recorded that can give rise to a false HIV-positive reading. These separate conditions include flu, flu vaccination, malaria, tetanus vaccination, hepatitis A and B, hepatitis vaccinations, fungal infections, alcohol and drug use, recent viral infections and even pregnancy.[11] Receiving a spurious but wholly devastating diagnosis of HIV-positive will prompt your doctor to recommend a course of 'anti-HIV' drugs. Known as protease inhibitors or anti-retrovirals, these drugs are highly toxic. They have the well-documented capacity to harm the mother, and also severely to deform and even kill the unborn child.[12]

The current levels of spending on AIDS drugs in the western world are phenomenal. So too are the profits enjoyed by the AIDS drug manufacturers. As a result, the information contained in this advisory is largely being ignored by the medical establishment. Sadly, this is not an unexpected reaction. The pursuit of profit at the expense of health, the wilful employment of flawed medical procedures, the administration of dangerously toxic drugs to expectant mothers, the disregard for the plight of thousands upon thousands of wrongly diagnosed people, and a refusal by the medical establishment to listen to sound contrary evidence or to admit medical negligence - all are the hallmarks of that once-respected drug, thalidomide. Do not allow either yourself or your child to face the possibility of becoming another heartbreaking medical statistic. For more information on AIDS, please obtain a copy of *World Without AIDS*, available through Credence Publications.

Take action♥

If you have been diagnosed with 'HIV infection' or 'AIDS', the following protocol may be beneficial. Please note that conditions diagnosed as AIDS are dangerous and life-threatening. The following

---

[11] **Johnson, Christine**, *Continuum Magazine*, September 1996. **Maggiore, Christine**, *What if Everything You Knew about AIDS was Wrong?* An Alive and Well Publication, April 2000; **Ransom & Day**, *World Without AIDS*, Credence Publications, July 2000. www.credence.org

[12] **Kumar et al**, *Journal of Acquired Immune Deficiency Syndromes*, 7; 1034-9, 1994. *JAMA* Journal of American Medical Association, 5th January 2000, Incidence of liver damage. *World Without AIDS*. AZT and enlarged craniums in infants. Refer to www.virusmyth.com for a more comprehensive list of scientific references which catalogue the damage caused by AIDS drugs.

regimen, if you choose to follow it, must be rigorously adhered to, preferably under supervision of a doctor acquainted with nutritional and detoxification protocols:

- **TIP:** Hire the services of a medical doctor (MD) or naturopathic physician (ND), trained in nutrition and aware of the AIDS/HIV deception
- **TIP:** Take no further 'AIDS tests'
- **PREVENTION:** Consider immediately dropping the use of AIDS medications, especially nucleoside analogues and DNA chain-terminators. These are heavily immuno-suppressive and carcinogenic, bringing on the very symptoms of the problem you are trying to conquer
- **PREVENTION:** Cease taking ALL recreational drugs, including the sex-stimulant amyl nitrite (poppers) (known to cause Karposi's sarcoma). If you have a drug addiction, a suitable clean-up program should be sought out and rigorously adhered to
- **PREVENTION:** If you are a homosexual, avoid sex and the lifestyle that goes with the 'fast-track' homosexual community. Unprotected sex with multiple partners heightens the chances of contracting sexually transmitted diseases, such as herpes, gonorrhoea, syphilis, etc., along with the incessant drinking, taking of drugs, the ongoing regimens of antibiotics, not eating properly, etc., problems which themselves will generate antibodies that can be interpreted as AIDS-specific (they are not). Once you have triggered a positive AIDS test, physicians will usually then prescribe dangerous cell toxins, such as AZT
- **DIET AND DETOXIFICATION:** Follow the regimen for cancer explained in the appropriate section of this book. This regimen addresses fungal/yeast infections, cancer, immuno-suppressant problems, detoxification, nutritional support and a correct and cleansing diet. With AIDS, it is also *what you give up* that will make the difference between life and death.

Further resources
World Without AIDS by Steven Ransom and Phillip Day

ADD/ADHD

Attention deficit disorder, attention deficit hyperactivity
disorder, learning disorder, conduct disorder, etc.

Profile

In 1987, Attention Deficit Hyperactivity Disorder (ADHD) was
voted into existence by members of the American Psyychiatric
Association (APA) during the compilation of its DSM-III-R mental
illness register. Within one year, 500,000 children in America alone
had been diagnosed with an affliction, created by a show of hands,
which had no apparent corresponding physical brain disorder. Many
children have subsequently been prescribed dangerous, mind-
altering drugs to control their behaviour. By 1997, 4.4 million
citizens had been labelled ADHD.

In 1975, US federal law had provided funding and psychology-
based education for 'learning disabilities'. By 1989, 1.9 million had
been diagnosed as having Learning Disorder (including Attention
Deficit Disorder). At the end of 1996, 2.6 million American children
had been branded 'special needs'. Did funding play a factor in this
mass diagnosis? Today, ADHD is said to account for a third to half of
all child mental health referrals.

In my book *The Mind Game*, I expose the cynical manipulation
and deceit practised by psychiatry on the public, and reveal the truth
behind what 'mental illnesses' actually are. They are physical
problems that affect the way we think and behave, and the
phenomena of ADD and ADHD are no exception. If you, or someone
you know, suffers from behavioural abnormalities that have been
diagnosed ADD/ADHD, before you or your family resort to the
proffered drug treatments, which include mind-altering substances
such as Ritalin and Prozac, often provoking mental aberrations of
their own, please read the remainder of this chapter.

Symptoms

Little Billy has a problem. He doesn't finish his homework. He is
rowdy in class. He can't sit still at mealtimes and fidgets constantly.
When his parents buy him a new toy, he smashes it or wears it out.

He is a beast with the furniture, tumbling around the room and getting into things with boundless energy.

But Billy's temper tantrums have caused problems at school as well as home. He is unpopular with his peers, defiant of authority, sometimes exhibits a speech impediment and lies to get out of trouble. Billy's parents have been warned by the principal to 'get something done' or Billy won't be allowed to return to school to disrupt others. *"Billy needs help,"* the head intones sombrely. He gives them a telephone number to call. Drugs such as Ritalin, Halcion, Xanax, Dexedrine and Prozac are routinely prescribed.

Physiological indicators to watch for in a child labelled ADD/ADHD are those symptoms usually associated with allergy: excessive mucus, ear infections, skin rashes, facial swelling, tonsillitis, discolouration around the eyes, bloating and digestive problems, bad breath, bedwetting, eczema and asthma. Most of these are associated with prostaglandin imbalance - chemical modulators that affect the brain, inflammatory reactions and water balance. This in turn led some researchers to wonder whether the body sometimes has problems converting essential fats into prostaglandins and neurotransmitter hormones.

Why ADD/ADHD are not 'diseases'

In millions of households across the world, parents have noticed behaviour in their children far more aberrant than expected with their particular age-group. These traits, as we have seen, have been prescribed medical epithets or disease classifications by psychiatry. But are these 'mental diseases', or do they have more straightforward explanations? How likely is it that millions of children have suddenly become 'mentally ill'?

Retired California neurologist Fred A Baughman Jr sent a letter in January 2000 to US Surgeon General David Satcher in response to Satcher's Report on mental illness. *"Having gone to medical school,"* Baughman wrote, *"and studied pathology — disease, then diagnosis — you and I and all physicians know that the presence of any bona fide disease, like diabetes, cancer or epilepsy, is confirmed by an objective finding — a physical or chemical abnormality. No demonstrable physical or chemical abnormality: no disease!"*

"You also know, I am sure," Baughman continued, *"that there is no physical or chemical abnormality to be found in life, or at autopsy, in 'depression, bipolar disorder and other mental illnesses.' Why then are you telling the American people that 'mental illnesses' are 'physical' ...?'"*

Baughman concluded his six-page letter to Satcher by declaring that *"your role in this deception and victimization is clear. Whether you are a physician so unscientific that you cannot read their [the American Psychiatric Association's] contrived, 'neurobiologic' literature and see the fraud, or whether you see it and choose to be an accomplice — you should resign."*

Researchers Bunday and Colquhoun tested the theory to see whether supplementing with essential fatty acids would make any difference. They tested evening primrose oil, a rich source of gamma-linolenic acid (omega 3), on children who had been diagnosed ADD/ADHD. The following, provided by the Hyperactive Children's Support Group, is typical of such anecdotal reports:

"Stephen, aged 6, had a history of hyperactivity, with severely disturbed sleep and disruptive behaviour at home and at school. Threatened with expulsion from the school because of his impossible behaviour, his parents were given two weeks to improve matters. They contacted the Hyperactive Children's Support Group, and evening primrose oil was suggested. A dose of 1.5g was rubbed into the skin morning and evening. The school was unaware of this, but after five days the teacher telephoned the mother to say that never in 30 years of teaching had she seen such a dramatic change in a child's behaviour. After three weeks, the evening primrose oil was stopped, and one week later the school complained. The oil was then introduced to good effect."[13]

Scientists at Purdue University in the US have found that children exhibiting hyperactivity have altered fatty acid metabolism

---

[13] Provided by the Hyperactive Children's Support Group, www.hacsg.org.uk

and lowered levels of these essential nutrients in their blood, compared to controls. One fatty acid, DHA, has shown to be low in children marked with low mental performance. Fish oils are rich in DHA. Other evidence however demonstrates that genuine hyperactivity and attention deficit may not be caused by poor nutrition alone. Two other elements play large in causation – that of chemical toxins and food allergies.

Homing in on the problem – Diet

Essential fats can only be converted into prostaglandins by two enzymes, which themselves are dependent upon the presence of vitamins B3 (niacin), B6, biotin, zinc and magnesium. Dr Abram Hoffer explored the possibility of a link between B3 and B6 deficiencies and ADD. Hoffer gave 3 g of vitamin C and over 1.5 g of B3 (niacinamide) to 33 children. Only one failed to respond favourably. Children with low levels of the essential neurotransmitter hormone serotonin have been helped with B3 and B6 supplementation. Zinc and magnesium deficiencies are well known to cause immune system problems, coupled with excessive fidgeting, anxiety, loss of co-ordination and learning difficulties in the presence of a normal intelligence. The magnesium, zinc, copper, iron and calcium levels of plasma, erythrocytes, urine and hair in 50 children aged 4 to 13 years with hyperactivity were examined by atomic absorption spectrometry. The average concentration of all trace elements was lower when compared with the control group.[14]

Homing in on the problem – Chemical toxins

Certain chemicals, now extremely common in our environment, can act as 'anti-nutrients' – that is, they bleed away or bind essential nutrients in the body. Lead produces symptoms of aggression, poor impulse control and attention span. Refined sugar and sugary foods produce a kaleidoscope of problems with poisoning and hyperactivity. Excess copper and aluminium cause hyperactivity and have been found in significant amounts in children with behavioural disorders. *"Copper and lead deplete zinc levels and may contribute*

---

[14] **Kozielec, T, et al**, "Deficiency of Certain Trace Elements in Children with Hyperactivity", *Psychiatr. Pol.* 28, pp.345-353, 1994

to deficiency," Dr Pfeiffer remarks.[15] Monsanto's infamous artificial sweetener aspartame is another major causative factor (contained in products such as chewing gums and foods and drinks sweetened with Nutrasweet, Equal and Canderel (see **Aspartame Disease**).

Perhaps one of the most dangerous pastimes a child can indulge in is the consumption of soda beverages. These contain high levels of phosphoric acid and up to seven teaspoon equivalents of refined sugar in one aluminium can. Children drinking 6-8 sodas a day may be ingesting over 50 teaspoons of sugar just from the soda drinks alone. In addition, there are the excess sugars found in their processed foods and candies to consider.

Homing in on the problem – Allergies

Perhaps the leading cause of ADD/ADHD worthy of investigation is in the realm of food toxins and allergies. Dr Neil Ward is a scientist who has been at the forefront of additive research. A press release from his university in Guildford, UK, reports:

Children's disruptive behaviour can be linked to food choice. Hyperactivity, attention deficit disorder... and antisocial or aggressive behaviour in children can be traced back to what they eat. According to Dr Neil Ward, from the University of Surrey's Chemistry department, some children can react to the additives, preservatives and colourants in food products, causing certain behavioural problems. "Parents should identify the products which cause the reaction and eliminate them from the child's diet," he said.

Dr Ward monitored groups of children in schools. He aimed to find out whether behavioural disturbance linked to chemicals appeared in isolated groups or if all children were at risk. He found that certain colourants could lead to an adverse reaction within 30 minutes of consumption. He identified toxic metals like lead and aluminium and food colourants as the main culprits. Reactions to these chemicals included behavioural or body reactions like rash or physical impairments.

---

[15] **Pfeiffer, Carl & Patrick Holford**, *Mental Illness – The Nutrition Connection*, ION Press, London: 1996. p.153

The soda additive tartrazine is a known problem. Dr Ward discovered that adding tartrazine to drinks increased the precipitation of zinc in the urine. Ward speculated that tartrazine was binding to zinc, rendering it unavailable to the body, which then excreted it. Ward found behavioural changes *in every child who consumed the drink containing tartrazine.* Four out of ten children in the study had severe reactions, three developing eczema or asthma within 45 minutes of ingestion. Ward concludes in the above press release:

"Children in primary schools are under a lot of peer pressure to consume certain products, and they tend to favour products containing a lot of sugar. The problem is that these products often also contain some 'nasty' chemicals. Consumers often don't understand the information on food labels. They were a bit more conscious of labels when concerns about e-numbers were first raised, but since organic food hit the shelves, people seem to think everything is safe now. It is very important that not only children but in many cases their parents should be encouraged to learn more about the foods they choose to consume, how they are stored, prepared and cooked in terms of providing optimum nutritional value to their diet."[16]

Homing in on the problem – Fungi, yeast and parasites

High-sugar diets also have another downfall for the child. They feed opportunistic fungi and yeasts within their body, resulting in a release of potentially hazardous mycotoxins into the child's bloodstream. Reactions may range for the annoying rashes and skin blemishes through to serious side-effects and illnesses. These problems may be cleared up with, once again, a consistent and permanent change in diet, along with simple herbal treatments (see **Candidiasis**).

---

[16] Press release, 12th April 2002, University of Surrey at Guildford. Enquiries: Liezel Tipper, Press Officer, Tel: +44 (0)1483 689314 or E-mail: press-office@surrey.ac.uk

Other somatic indicators

Gluten allergies to wheat, barley, rye and oat products are very common and lead to bloating and an auto-immune reaction known as coeliac disease (see **Inflammatory Bowel Disease**). Studies show that 1 in 33 of us may be susceptible. Others indicate that the incidence of gluten/gliaden intolerance may be as high as 1 in 10.[17] The unmanageable, sticky gluten protein can disrupt the lining of the intestinal wall, destroying villi which absorb nutrients, and allow the permeation of food particles and toxins through the intestinal wall and into the bloodstream. Resultant immune system reactions to this range from self-poisoning conditions, such as chronic fatigue syndrome and leaky gut syndrome through to the symptoms listed earlier.

In 1975, Dr Ben Feingold reported successful treatment of ADD by removing chemical additives, dyes from the diet, as well as foods containing salicylates, coffee, tea, as well as some fruits, nuts and berries. Sensitivity, even to some natural foods, is believed to be the result of auto-immune reactions to known chemical antagonists found in processed problem foods, such as junk foods, pizzas, sweets, candy, sodas and their 'diet' equivalents. Dr Schoenthaler found an empirical connection between sugar/junk food intake and anti-social and criminal behaviour.[18] Other problem foods connected with ADD/ADHD may involve eggs, chocolate, rape oil (canola) and unfermented soy food derivatives (soya 'milk' and meat substitute foods).[19]

Nutritional versus drug approach

The optimal approach to helping a child, or indeed any adult, with hyperactivity problems involves a strategy which tackles all the above factors. But first, let's see whether true hyperactivity exists by asking some interesting questions:

1)   Is the child really hyperactive, or is this a simple case of 'a kid just being a kid'?

---

[17] www.mercola.com. Search on 'gluten' and 'celiac'

[18] See section on *Criminal Violence*

[19] For more information on the harm wrought by unfermented soy ('milk' and 'meat'), please see **The Shadow of Soy**

2)   Was the 'hyperactivity' label put on your child by a teacher who simply cannot keep control of their classroom, and so the children took advantage of the uncontrolled environment?

3)   Is the school your child attends part of a grant system where it can earn money from the government for every child given a 'mental illness' label?

4)   Do YOU, as a parent, think there is anything wrong with your child?

To me, the parent is sovereign over their children, in spite of the steadily encroaching nanny state. And yet many mothers, who unwittingly assume the role of the family nutritionist, tacitly allow their children to wander aimlessly through a nutrient-deficient and chemical minefield with the diets they consume today. Many parents also, cramming white bread, biscuits, doughnuts, hot dogs and pizza down the throats of their co-operative brood, still believe the old adage that if the kids are 'full', they have eaten well. As this book pointedly demonstrates, bad food always has consequences.

One of the first measures recommended by specialists like Dr Pfeiffer and nutrition expert Patrick Holford, founder of London's Institute of Optimum Nutrition (ION), is to have a problem child undergo a full medical examination. Pinpointing problem foods and chemicals in the early stages precludes the need for a trial and error approach with diet. Removal of potentially harmful foodstuffs from the diet for a period of time (60 days) will highlight whether these food(s) are the 'trigger' for any food sensitivity problems.

ADD/ADHD – the nutritional approach

There are a number of well-designed studies showing the efficacy of nutritional supplementation for learning and hyperactive disabilities. There is also abundant evidence for the addictive and psychological damage drugs prescribed to children can do, with little appreciable upside, save that of *altering the child's behaviour*, or, in the case of Prozac, drugging the patient so they cannot remember what they were worried about in the first place. Yet the American Academy of Pediatrics overwhelming endorses the use of these drugs as first resort for ADD/ADHD conditions.[20] There is not one mention of nutrition in the American Academy of Pediatrics position paper on ADHD.[21] In 1995, the AAP did produce a video on nutrition however. It was funded by the Sugar Association and the Meat Board.[22]

The title of a fact sheet promoted by the American Dietetic Association, focussing on ADHD, is "Questions Most Frequently Asked About Hyperactivity". The fact sheet asks two questions: *"Is there a dietary relationship to hyperactivity?"* and *"Should I restrict certain foods from my child's diet?"* These were answered with the same word – *"No."* [23] The source quoted for the fact sheet is The Sugar Association (again), which also produced its own consumer guidelines, including the laughably asinine statement: *"Sugar has a mildly quieting effect on some children."* [24] [25]

Researcher Egger showed that 79% of hyperactive children improved when artificial colourings, flavourings and sugar were eliminated from their diet. In fact 48 different foods were found to be allergy-positive, producing medical symptoms among the children tested. For example, 64% reacted to cow's milk, 59% to chocolate, 49% to wheat and gluten-bearing products, 45% to oranges, 39% to eggs, 32% to peanuts and 16% to sugar.[26] Researcher Schoenthaler's immense work in this area indicated that 47% of his juvenile delinquent subjects noticeably improved their problem behaviour (theft, insubordination, violence, hyperactivity, suicide attempts, etc.) when artificial colourings, flavourings and sugar were eliminated from their diet.[27] (see **Criminal Violence**)

---

[20] "Medication For Children With An Attention Deficit Disorder (RE 7103)", American Academy of Pediatrics, Committee on Children With Disabilities, Committee on Drugs; *Pediatrics*, 80(5), November 1987

[21] Ibid.

[22] **O'Connor, Amy**, "In The News", *Vegetarian Times*, October 1995, p.20

[23] *Journal of the American Dietetic Association*, September 1994, p.975

[24] "Questions Most Frequently Asked About Hyperactivity," Produced by the Sugar Association, Inc., Washington, D.C.

[25] "Consumer Fact Sheet: Diet and Behaviour," The Sugar Association Inc., Washington, DC.

[26] **Egger, J, et al**, "Controlled Trial of Oligoantigenic Treatment in the Hyperkinetic Syndrome," *Lancet*, 1985, p.540

[27] **Schoenthaler, Stephen**, "Institutional Nutritional Policies and Criminal Behavior," *Nutrition Today*, 20(3), 1985, p.16; see also: **Stephen Schoenthaler**, "Diet and Crime: An

Take action ♥

Dr Carl Pfeiffer and Patrick Holford recommend the following dietary changes for those diagnosed with ADD/ADHD. In addition, I have added further protocols that will benefit the child immensely. This routine is also great for teenagers and adults experiencing behavioural problems.

Please note that a qualified health practitioner should supervise each individual case to ensure protocols and safety measures are observed. *Patients MUST NEVER discontinue any psychiatric medications unsupervised*:

- **DIET: COMMENCE THE *FOOD FOR THOUGHT* LIFESTYLE REGIMEN**
- **DIET:** Eliminate chemical additives
- **DIET:** Discontinue junk foods, especially sodas and other chemically-laden, high-street food attractions
- **DIET:** Avoid sugar, refined flour and polished (white) rice
- **DIET:** Avoid pork, aspartame, saccharin, synthetic/fake fats, sweets/candy and fluoridated water
- **DIET:** Eat good quality fish, rich in oils
- **DIET:** Ensure that 70% of the diet comprises high-water-content, high fibre, living, whole organic foods
- **DIET:** Drink 3-4 pints of clean, non-chlorinated, non-fluoridated water a day
- **DETOXIFICATION:** Test for and detoxify toxic elements
- **RESTORE NUTRIENT BALANCE: COMMENCE THE BASIC SUPPLEMENT PROGRAM,** ensuring:
- Flax seed oil, 1 tbsp per day

Empirical Examination of the Value of Nutrition in the Control and Treatment of Incarcerated Juvenile Offenders," *International Journal of Biosocial Research*, 4(1), 1983, pp.25-39. **Stephen Schoenthaler**, "Types of Offenses Which can be Reduced in an Institutional Setting Using Nutritional Intervention: A Preliminary Empirical Evaluation," *International Journal of Biosocial Research*, 4(2), 1983, pp.74-84. Stephen Schoenthaler, "The Los Angeles Probation Department Diet Behavior Program: An Empirical Evaluation of Six Institutions," *International Journal of Biosocial Research*, 5(2), 1983, pp.88-98

- B-complex (inc. B1, B3, B5, B6), calcium, magnesium, zinc and other key nutrients
- **PREVENTION:** ENSURE ADEQUATE EXERCISE to burn off excess energy
- **PREVENTION:** Avoid foods that may contribute to allergies. These are typically wheat, dairy, sugar, eggs, oranges and chocolate
- **PREVENTION:** Examine and evaluate high lead levels in the child's environment, together with any other chemical factors which may be relevant
- **PREVENTION:** Watch for somatic, allergic reactions in the child, including bloating or irregular bowel movements, excessive mucus, ear infections, skin rashes, facial swelling, tonsillitis, discolouration around the eyes, bloating and digestive problems, bad breath, bedwetting, eczema and asthma
- **TIP:** Apply a firm but loving discipline to the child
- **TIP:** Ensure that the child is co-operative with dietary changes. Obviously, in more than a few cases, this is not easy. Ensure consistency in applying dietary amendments. Discontinuing psychiatric drugs may be considered by a qualified health practitioner familiar with an orthomolecular (nutritional) approach to these conditions. <u>Discontinuing psychiatric medication must never be undertaken without professional supervision</u>

Addictions

Profile

A classically undernourished person seeks a 'lift' to improve how they feel. Often substance abuse or addictions are the result. Repetitive behaviour carried out in a state of emotion will establish the cycle as a comfort zone in the brain, especially if the addictive activity results in a perceived improvement of mood. "Alcohol makes me forget…" is an improvement of mood to the alcoholic, who might be seeking refuge from emotional, financial or professional problems.

Once the addiction sets in, there are biochemical and nutritional implications that need to be dealt with, along with the psychological factors. These are best treated side by side.

Symptoms

Insomnia, nightmares, violent mood swings, feelings of doom, hallucinations, craving for sweets and alcohol, fluctuating weight, hypoglycaemia, compulsive workaholic behaviour, extreme anxiety and nervousness. Once again a downward spiral is created when alcohol or drug abuse depresses appetite, which leads to malnutrition, which leads to a need to improve mood, which leads to alcohol and drug abuse, which leads to a further depression of appetite, and so on.

Addiction and hypoglycaemia

Alcoholics and drug addicts invariably have chaotic blood sugar (see **Hypo/Hyperglycaemia**). Dr Carl Pfeiffer reports that in 1973, when a group of 200 alcoholics was tested for glucose intolerance. 97% of them came up positive.[28] Those addicted to alcohol, drugs (recreational or pharmaceutical) and junk foods can manipulate their blood sugar and hence mood with their habits. This creates a dependence on the substances to improve mood.

---

[28] Pfeiffer, Carl & Patrick Holford, op. cit. p.165

Addiction and allergies

Often the addict can test positive for allergy with the substance to which they are addicted or drawn. Pfeiffer, Philpot and Kalita discovered that over 75% of tobacco smokers showed a positive allergy for tobacco on skin tests.[29] Typically all addicts require a normalisation of blood sugar, a nutrient-dense, organic diet (the majority eaten raw to preserve amino acids and enzymes) and optimum supplementation.

Libby and Stone pioneered the use of mega-doses of intravenous vitamin C in detoxifying heroin and methadone addicts. 30-85 grams a day were administered to 30 heroin addicts with 100% success.[30] Pawlek achieved significant results using 3 grams of vitamin C and high doses of niacin (up to 2 grams/day).[31] Alkali-forming diets are essential for the recovering alcoholic. In 1973, Blackman gave 19 heroin addicts sodium and potassium bicarbonate every half an hour for two hours, followed by a two-hour break, and repeated the cycle until withdrawal had been completed. The volunteers reported that withdrawal symptoms were either completely or considerably reduced.[32]

Narconon

The highly successful Narconon program claims a 70% success rate with substance abuse withdrawal and detoxification over two years. The program makes the point that withdrawal is not the same as detoxification. Drug residues may stay within the body for several months after withdrawal before the patient is 'clean'. Optimum nutrition and the guidelines below are used by Narconon to assist the patient in a full and, as far as possible, hassle-free detoxification. Kirsty Alley, star of Cheers, was formerly an alcohol and cocaine addict who recovered through the Narconon program. The three-step program used by Narconon involves:

---

[29] Ibid.

[30] **Libby, AF & I Stone**, "The Hypoascorbemia-Kwashiorkor Approach to Drug Addiction Therapy: Pilot Study", *Orthomolecular Psychiatry*, 6(4),300-308:1977

[31] Pfeiffer, Carl & Patrick Holford, op. cit. p.166

[32] Ibid.

1) Withdrawal from addictive drugs and substances. The patient is given a comprehensive mineral and vitamin program, sometimes the latter is administered intravenously. This is backed up with a special magnesium and calcium drink, which assists in eliminating the cramps, twitches and nerve pain which often accompany opiate withdrawal

2) Purification involves the use of a combination of niacin (vitamin B3) saunas and exercise to sweat out the drug and substance residues. Niacin is steadily increased up to 2 g a day, accompanied with a comprehensive exercise regimen and prolonged sessions in the sauna. The patient is constantly drinking purified water to hydrate their system

3) Full 24-hour counselling support is given during the program duration

The fungi conspiracy

A dependence on sweet things, including alcohol, may be an indication that the patient is suffering from a yeast or fungal infestation, such as *Candida albicans*. Search for other indicators, such as rashes around the genitalia (jock itch and vaginal yeast infections), toe-nail fungus, athlete's foot, etc. A craving for sweet things can often be as a result of fungi getting hungry and increasing the discharge rate of their mycotoxins, which gives the patient a depressed, 'there's something missing' mood. Sweets, alcohol and other foods seem to lift these cravings since you solve the hunger problem of 'Those Within'. Critters, as I call them, will feature quite prominently with many diseases we will look at, as they infest, multiply and cause damage within a body that has abused itself to such an extent with modern, 'convenience' foods and liquids.

Breaking patterns – the carrot and the stick

Addictions and habits also have another angle to them which must be dealt with, namely patterns. The human brain uses patterning in order to establish behaviour it believes will assist it in surviving. Any behaviour repetitively carried out over a 15- to 30-day period in a state of positive emotion will be established by the brain as a pattern ('comfort zone'). Unfortunately bad patterns, or addictions, can begin this way. The key to patterning revolves around understanding that the brain's most dominant human dynamic is survival. The two key elements the brain uses to survive are:

> The need to avoid pain (the stick)
> The desire to gain pleasure (the carrot)

Pleasure

These elements are invariably used, for example, in advertising, where a client's product is presented to the public with tremendous pleasure linked to it; in practising a skill, over and over, in order to master it; educating a child at home using pain and pleasure, scolding if naughty, rewarding if good. Animals, such as dogs, are also trained the same way, where they are taught repetitively to carry out an action, and are then rewarded each time they perform it satisfactorily, or scolded if they do not. The dog will link fetching a stick to the pleasure of receiving a food treat, and will then perform the task when required.

Ivan Pavlov and Vladimir Bekhterev experimented with dogs, where they were able to induce salivation at the ring of a bell. Donald Ewen Cameron used electroshock to 'de-pattern' his subjects, attempting to change their behaviour. Repetitive patterning may have been installed in a person quite accidentally. A person tries smoking because he has heard it is 'cool' and relaxes you. He coughs and chokes over the first few, but PERSISTS. Thereafter his body 'learns' the technique, because the behaviour has been repeated persistently for a period of time in a state of emotion.

Pain

From birth, our brain has been evaluating survival threats in the outside world and linking pain or pleasure to the various activities in which we engage. If we fall off our bike and hurt ourselves, our brain may be reluctant to try the activity again as it seeks to avoid pain in order to survive. A number of activities can cause people 'brain-pain'. Here are a few:

- Speaking in public
- Parachuting
- Bungee-jumping
- Viewing sharks underwater while in a cage
- Handling snakes
- Handling cockroaches and spiders
- Dieting
- Giving up smoking
- Giving up alcohol
- Giving up drugs
- Moving out of a comfort zone

Some of these, such as parachuting, bungee-jumping and swimming with sharks are perceived as a survival threat by the brain, and so our trusty, cerebral organ will give us the appropriate, uncomfortable, emotional state to warn us from undertaking the activity. Giving up things, such as cigarettes, drugs, alcohol or certain types of food, moves us out of the mental comfort zones our brains created when we repeated this behaviour persistently in a state of emotion. Thus the brain has been educated to perceive that ceasing these activities constitutes a survival threat.

Breaking the pattern

It is relatively straightforward to re-educate the brain into dumping unwanted addictions and habits (mental patterns) and installing beneficial ones. The method is a three-step process:

- Gain leverage on the problem
- Break the unwanted pattern/habit/addiction
- Install the new pattern/habit

Step 1 - Gaining leverage on the problem

How badly do you want to give up smoking, alcohol or drugs? So badly that you will do anything? Gaining leverage is all about getting the mind to the point of critical mass where you are prepared to do whatever it takes to dump the habit or addiction. How many people tried to diet when they didn't want to? Or attempted to quit smoking when their heart wasn't in it? It is absolutely necessary to *gain leverage* on your habit prior to breaking the pattern associated with it. Below are some questions you might find helpful in gaining the necessary leverage on your situation:

> ➤ In order to arrive at the solution, have I examined the problem?
> ➤ Do I actually know what I want out of life?
> ➤ Am I willing to move out of my comfort zone?
> ➤ Am I prepared to cease routinely doing what I know is harming myself and others?
> ➤ What do I *have* to change in my life?
> ➤ Am I prepared to change these things RIGHT NOW?
> ➤ What am I doing correctly at the moment?
> ➤ What will be the consequences to myself and others if I DON'T change?

The problem with bringing 'positive thinking' to bear on an addiction is simple – you have to think! As most nail-biters, drinkers, drug-takers or smokers will tell you, the brain will automatically trigger the pattern to indulge these activities without conscious thought. Positive thinking is crucial for gaining leverage on the problem, but alone won't often achieve the goal. Two other steps are required.

Step 2 - Breaking the pattern

Nail-biters will pop down to the pharmacy for some of that revolting gunk they paint on their nails. Next time the brain decides to trigger their nail-biting pattern, they end up with a mouthful of the noxious liquid. This causes the brain some pain. When done repeatedly in a state of emotion over a period of time, the brain will forget the old pattern.

I was a cigarette smoker for 15 years and was able to quit using a bag of lemons! Every time I felt like a cigarette, I would cut a lemon in half and squeeze it into my mouth instead. The brain didn't think much of this pattern-breaking method. Neither did my eyelids, which flickered several hundred times a second! Over a period of time though, the brain finally gave up with the smoking pattern, as the lemons were causing it too much consternation and ....pain.

Breaking patterns is also dependent on location. If you go to a bar or pub and that is where you smoke and drink, you must break the pattern of going there if you want to drop these activities. If you want to change your eating habits, often the restaurant which serves the food that gets you into trouble beckons all the more! Avoid it and set up a new regime or pattern that avoids old routines or haunts. The brain only needs time and repetition in order to learn a new way.

Step 3 – Installing the new pattern

World-class motivator Anthony Robbins has a great system for teaching pattern installations, which I highly recommend. Installing new and beneficial patterns enables a person to 'customise' their lifestyle and remove the junk patterns at the same time. All it takes to do this is persistence, persistence, persistence and persistence! Simply link mental pain and anguish to the pattern or activity you wish to banish, then link a huge amount of pleasure to the incoming pattern and then *keep doing this for the required period of time*. While I was quitting smoking, I used to drive around in my car with an unlit cigarette hanging from my lips, so I could smell the tobacco and feel the texture of the cigarette in my mouth while I was imagining diseased lungs in hospital buckets, coughing paroxysms, a tight chest and burnt clothing. Thus I was linking extreme pain to my cigarette habit.

After routinely torturing my brain with these images for around five minutes or so at a time, I would then take the cigarette, break it, and spend ten minutes linking a huge amount of pleasure to NOT SMOKING! I breathed in the fresh, clean air; felt how wonderful it was to be a non-smoker, and revelled in the success of the victory. And sure enough, after a number of attempts at getting me to repeat the pattern (for which my brain received its obligatory lemon), I proved to be more persistent than my amorphous brain curds, which subsequently caved in under the assault of lemons and fresh air and accepted the new pattern of NOT SMOKING.

Notice that you can also teach your brain to build a pattern that will override your brain's natural survival instinct and indulge in a dangerous activity, if that is what you want. Soldiers are trained to think coolly in life-and-death, survival situations. People do swim

37

with sharks and bungee-jump and sky-surf and hunt snakes. If this is really what you think you have been called to Earth to do, then patterning can achieve it... and much more besides.

Revision

Old patterns go, but the brain still files them away to see if they can be used at a later date. Some ex-smokers still crave cigarettes if they are in a location-sensitive part of their old pattern, in a state of emotion, and then get a whiff of tobacco smoke. Repeat steps 1-3 above every three months or so following the ceasing of a pattern to hammer home to the brain just how things are going to be done from now on.

Take action♥

Those suffering from addictions may benefit from the following:

- **TIP:** Seek the help of a physician acquainted with metabolic and anti-parasite approaches to alcoholism
- **DIET: COMMENCE THE ANTI-*CANDIDA* DIETARY REGIMEN,** ensuring anti-*Candida*/fungal supplements are taken consistently and regularly. Once addiction is broken, transfer to **THE *FOOD FOR THOUGHT* LIFESTYLE REGIMEN**
- **RESTORING NUTRIENT BALANCE: COMMENCE THE BASIC SUPPLEMENT PROGRAM,** ensuring:
- Thiamine (B1), 150 mg per day
- Niacin (B3), 500 mg, twice per day
- Pantothenic acid (B5), 500 mg, twice per day
- Vitamin B6, 100 mg, twice per day
- Vitamin C (ascorbates plus bioflavonoids), 10 g a day, spread throughout the day
- L-glutamine powder, 5 grams, twice per day
- Essential fatty acids, including GLA
- Break the addiction pattern
- **REGULAR EXERCISE AND REST – V. IMPORTANT. DO NOT SKIP, FUDGE, MISS OUT OR OTHERWISE SHIRK!**

Alcoholism

Profile

Perhaps no more destructive condition afflicts our society today than alcoholism. In a 'free' society, where people are able to make their own choices, many have, and the damaging and tragic consequences of their alcoholism and drinking benders spread far beyond just the individual affected: physical violence on family members and friends, drink-driving deaths, crime, physical sickness, losing your job.

In America alone, it is estimated that 10% of adults have a drink problem alone, with loss of productivity costs amounting to $15 billion, health costs $8.3 billion, accidents and other losses, $5.0 billion.... It's estimated that alcoholism costs the United States $136 billion a year. Some free choice.

Symptoms

Visible signs of excessive alcohol consumption. Depression. Unexplained days off work, loss of friends, accident-prone. Violent fits. Drinking alcohol before breakfast. Tremors, delirium, hallucinations and blackouts. Poor physical condition. Alcoholic odour on breath or oozing out of pores. Flushed face. Unexplained bruises or contusions on body.

Commentary

The causes of alcoholism, as with drug abuse, are multi-factorial and so the remedies must 'turn off the tap' for each of these causes or the patient will re-offend. As mentioned in the previous section on addictions, initially people take mind-altering substances to improve mood. It is the visible shifting of mood experience that provides the pleasure, relief or oblivion from life's circumstances that initiates the addiction pattern in the subject. The programs that work best for an alcoholic or drug addict depend heavily on removing the patient to a different environment and giving them a completely new set of positive priorities on which to focus. This breaks the patterning of the addiction over a period of time. Notice that any re-offending merely re-establishes the pattern (see **Addictions**).

Physical problems

Alcoholism is, needless to say, a very physical problem too. In many ways, the disorder represents the quintessential hook-up of the mind relentlessly driving the body.

Alcoholics generally have a disturbed metabolism, chaotic blood sugar patterns, low zinc action, and vitamin deficiencies, primarily A, B's, C and E. Hypoglycaemia and cravings for sugar are common, as are the yeast/fungal infestations that invariably drive them. Liver fatty damage too occurs quite early on in the patient's drinking. Alcoholics are characterised by aberrant neurotransmitter production – hormones that affect and stabilise mood. Low levels of tryptophan, an amino acid required for the production of serotonin, are also in evidence. Alcoholics will also have immune system problems manifesting themselves as food intolerances (see **Allergies**).

Take action♥

One of the very first tasks is for the alcoholic to admit they have a problem and be resolved to take action and take it consistently. The following measures will not work unless consistency is the watchword and the patient really wants to overcome their disability. Family and friends are extremely important in this regard in providing a positive, nurturing environment during withdrawal and recovery rather than one of condemnation:

- **VITAL:** Read the **Addictions** and **Allergies** sections of this book
- **VITAL:** Find a doctor (MD) or naturopath (ND) familiar with nutrition and detoxification procedures
- **VITAL:** Sign up to regular counselling sessions. Before atheistic/agnostic Alcoholics Anonymous campaigners began dismantling the famous 12-step program because of its biblical connections, this was a fine system for re-concentrating the mind of the alcoholic on positive and dynamic personal intervention
- **VITAL:** If you are an alcoholic reading this, put feelings of failure and shame behind you and resolve to get the problem sorted. Don't TELL others what you are going to

do, SHOW them your success and faith in yourself by your actions, *one day at a time*

- **DIET: COMMENCE THE ANTI-*CANDIDA* DIETARY REGIMEN.** You have a fungal/yeast/ bacteria problem that will need to be dealt with over a protracted period. Run this dietary regimen for three months, then transfer onto the more liberal ***FOOD FOR THOUGHT* LIFESTYLE REGIMEN** thereafter
- **DETOXIFICATION:** Follow the entire course of action explained in the **Candidiasis** section of this book
- **RESTORING NUTRIENT BALANCE: COMMENCE THE BASIC SUPPLEMENT PROGRAM**, ensuring:
- **ANTI-*CANDIDA*/FUNGAL SUPPLEMENTATION**
- 'Ingenious' (Neways Int'l), as directed (see **A Guide to Nutritional Supplements**)
- Vitamin A emulsion, as directed
- Silymarin (milk thistle extract), 140-210 mg, three times per day
- Vitamin C (ascorbates plus bioflavonoids), 2-3 g, twice per day
- Carnitine, 300 mg, three times per day
- Magnesium, 200–400 mg, three times per day
- Glutamine, 1 g per day
- Establish a regular, consistent exercise regimen at a local gym. Use a personal trainer in order not to shirk all that hard work!

A final note on stress

To all alcoholics and drug addicts out there, life is beautiful and yours for the taking. It is your birthright to live a long and happy life as one of God's children. Maybe a comprehensive re-think on your priorities in life is long overdue. Maybe you are your own worst enemy. Maybe you have been the one stressing yourself out. Have you been giving yourself task after task after task to perform which has driven you into a corner? Is alcohol really the answer to those money problems, or is not the answer to a money problem... money? Please remember that I never yet met anyone whose last words were, *"Darn, I wish I'd spent more time at the office."*

41

If you are a recovering alcoholic, or one who is now committed to getting cleaned out, go out there, get busy, and have a nice rest of life. There are people like us within easy reach who are batting on your team. Don't hesitate to ask for help. I never do!

Live.

Allergies

Profile

In this book, we examine some of the problems of allergies/sensitivities and food intolerances, and how they affect the mind. Common food intolerances, such as those for wheat (gluten), milk (casein), chocolate, eggs, oranges and other salicylates may disrupt hormone levels, resulting in mental symptoms that can range from depression to schizophrenia and the classic 'straitjacket' problems.

Symptoms

Many of these disorders occurring later in life, described as mental illnesses, may begin early in childhood and show up as eczema, infantile colic, rashes, fits and temper tantrums, excessive mucus formations, frequent rapid colds, hyperactivity, speech difficulties, anxiety, seasonal allergies and coeliac disease (malabsorption of food). In *Health Wars*, we examined the problems brought on by infants fed cow's milk during their first two years' of life. This is a vulnerable period for a small child, whose immune system usually has not fully developed until the third year. Assaulting the child with multiple vaccinations, foreign and often hostile proteins, such as those found in wheat and cow's milk, can lead to all sorts of problems, like autism and type 1 diabetes, especially when the child has not been adequately breast-fed to ensure the full spectrum of immune factors are taken in to begin with.

Once the immune system is formed, there may be imperfections in how the system performs when assaulted with particles the body identifies as toxins. Damage and scarring to the intestinal wall by gluten/gliaden in wheat, barley, rye and oats, for instance, destroys the finger-like villi which absorb nutrients, leading to coeliac disease, where the food can pass unprocessed through the small intestine. Leaky gut syndrome, where undigested food particles permeate the damaged intestinal wall and enter the bloodstream, is typified by systemic poisoning and a chronic-fatigue reaction of lethargy, listlessness and depression (see **Inflammatory Bowel Disease**).

Experimental double-blind studies and control trials conclusively show that wheat, milk, cane sugar, eggs (often the whites), tobacco and food additives are the chief culprits. In one control study, 96 patients diagnosed as suffering from alcohol dependence, major depressive disorders and schizophrenia were compared with 62 control subjects selected from adult hospital staff members for possible food/chemical intolerances. Those suffering as 'depressives' were found to be the highest suffering from allergies: 80% were found to be allergic to barley and 100% were allergic to egg white. Over 50% of the alcoholics were found to be allergic to egg white, milk, rye and barley. Of the schizophrenic group, 80% were found to be allergic to both milk and eggs. Only 9% of the control group were found to suffer from any allergies.[33]

Schizophrenics, routinely treated with drugs, were randomly assigned milk- and gluten-free diets while on the locked ward. They were discharged nearly twice as rapidly as control patients assigned a high-cereal diet. Wheat gluten secretly added to the cereal-free diet undid this effect, showing that wheat gluten was a player in the behaviour of these schizophrenic patients.[34]

Elimination/challenge testing

Removing problem foods and then reintroducing them one by one under controlled conditions to see if the problems reoccur is known as elimination/challenge testing. This should always be done under clinical supervision, especially when side-effects may be quite severe, such as fits, asthma, anaphylactic shock, severe depression and violent, psychotic episodes.

The antihistamine effect

In *The Mind Game*, we examine the effects of histadelia, or excess histamine, in the body, and its association to mental illness. It is interesting to note that many psychiatric medications are very similar in their chemical profiles to antihistamines, and indeed are designed to suppress brain histamine receptors. Tricyclic and antidepressant drugs, such as imipramine (Tofranil) and amitriptyline, are in this group. Other drugs, such as chlorpromazine

---

33 Pfeiffer, Carl & Patrick Holford, op. cit. p.139
34 Ibid.

and promazine, are designed to inhibit histamine production and promazine is used to treat allergies. This seems to confirm the role of histamine excess in related emotional disorders and therefore Pfeiffer, Holford and Hoffer encourage physicians to adapt their patients' diets before resorting to potentially debilitating medication. Carl Pfeiffer has also devoted much of his professional research time to examining B6 (pyridoxine), zinc and manganese deficiencies, and their role in restoring his patients to health:

"Several vitamins are noted for their effectiveness in reducing allergic symptoms. Vitamins C and B6 are probably the most effective. Dr William Philpott has used both of these vitamins intravenously to turn off allergic symptoms provoked by testing for allergies. The patients on adequate vitamin C will have fewer allergic symptoms. B6 should be given to the point of nightly dream recall and the minerals calcium and potassium should be plentiful in the diet. Zinc and manganese are also needed by the allergic patient. Elimination of the offending foods may be needed for several months. For multiple food allergies, in which this approach would severely limit the diet, a four-day rotation diet in which each food is eaten only once every four days should be tried. If this approach is unsuccessful, intradermal allergy testing to determine the degree of allergy and the neutralising dose of each allergen is recommended." [35]

Most patients suffering from food allergies also have pyroluria, where excessive pyrrole chemicals are found in the urine, binding vitamin B6 and zinc (see **Pyroluria**). Since coeliac damage to the intestinal wall may result in malabsorption of nutrients into the body, while often allowing undigested food proteins into the blood creating allergy, healing of the intestinal system is vital to a restoration of the patient to full nutritional homeostasis.

---

[35] Ibid.

Take action♥

Those suffering from allergies may benefit from the following:

- **TIP:** Avoid foods or areas that trigger allergies. Allergy test to determine foods to which the patient is sensitive
- **DIET: COMMENCE THE *FOOD FOR THOUGHT* LIFESTYLE REGIMEN**
- **DETOXIFICATION:** Magnesium oxide bowel cleanse
- **RESTORE NUTRIENT BALANCE: THE BASIC SUPPLEMENT PROGRAM**, ensuring:
- Methionine, 500 mg, twice per day
- Calcium, 500 mg, twice per day
- Magnesium, 400 mg a day
- Zinc, 25 mg, twice per day
- Manganese, 10 mg, twice per day
- Essential fatty acid supplement or 1 tbsp flaxseed oil
- Vitamin B6, 100 mg, twice per day (enough for nightly dream recall. Absolutely no more than 600 mg a day)
- Vitamin C (ascorbates plus bioflavonoids), 1-2 g, twice per day

Alzheimer's Disease, Senile Dementia

Profile

Mental impairment problems are devastating our cultures today, and yet this has not always been the case. Clearly, toxicity issues are at the fore. As many as a third of all hospital beds in the UK are taken up with geriatric patients suffering a host of disorders, a large proportion of them institutionalised because of senility. The cost to healthcare runs to billions.

With mental impairment problems, the following questions should be asked and the conditions addressed FIRST:

- Is the patient eating organic, whole, non-pesticide-laden foods?
- Is the patient nutritionally deficient?
- Is the patient drinking up to 4 pints of clean, fresh water a day?
- Does the patient have chaotic blood sugar levels?
- Is the patient on any psychiatric medication which might be giving the appearance of senility or slow cognitive ability?
- Does the patient suffer from food allergies?
- Has the patient any evidence of yeast or fungal infections?
- Does the patient live in a toxic environment?
- Does the patient eat junk food and drink sodas?
- Has the patient been mentally unchallenged for a period of time?

Memory problems – potential causes

Several factors influence memory:

- Use it or lose it!
- Impaired blood supply to the brain

- Nutritional intake, especially minerals such as zinc and manganese, vitamins, especially the 'B' group, and essential fatty acids
- Food allergies
- Toxins
- Abnormal blood sugar levels (glucose intolerance)

Use it or lose it!

In my view, retirement is the single most damaging thing for a person, when they are persuaded to end their productivity and bow out of the work ethic until they expire. It is in the nature of humans to produce and be mentally active. Depression, listlessness and despair often set in when brains are put in mothballs and the person vegetates in a chair in front of the TV for the rest of their lives.

In *Health Wars*, we take a look at cultures who routinely live past 100 and remain active. If you are 70-80, start looking around for another career! Think of the skills and knowledge you have amassed that could benefit others. If your brain is busy and well fed, it is a happy brain. And so you will be too.

Blood supply to the brain

One of the most common medical conditions we suffer from over the age of 50 is atherosclerosis, or lipoprotein plaque in the arteries. In *Health Wars*, we devote two chapters to affairs of the heart and the cardiovascular system, showing that heart disease, in almost all its forms, may be traced back to nutritional deficiencies, including an early form of scurvy.

Scurvy

Scurvy occurs when collagen breaks down in the body. Collagen is a tough, fibrous material the body uses to clad arteries, veins and capillaries, as well as organs and the skin, to give them structure. Collagen is a lot like the steel girders you see when builders are erecting a new skyscraper. Each collagen fibre has been calculated to be far tougher and stronger than an iron wire of comparable width. In the absence of adequate nutrition, specifically vitamins C, E and the amino acids lysine and proline, collagen begins to dissolve. When sailors went off to sea and eschewed their usual diet of fruits

48

and vegetables in favour of the non-perishable foodstuffs used during long voyages, scurvy invariably set in within a matter of weeks, the collagen dissolved, and the sailors literally fell apart. The cure was to recommence consumption of living, whole fruits and vegetables rich in the nutrition required to repair collagen and nourish the whole body.

Atherosclerosis

With heart disease, the process is much slower, sometimes taking years to develop, since very few in the western world today suffer from vitamin C depletion. Like scurvy, a chronic vitamin C deficiency causes the beginning of a collapse in the arterial walls, necessitating a healing process to commence, in the form of lipoprotein(a) fats which the body attempts to use to bond the thousands of tiny breaches in the arterial walls.

These lipoproteins are Nature's perfect Band-Aid. They are extremely sticky and form the majority of the atherosclerotic deposits associated with advanced forms of heart disease today. Cardiovascular medicine, unaware or willingly ignorant of the underlying nutritional deficiency cause of atherosclerosis, focuses its attention on vilifying the lipoprotein's LDL (low-density lipoprotein) cholesterol content as one of the primary *causes* of heart diseases, when it is in fact the healing (survival response) precursor, *brought on by a chronic vitamin C deficiency*. Today the drug industry has mobilised a multi-billion-dollar business of anti-cholesterol drugs, which have wrought devastating results in cardiac patients, necessitating a further $20 billion drug program to combat all the side- effects.[36]

Most people have accumulated Lp(a) in their arteries after age 50, bringing on the usual problems with sticky blood, thrombosis, atherosclerosis and high blood pressure. Strokes too are caused when Lp(a) clogs the brain artery, impairing vital blood flow to the brain. And it is here that our interest in memory loss focuses. Impaired blood flow to the brain will cause death or partial paralysis. Patrick Holford writes:

---

[36] **Sellman, Sherill**, *Hormone Heresy*, GetWell Int'l, Inc. 1998; also **Seaman, Barbara**, *The Doctors' Case against the Pill*, Hunter House, USA, 1995, p.7

"When cells are starved of oxygen, they switch to a more primitive mode of operation called anaerobic respiration. The cells begin to divide and spread – unless they are nerve cells.... Nerve cells can't regenerate. So what happens to them? They just stop working. The result is senility."[37]

Aluminium and toxic metals

Another common finding in premature senile dementia, known as Alzheimer's disease, is an entanglement of nerve fibres. When these nerve clusters are found in the frontal and temporal regions of the brain, they are frequently saturated with aluminium.[38] Many theories abound on how this aluminium accumulates. Aluminium can be taken into the body through the water supply, cooking utensils, toothpastes (the tube), aluminium foil packaging, soft drinks and antacids. Detoxification regimens, such as those expounded on in this book (also in *Food For Thought* and *Health Wars*), will assist the body in ridding itself of unwanted accumulations of heavy metals. Chelators, natural substances that attach themselves to toxic elements and escort them out of the body, are used to remove aluminium.

Excess amounts of the following metals are known memory disruptors and inhibitors:

Lead: leads to hyperactivity and aggression. Taken in from traffic fumes and industrial pollution. Chelated using vitamins C, B1 and zinc.

Aluminium: leads to memory loss and senility. Derived from cooking utensils, water, etc. Chelated using zinc and magnesium.

Cadmium: leads to aggression and confusion. Derived from cigarettes. Chelated with vitamin C and zinc.

Copper: leads to anxiety and phobias. Derived from water piping. Chelated with zinc.

Mercury: leads to headaches and memory loss. Derived from pesticides, some vaccinations and mercury amalgam dental fillings. Chelated with selenium.

---

[37] Pfeiffer, Carl & Patrick Holford, op. cit. p.176

[38] **Martyn, C, et al**, "Geographical relation between Alzheimer's disease and aluminium in drinking water", *Lancet*, 14th January 1989

Food sensitivities

Those with memory impairment problems may also be suffering from the effects of food sensitivities, as discussed earlier (see **Allergies**). An allergy test may determine an underlying, treatable food allergy problem, which may be contributing to the patient's condition.

Pellagra

As discussed in the section entitled **Schizophrenia**, an old nutritional problem named pellagra is haunting us still. Pellagra is a niacin (B3) deficiency which will result in the four 'D's – dizziness, diarrhoea, dementia and death. Vitamin B3 is essential for oxygen utilisation in the body. It is incorporated into the coenzyme NAD (nicotinamide adenosine dinucleotide). Low amounts of B3 will invariably bring on symptoms that can be interpreted as dementia, Alzheimer's, etc.[39]

Boosting the memory

Those suffering memory impairment have a veritable arsenal of nutritional weapons at their disposal, as we shall see.[40] The neurotransmitter acetylcholine is the brain hormone responsible for memory retention. Experiments done at Palo Alto Hospital in California showed that drugs which boost production of acetylcholine produced 'super-memories'. Natural nutrients however can effectively boost acetylcholine production. These are choline, glutamine, DMAE (a nutrient found in fish), and its salt, Deanol. Pyroglutamate is also excellent, and many 'memory' supplements on the market today contain a mix of these nutrients which work better when used synergistically.

---

[39] For more information on pellagra, see *Health Wars*
[40] See **A Guide to Nutritional Supplements**

Elderly nutritional failures

One US study in 1975 failed to find one geriatric patient with a normal nutritional profile.[41] Alzheimer's and senility in general may be no more than decades of sub-optimal nutritional abuse, combined with a slow toxicity through foods and the environment. Boosting the nutritional intake of the elderly is of course rarely done in care homes and hospitals, where nutritional education among doctors and nurses is sadly lacking. The regimen at the end of this section will be beneficial for all who are suffering from these types of problems.

Self-poisoning through personal care and household products

Household and personal care products contain chemicals, which, over time, can build systemically in the body, causing mental impairment and other serious health problems. A special section on these is included at the end of this book (see **Environmental Toxins**). Shampoos, conditioners, make-up, antiperspirants, mouthwash, baby oil, fly spray and a dozen other offenders are used by the population daily with scant regard for the long-term hazards, which are only now becoming known.

Take action♥

- **DIET: COMMENCE THE *FOOD FOR THOUGHT* LIFESTYLE REGIMEN**
- **TIP:** In the event the patient exhibits yeast or fungal problems, adopt the measures described in the section on *Candida* and replace **THE *FOOD FOR THOUGHT* LIFESTYLE REGIMEN** with **THE ANTI-*CANDIDA* DIETARY REGIMEN** (with appropriate anti-fungal supplementation)
- **DIET:** Eliminate all junk or processed foods, including sugar-based foods and the high-glycaemic food group which breaks down into glucose in the body (bread, pasta, cereals, potatoes, pastries, etc.)

---

[41] Pfeiffer, C & Patrick Holford, op. cit. p.178

- **RESTORE NUTRIENT BALANCE: COMMENCE THE BASIC SUPPLEMENT PROGRAM**. This will boost oxygen to the cells and prevent deficiency in any one of over 60 different nutrients. Ensure intakes of:
- Vitamin C (ascorbates plus bioflavonoids), 2 g, twice per day
- Thiamine (B1), 100 mg per day
- L-carnitine (Vitamin B_T), 400 mg, three times per day
- Deanol – 100 mg per day
- DMAE – 500 mg per day
- 'Ingenious' complex, containing 'smart' nutrients, such as 5-HTP, pyroglutamate, glutamine, phosphatidylcholine and pantothenic acid (B5)
- Essential fatty acid intake. Omega 6 fat intake should be twice that of Omega 3's. (see **A Guide to Nutritional Supplements**) These can be taken in supplement form or by grinding up one measure of sunflower seeds, sesame and pumpkin seeds and two measures of flax seeds, taking two tablespoons of this mixture every morning. Ensure you buy fresh seeds!
- **DETOXIFICATION:** Magnesium oxide bowel cleanse
- **DETOXIFICATION:** Change out potentially harmful personal care and household products for safe alternatives (see **Environmental Toxins**)
- **DETOXIFICATION:** Removal of dental amalgams (not all at the same time!)
- **TIP:** Ensure 4 pints of clean, fresh water per day (2 litres)
- **TIP:** Stay enjoyably busy and productive until your need for oxygen ceases ☺

Anorexia/Bulimia

Profile
These eating disorders have gained prominence over the past twenty years. Anorexia is characterised by a lack of appetite, almost invariably accompanied by psychological stresses and significant weight-loss. Patients literally begin to starve themselves.

Patients suffering from bulimia feel a compunction to binge-eat and then enforce vomiting in order not to put on weight. Traditional treatments have included psychotropics such as chlorpromazine, sedatives, anti-depressants and electroshock. British child singing star Lena Zavaroni was given a lobotomy for her anorexia at Cardiff Hospital. She died two weeks later of an infection.

Anorexia symptoms
Loss of appetite, weight loss, impotency in males, nausea, skin lesions, depression, anxiety amenorrhoea. Anorexia is also exacerbated by the subject having a compulsion to be lean and thus fashionably attractive.

Anorexia commentary
In the 1980's, Professor Bryce-Smith reported in Britain's *Lancet* that anorexics were invariably zinc-deficient. Studies were showing that zinc-deficient animals lost their desire for food and that the small intestinal mucosa were abnormal as a result.[42] When force-fed a zinc-deficient diet, anorexics can become seriously ill.[43] With lack of nutrient absorption invariably accompanying the condition, a downward spiral is created when loss of food creates a deepening zinc deficiency which in turn further suppresses appetite, creating more zinc deficiency.

Bryce-Smith and Dr Simpson treated a 13-year-old girl who was anorexic, tearful and depressed. After treatment with a basic supplement program, antioxidants and zinc, she had recovered to

---

[42] **Akar**, *Lancet*, 13th October 1984, p.874
[43] **Flanagan**, *J. Nutr.* 114, 493-502: 1984

'normal' within two months, was cheerful again, and had increased her body weight by almost 45%.[44]

Hambridge and Silverman advise that *"...whenever there is appetite loss in children, zinc efficiency should be suspected."*[45] Bakan concluded that *"...the symptoms of anorexia and zinc deficiency are similar in a number of respects.... It is proposed that clinical trials be undertaken to test its effectiveness in treatment."*[46] Horrobin et al discovered that *"...there is substantial evidence to suggest that anorexia nervosa is due to a combined deficiency of zinc and EFA's* [essential fatty acids]*"*[47]

Many other studies confirm the connection between zinc deficiency and appetite loss. Normalising of menstruations also occurred with anorexics supplemented with zinc.[48] Cigarette smoking and other substance abuses have also been linked to eating disorders.[49] Ward concluded from his trial that *"...the urinary element of a 21-year-old female suffering from anorexia nervosa exhibits highly significant decreases in Ca, Co, Cr, Cu, Fe and Zn, when compared to an age-matched female control. Zinc, and possibly calcium imbalance, is shown to be associated with anorexia nervosa."*[50]

Safai-Kutti reported: *"During a follow-up period of 8-56 months, 17 out of 20 patients increased their body weight by more than 15%. The maximal weight gain was 57% after 24 months of zinc therapy. The most rapid weight gain was 24% over 3 months. None had weight loss after the administration of zinc therapy. None of our patients developed bulimia."*[51]

[44] **Bryce-Smith & Simpson**, *Lancet*, 11th August 1984, pp.350-351

[45] **Hambridge & Silverman**, *Arch. Dis. Child.*, 48, 567: 1973

[46] **Bakan**, *Med. Hyp.*, 5, 7: 1979

[47] **Horrobin, et al**, *Med. Hyp.*, 6, 277-296: 1980

[48] **Safai-Kutti**, *Am. J. Clin. Nutr.*, 44, 581-582: 1986

[49] **Jonas & Gold**, *Lancet*, 15th February 1986, p.390

[50] **Ward**, *J. Mircronutr. Anal.*, 2, 211-231: 1986

[51] **Safai-Kutti**, *Acta. Psychiatr. Scand. Suppl.*, 361, 14-17: 1990

Bulimia symptoms

The patient binge-eats and follows with self-induced vomiting, the use of laxatives, diuretics, strict fasting and compulsive exercise in order to avoid gaining weight. Not all bulimics are anorexic. The patient often complains of a lack of control when around food. Other factors to consider with anorexia and bulimia are hypoglycaemia (glucose intolerance), food allergies and candidiasis. The patient should seek qualified nutritional and emotional counselling while undergoing treatment.

Take action♥

Anorexics and bulimics may benefit from:

- **DIET: THE *FOOD FOR THOUGHT* LIFESTYLE REGIMEN**, adapted to provide a protein-rich, organic, whole-food diet, which includes fruits, vegetables, lentils, beans, ground seeds (sesame, sunflower, flax and pumpkin), quinoa and lightly broiled fish. Avoid all fried foods
- **DETOXIFICATION:** Avoid junk food, sodas, and confectionary
- **RESTORE NUTRIENT BALANCE: COMMENCE THE BASIC SUPPLEMENT PROGRAM,** ensuring:
- Zinc (gluconate), 25 mg, twice per day
- Vitamin B6, 100 mg, twice per day
- Pancreatic (digestive) enzyme supplement
- **TIP:** Good, consistent counselling from someone the patient trusts and respects
- **TIP:** Curtailment of substance abuse, including tobacco and street drugs
- **TIP:** Check for yeast and fungal infections. If positive, replace **THE *FOOD FOR THOUGHT* LIFESTYLE REGIMEN** with **THE ANTI-*CANDIDA* DIETARY REGIMEN** plus anti-fungal supplementation

Arthritis
Osteoarthritis, rheumatoid arthritis,
ankylosing spondylitis, etc.

Profile
Everyone knows someone who suffers from the degenerative condition of arthritis. Stiffness, pain in the early morning upon rising, incapacitation, joint swelling, bony fingers, bone spurs, hip and knee problems – those aluminium walkers.

Arthritis in all its manifestations has traditionally been regarded as an old person's disease, and yet, more and more, children and teenagers are afflicted. Arthritis, as we shall see, is <u>the most treatable of illnesses</u>, and extremely easy to prevent. Once again, cultures adhering to an adequate agrarian diet full of fresh whole-foods free of pesticides, sugar and other contaminants DO NOT GET ARTHRITIS.

There are several forms of the disease we can review. Firstly, the extremely common...

Osteoarthritis: First manifests with stiffness or pain in the wrist, fingers, knees, hips, etc. Joint crepitus, stiffness after periods of inactivity, narrowed joint spaces, cartilage erosion, bone spurs, etc. Over 45 million Americans suffer from osteoarthritis, many undergoing joint replacement surgery after many years of pain killers and other drugs.

Primary osteoarthritis is the manifestation that leads one to believe that this form of arthritis is simply a disease of old age. Science believes that a breakdown in the cartilage matrix forming the cartilage, the gel-like material that acts as the shock-absorber layer between the joints, provokes an enzyme reaction which destroys further cartilage formation, causing bones to abrase, creating pain and extreme discomfort.

Secondary osteoarthritis is the term usually given to osteoarthritis which has occurred as a result of some primary incident trigger, usually an accident, surgery, hormonal irregularities, gout, previous fractures, etc.

Problems with the official treatments

Drs. Murray and Pizzorno report that in many cases, osteoarthritis, if left alone without any nutritional or therapeutic intervention, will clear itself.[52] One study catalogued the natural progression of the disease in the hip over a ten-year period with no therapeutic intervention. X-rays were taken to confirm that the disease was in its advanced stages in the subjects to be studied. Later, after the patients were left alone with no therapeutic intervention, X-rays taken later confirmed that improvements did occur over time, with complete recoveries being experienced in fourteen of the thirty-one hips studied.[53] This microcosmic look points the finger of suspicion once again at the bankrupt methods medicine has been using to contain or reverse the condition on an international scale.

Usually, arthritis sufferers are treated with aspirin and non-steroidal anti-inflammatory drugs (NSAIDS), such as ibuprofen derivatives (Motrin, Advil, etc.). Many of these drugs have side-effects which include gastro-intestinal upsets, headaches, dizziness, ulcers, and a disconcerting propensity to inhibit cartilage synthesis and promote further cartilage disintegration.[54] As Murray and Pizzorno conclude, *"NSAIDS appear to suppress the symptoms but accelerate the progression of osteoarthritis."*[55] Eventually, the patient either has to opt for joint-replacement surgery, where applicable, or simply 'put up with it', and suffer progressive degeneration with the help of a constant diet of painkillers.

The hormone connection

In females, increased incidences of osteoarthritis coincide with estrogen dominance, provoking menopausal symptoms of flushing, mood changes, sweats, etc. (see **Menopausal Problems**). Tamoxifen, an estrogen suppressor and chemotherapy drug used in the treatment of estrogen-positive breast cancers, appears to

---

[52] **Murray, M & J Pizzorno**, *Encyclopaedia of Natural Medicine*, Little, Brown, UK, p.696

[53] **Perry, GH, Smith, MJG & CG Whiteside**, "Spontaneous recovery of the hip joint space in degenerative hip disease", *Ann Rheum Dis* 31 (1972): pp.440-8

[54] **Shield, MJ**, "Anti-inflammatory drugs and their effects on cartilage synthesis and renal function", *Eur J Rheumatol Inflam* 13 (1993): pp.7-16

[55] Murray, M & Joseph Pizzorno, *Encyclopaedia of Natural Medicine*, op. cit. p.697

decrease the erosion of cartilage, yet Tamoxifen is a known liver carcinogen.[56] Osteoarthritis in women is clearly linked to hormonal irregularities, which is why the most effective natural and non-toxic protocols for menopausal problems work so well with arthritis in women. As proof of this, estrogen dominance also coincides with hypothyroidism (underactive thyroid) (see **Hypothyroidism**). Those with hypothyroidism are known to have an increased risk of developing osteoarthritis as time proceeds.

Causes of primary osteoarthritis

- Diets predominant in sucrose, white flour products and refined processed foods
- The nightshade family (*Solanaceae*) of vegetables have been known to trigger osteoarthritis. These include tomatoes, potatoes and eggplant. Some speculate that it is not the vegetables themselves but pesticides residues on the plants that are to blame
- 'Junk in the joints'. Leaky gut syndrome is a condition where excessive wear on the intestinal membranes (usually by gluten and other antagonists), render them permeable to undigested food proteins passing from the digestive tract into the bloodstream, thickening up the blood (a condition known as 'Rouleau'). The body attempts to stash the junk, sometimes into the joint area, provoking an immune system reaction. Excess acid is a common by-product of 21st century diets, which inhibits the formation of new cartilage.[57]

Causes of secondary osteoarthritis

These, as mentioned in the 'secondary osteoarthritis' section above, will include 'primary events' that trigger the condition. This could be a fall, hormonal problems, or other conditions usually revolving around an overly acidic body system.

---

[56] Ransom, Steven, *Great News on Cancer in the 21st Century*, op. cit.
[57] See index: Molecular mimicry

Rheumatoid arthritis

Rheumatism involves fever, weakness, swollen and 'warm' joints, deformities of the joints in hands and feet. Rheumatoid arthritis has long been termed an 'auto-immune disease', wherein the immune system appears selectively to destroy connective tissue, tendons, joint muscles and bone. Traditional medicine points to a specific genetic marker, HLA-DRw4, which allegedly predisposes the subject to RA. In reality, RA cannot thrive without key environmental factors being present.

Other related conditions include:

Systemic lupus erythematosus (SLE): A chronic, inflammatory disease involving connective tissue and other organs of the body. Symptoms include a red, scaly rash on the face, affecting the nose and cheeks. Mouth sores, arthritis, progressive damage to the kidneys and heart, low white cell count and anaemia. The condition is diagnosed by the presence of abnormal antibody activity. Lupus is described as an 'auto-immune' condition. Fungal involvement producing these antibodies is suspected and should be verified.

Ankylosing spondylitis: An inflammatory disorder of the joint capsules which affects young men, mostly damaging connective tissue around the spine and large joints.

Scleroderma (systemic sclerosis): A chronic disorder affecting skin, internal organs and joints, presenting waxy, scaly skin, ivory in colour, due to blood vessel abnormalities. The illness can extend to other organs of the body, changing the character of tissue and presenting a whole range of symptoms from mild to fatal. Abnormal cell growth in the esophagus is characteristic of about one third of cases. Again, fungal involvement is suspected.

Critters... again

All rheumatoid arthritis sufferers demonstrate an altered microbial flora and small intestine bacterial overgrowth (SIBO)... sound familiar?[58] In fact, the severity of RA in a patient correlates to the degree of fungal overgrowth in the body.[59] Medicine has fixated

---

[58] See **Inflammatory Bowel Disease**

[59] **Henriksson, AEK, et al**, "Small intestinal bacterial overgrowth in patients with

on the presence of antibodies in RA sufferers without really zeroing in on why they are there in the first place. Mycoplasmic microbes are known to infect joints which trigger specific attacks on them by immune factors. A major part of the nutritional treatments for arthritis therefore centre around detoxification and parasite cleansing, ensuring that the digestive system is restored to normal function as far as possible. The use of digestive (pancreatic) enzymes is usually warranted.

Summary of arthritis

All the evidence from science and practical application in clinics around the world indicates the following:

- Traditional medicine is of limited help with arthritis of all kinds, and can actively promote the disease with the use of NSAIDS, aspirin and other drug interventions
- Diet and lifestyle are primary factors in the development of the conditions. Food sensitivity problems and heightened ingestion of junk trans-fats are key areas for investigation
- Yeast, fungi and their associated waste products are also implicated in rheumatoid arthritis
- Impaired or dysfunctional digestion must be corrected

Take action♥

Patients suffering from any manifestations of arthritis may benefit from the following:

- **SUPERVISION:** Secure the services of an MD or ND knowledgeable in nutritional treatments for arthritis
- **DIET: COMMENCE THE ANTI-*CANDIDA* DIETARY REGIMEN.** High quality food is the key here, as always, eaten four or five times per day. Fresh and organic food, most of it eaten raw to preserve enzyme activity
- **DIET:** Drink 4 pints (2 litres) of clean, fresh water per day

- **DETOXIFICATION:** Magnesium oxide bowel cleanse
- **DETOXIFICATION:** Ensure anti-yeast and -fungi herbal controls are used in the **ANTI-*CANDIDA* DIETARY REGIMEN**
- **RESTORE NUTRIENT BALANCE: COMMENCE THE BASIC SUPPLEMENT PROGRAM**, ensuring:
- Glucosamine sulphate, 1,500 mg per day
- Vitamin B3, niacinamide, no-flush, 500 mg, four times a day (liver enzymes will need to be periodically checked). Do not continue the supplementation of this nutrient longer than your physician recommends
- Vitamin C complex (ascorbates plus bioflavonoids), 2 g, twice per day
- Vitamin B3, 150-300 mg per day
- Boron, 6 mg per day
- Selenium, 200 mcg per day
- Digestive enzyme supplement, as directed, taken between meals on an empty stomach
- **TIP:** Essential fatty acid intake is vital (this is part of **THE BASIC SUPPLEMENT PROGRAM**). Ideally, increased intakes of fish oils and flaxseed oil (1 tbsp per day) meal should be included. The diet can also include oily fish such as mackerel, herring, halibut and salmon (not farmed, but cold caught)
- **TIP:** Pay special attention to foods that need to be avoided in **THE ANTI-*CANDIDA* DIETARY REGIMEN**. These will also include the nightshade family, e.g. potatoes, peppers, tobacco, eggplant and tomatoes

Aspartame Disease

Profile

Today, the sweeteners sucrose and saccharin remain as controversial as ever, and the debate over whether or not they represent a cancer hazard to the public continues to rage. And yet, people who have turned to another alternative to saccharin and sugar over the past 20 years have become equally dismayed at a parallel fur-fight over aspartame, decked out in the garb of a light blue sachet, which began adorning restaurants and diners the world over under the brand names Nutrasweet, Canderel, Equal, Spoonful and Equal-Measure.

Aspartame was discovered by accident in 1965 by James Schlatter, a chemist working for G D Serle Company, who was testing anti-ulcer compounds for his employers. Aspartame's original approval as a sweetener for public consumption was blocked by neuroscientist Dr John W Olney and consumer attorney James Turner in August 1974 over concerns about both aspartame's safety and G D Serle's research practices. However, aspartame duly received its approval for dry goods in 1981 and its go-ahead as a sweetener for carbonated beverages was granted in 1983, despite growing concerns over its neurological effects.[60] In 1985, G D Serle was purchased by pharmaceutical giant Monsanto, and Serle Pharmaceuticals and The NutraSweet Company were created as separate corporate identities.

According to researcher Alex Constantine in his essay entitled "Sweet Poison", aspartame may account for up to 75% of the adverse food reactions reported to the US FDA, due primarily to its reported ability to affect neurological processes in humans. Dr Olney found that an excess of aspartate and glutamate, two chemicals used by the body as neurotransmitters to transmit information between brain neurons, could kill neurons in the brain by allowing too much

---

[60] Two FDA scientists, Jacqueline Verrett and Adrian Gross, reviewed data from three studies which highlighted alleged irregularities in G D Serle's research procedures. The two government scientists declared that the irregularities they had uncovered were serious enough to warrant an immediate halt to aspartame's approval for use. *Food Magazine*, "Artificial Sweetener Suspicions", Vol. 1, No.9, April/June 1990.

calcium to collect in the neuron cells to neutralise acid. This neurological damage led Olney to label aspartate and glutamate 'excitotoxins', in that they, according to Olney, 'excite' or stimulate the neural cells to death.[61]

Symptoms

Side-effects laid at the door of aspartame poisoning include fits, convulsions, multiple sclerosis, Alzheimer's disease, ALS, memory loss, hormonal problems, hearing loss, epilepsy, Parkinson's disease, AIDS dementia, brain lesions and neuro-endocrine disorders. Risks to infants, children and pregnant women from aspartame were also underscored by the Federation of American Societies for Experimental Biology, a research body that traditionally follows FDA policy and adopts a softly-softly approach to chemical problems. The Federation declared: *"It is prudent to avoid the use of dietary supplements of L-glutamic acid by pregnant women, infants and children. The existence of evidence for potential endocrine responses... would also suggest a neuroendocrine link and that... L-glutamic acid should be avoided by women of childbearing age and individuals with affective disorders."* [62]

Commentary

Aspartame comprises two chief trouble-makers:

Phenylalanine: The amino acid L-phenylalanine, used by the brain, comprises 50% of aspartame. People suffering from the genetic disorder phenylketonuria (PKU) cannot metabolise phenylalanine and so an excess of this amino acid builds up in parts of the brain, leading to a decrease of serotonin levels, bringing on emotional disorders and depression.

Methanol: Also known as wood alcohol, the poison methanol is a 10% ingredient of aspartame, which is created when aspartame is heated above 86°F (30°C) in, for example, the preparation of processed foods. Methanol oxidises in the body to produce formic acid and the deadly neurotoxin, formaldehyde, also used as a prime ingredient in many vaccinations. Methanol is considered by America's Environmental Protection Agency (EPA) as *"...a*

---

[61] *The Guardian*, London, UK, 20th July 1990
[62] *Food Magazine*, op. cit.

cumulative poison, due to the low rate of excretion once it is absorbed. In the body, methanol is oxidised to formaldehyde and formic acid; both of these metabolites are toxic."[63]

A one-litre carbonated beverage, sweetened with aspartame, contains around 56 mg of methanol. Heavy consumers of soft drinks sweetened with aspartame can ingest up to 250 mg of methanol daily, especially in the summer, amounting to 32 times the EPA warning limit.

Dr Woodrow C Monte, Director of the Food Science and Nutritional Laboratory at Arizona State University, was concerned that human response to methanol was probably much higher than with animals, due to humans lacking key enzymes that assist in the detoxification of methanol in other creatures. Monte stated: *"There are no human or mammalian studies to evaluate the possible mutagenic, teratogenic, or carcinogenic effects of chronic administration of methyl alcohol."* [64]

Monte's concern about aspartame was so great that he petitioned the FDA through the courts to address these issues. Monte requested that the FDA *"...slow down on this soft drink issue long enough to answer some of the important questions. It's not fair that you are leaving the full burden of proof on the few of us who are concerned and have such limited resources. You must remember that you are the American public's last defense. Once you allow usage* [of aspartame], *there is literally nothing I or my colleagues can do to reverse the course. Aspartame will then join saccharin, the sulfiting agents, and God knows how many other questionable compounds enjoined to insult the human constitution with government approval."*[65]

Ironically, shortly after Dr Monte's impassioned plea, Arthur Hull Hayes, Jr., the Commissioner of the Food & Drug Administration, approved the use of aspartame in carbonated

---

[63] *Extraordinary Science*, Vol. 7, No.1, Jan/Feb/Mar 1995, p.39

[64] *The Guardian*, "Laboratory Animals Back from the Dead in Faulty Safety Tests", April/June 1990

[65] Ibid.

beverages. Shortly after, he left the FDA to take up a position with G D Serle's public relations company.[66] In 1993, the FDA further approved aspartame as a food ingredient in numerous process foods that would always be heated above 86ºF as part of their preparation.

Dr Joseph Mercola is no lover of aspartame. The well-known nutrition and health researcher itemises another catalogue of woes that have come to punctuate aspartame's hopeless legacy as a food additive:

"In 1991, the National Institutes of Health listed 167 symptoms and reasons to avoid the use of aspartame, but today it is a multi-million dollar business that contributes to the degeneration of the human population, as well as the deliberate suppression of overall intelligence, short-term memory[67] and the added contribution as a carcinogenic environmental co-factor.

The FDA and Centers for Disease Control continue to receive a stream of complaints from the population about aspartame. It is the only chemical warfare weapon available in mass quantities on the grocery shelf and promoted in the media. It has also been indicated that women with an intolerance for phenylalanine, one of the components of aspartame, may give birth to infants with as much as a 15% drop in intelligence level if they habitually consume products containing this dangerous substance." [68]

---

[66] Ibid.

[67] The FDA instigated hearings in 1985 on aspartame at the request of Senator Metzenbaum, when a sample case was heard, in which a woman's memory suffered almost complete collapse until she ceased taking aspartame-laced products.

[68] Mercola, Joseph, www.mercola.com; Also **Steinman, D**, *Diet for a Poisoned Planet*, University of California study, p.190

Asthma

Profile and symptoms

Wheezy exhalations and difficulty in breathing caused by the narrowing of the bronchial tubes (air-ways to the lungs). The condition is brought on variously by air pollution allergens (toxins and pollen), infections, food sensitivities, drugs such as Aspirin and non-steroidal anti-inflammatory drugs (NSAIDS), exertion (exercise), emotional outbursts, smoking, *Candida* infections, leaky gut syndrome, etc.

An acute asthma attack can be very serious, where breathing is impaired and can lead to asphyxiation through respiratory failure. The condition is most common in children under eleven years of age, among whom there is a two-to-one, male-to-female ratio which equalises by the age of thirty. Traditional treatments usually include the use of oral corticosteroids, bronchodilators and other inhalant aids.

That asthma is primarily caused by stress to a poor immune system has been established beyond doubt. The question is, what is doing the stressing and why is the immune system so poor to start with? There is evidence that the *pertussis* (whooping cough) vaccine is implicated as a primary causation in asthma (this is usually taken as part of the diphtheria, pertussis, tetanus (DPT) shot).[69]

Both types of asthma, extrinsic and intrinsic, are caused by the release of chemicals, including the neurotransmitter hormone histamine and factors known as leukotrienes. The production of excess histamine and leukotrienes is believed to be a secondary factor caused by dehydration, the reaction of a stressed and poorly performing immune system to challenging factors in the environment, and poor diet.

Hay fever, or seasonal allergic rhinitis, shares many common factors with asthma and is very prevalent today, its incidence

---

[69] **Odent, MR, Culpin, EE and T Kimmel**, "Pertussis vaccination and asthma: Is there a link?" *Journal of the American Medical Association*, 272 (1994): pp.592-3

increasing yearly. This has caused researchers to wonder what it is behind such a dramatic increase.

Our research indicates that the prevalence of asthma, hay fever and multiple chemical sensitivity today are primarily caused by a) a failure to breast-feed infants so that their immune systems form using the correct immune factors and b) the ongoing degradation of the immune system through poor diet and lifestyle.

Take action ♥

Most of the common, known causes for asthma are in fact secondary to the primary reason people develop these sensitivities in the first place, which is a poorly developed immune system then regularly challenged by environmental and dietary factors. Effective treatment of asthma involves a four-fold strategy: a) avoid asthma triggers, b) change diet to a vegan regimen (a 1985 study showed improvement in 92% of the participants)[70], c) eliminate any yeast and fungal infections[71], and d) use nutritional support to restore nutrient balance and boost immunity. This regimen must be conducted over a protracted period of time for the best results.

To the degree that the body can sort out defects in the immune system, the following regimen is recommended:

- **PREVENTION:** Avoid trigger foods, such as eggs, fish, shellfish, nuts, milk, chocolate, gluten products (wheat, barley, rye and oats), citrus and food colourings and additives
- **PREVENTION:** Avoid areas containing dust, mites, pollen, pollution, paint fumes and other causative factors
- **DIET: COMMENCE THE ANTI-*CANDIDA* DIETARY REGIMEN**, along with the recommended supplementation, ensuring a vegan approach, apart from cold caught, oily fish, i.e. salmon, mackerel, herring, etc.

---

[70] **Lindahl, O et al**, "Vegan diet regimen with reduced medication in the treatment of bronchial asthma", *MJA* 164 (1996) pp.137-40

[71] **Akiyama, K et al**, "Atopic asthma caused by C. albicans acid protease: Case reports", *Allergy*, 49 (1994) pp.778-81

- **DIET**: Take particular care to avoid the foods discussed in **Foods to avoid**, both in the **ANTI-*CANDIDA* DIETARY REGIMEN** and **THE *FOOD FOR THOUGHT* LIFESTYLE REGIMEN**
- **DIET:** Ensure additional intakes of flaxseed oil and other omega-3 essential fat food sources (see **A Guide to Nutritional Supplements**)
- **DETOXIFICATION:** Magnesium oxide bowel cleanse
- **RESTORE NUTRIENT BALANCE: COMMENCE THE BASIC SUPPLEMENT PROGRAM** (adjust for children according to body weight), ensuring:
- 'Ingenious' complex, as directed (see **A Guide to Nutritional Supplements**)
- Vitamin B6, 50 mg, twice per day
- Magnesium, 200-400 mg, three times per day
- Selenium, 200-400 mcg per day
- Vitamin B12, weekly injection
- Echinacea and astragalus, as directed
- Gingko biloba, 90 - 100 mg, three times per day
- **TIP:** Use a HEPA air filter (high efficiency particulate arresting) to assist in removing allergens from the patient's environment while recovering (these are available from heating and air-conditioning companies)
- **TIP:** Drink at least four pints (2 litres) of fresh, clean water each day
- **TIP:** Remove pets, dander, upholstery coverings and other media where allergens may collect

This regimen is *a long-term strategy* for all asthmatics, aimed at boosting immunity and allowing the body to adjust to environmental conditions gradually. Certain foods which trigger the condition should be avoided until asthma attacks appear to have diminished. Any reintroduction of trigger foods should be under the advice of your physician only after the condition has not been in evidence for a protracted period.

69

Autism

Profile

Dr Joseph Mercola reports: *"Autism is a spectrum of disorders that ranges in severity from bizarre, violent behaviour to an inability to communicate or interact socially, along with repetitive patterns of behaviour. Estimates of the prevalence of the syndrome in Britain range from 10 cases per 10,000 of the population with 'classic' autism, to 9.1 cases per 1,000 showing some signs of autistic behaviour. The National Autistic Society estimates that there are about 500,000 people with autism in Britain, 120,000 of them children. According to one recent study, there has been a tenfold increase among children between 1984 and 1994."*[72]

Autism and vaccines – the link

Much has been made in recent times of the potential for vaccines to cause autism. The world is currently experiencing a veritable autism epidemic, with one American child in 130, for instance, developing the condition.

Two main areas to consider are the problems caused by vaccine fillers, and the effects of vaccinations on the bowel and other organs.

Vaccine fillers

Vaccines can variously contain the following: .01-.025% each of formaldehyde, mercury (or substitute #6-pheno-oxyethanol, a protoplasmic poison), aluminium, paint thinner, coolant, antifreeze, dye, detergent phenols, solvent, borax, disinfectant, MSG, glycerol, sulfite & phosphate compounds, polysorbate 80/20, sorbitol, polyribosylribitol, betapropiolactone, Amphotericin B and other chemicals, plus hydrolysed gelatin, casein, dead animal tissue and blood (e.g. cow, chick embryo, monkey, sheep, pig, dog, etc.), aborted human foetus cells, mutated (more virulent) human viruses, contaminant animal viruses (e.g. SV40, which causes cancer in humans), bacteria, bacterial endotoxins and antibiotics.

---

[72] www.mercola.com

A parent might reasonably question how smart it is to inject *any* of the above into her infant, whose blood-brain barrier may not yet have fully developed. An immune system reaction may indeed be provoked by the vaccine, but perhaps not the kind for which the mother and father might be hoping.

To date, the US National Vaccine Injury Compensation Program or NVICP, established in 1986, has paid out in excess of $1 billion in injury awards to western vaccine recipients, with quite literally thousands of cases pending. This despite the fact that the former Health and Human Services Secretary Donna Shalala narrowed the definition of vaccine damage to such an extent that only immediate and severe reactions can now qualify. Seizures, disorders, brain damage, ataxia, paralysis, learning difficulties and deaths that occur many days or weeks following these vaccinations are now excluded.

Added to this, doctors have little incentive to report themselves to the government's Vaccine Adverse Event Reporting System or VAERS, prompting former director of the US Food and Drug Administration, David Kessler, to confess that *"...only 10% of vaccine injuries are ever reported."* [73] Lisa Jillani, of People Advocating Vaccine Education, has observed the growing number of children now suffering from 20/21st century behavioural disorders:

"So the injuries can even conservatively amount to tens of thousands of children, while doctors continue to diagnose and treat mysterious new illnesses and maintain the 'one in a million' adverse reaction myth taught in medical schools." [74]

Mercury – mad as a 'hatter'

Ever since hatters went mad from inhaling the vapours of the mercury-based compounds used to stiffen felt in the top hats they made, the warning sirens have always sounded with mercury. In vaccines, however, we are told mercury is safe. In the US, the Environmental Protection Agency's 'safe' level for mercury ingestion is set at .1 mcg/kg/day (that's a tenth of a microgram). Now witness the assault that comes against a child in the early period of its life,

---

[73] *Dayton Daily News*, 25th May 1993
[74] **Boykin, Sam**, *A Shot in the Dark*, 1998 www.creativeloafing.com

when its immune system is still developing and has not reached its full protective potential:

Day of Birth – hepatitis B – 12 mcg mercury (thimerosal)
30 times the safe level
At 4 Months – DPT and other shots – 50 mcg mercury
60 times the safe level
At 6 months – hepatitis B, polio – 62.5 mcg mercury
78 times the safe level
At 15 months – Further shots – another 50 mcg mercury
41 times the safe level

The Sunday Times reports: *"The number of vaccinations given to babies and children in Britain and America has increased significantly. In the United States the number given before the age of two has risen from 8 in 1980 to 22 now. In Britain in 1970, most children received diphtheria, tetanus, polio, whooping cough and BCG for tuberculosis; about half were also immunised against measles. In 1972 rubella was added; MMR in 1988, Hib (Haemophilus influenza type b), against a form of meningitis in 1992, MMR as a second dose in 1996, and meningitis C in 1999.*

The MMR first dose is given between 12 and 15 months, with diphtheria and tetanus and the second dose of MMR at three to five years. MMR does not contain thimerosal, though other child vaccines do. Thimerosal was introduced in the 1930's as a preservative and went into common use without review by America's Food and Drug Administration (FDA) because it was assumed to be safe." [75]

Thimerosal becomes organic mercury

Dr Tim O'Shea: *"Once it is in nerve tissue, thimerosal is converted irreversibly to its inorganic form. Thimerosal is a much more toxic form of mercury than one would get from eating open-sea fish; it has to do with the difficulty of clearing thimerosal from the blood.*

---

[75] *The Sunday Times*, 27th May 2001

Thimerosal is converted to ethylmercury, an organic form that has a preference for nerve cells. Without a complete blood-brain barrier, an infant's brain and spinal cord are sitting ducks. Once in the nerve cells, mercury is changed back to the inorganic form and becomes tightly bound. Mercury can then remain for years, like a time-release capsule, causing permanent degeneration and death of brain cells." [76]

Dr O'Shea also reports that the body normally clears mercury by fixing it to bile, but before six months of age, infants don't produce bile. The result: mercury cannot be excreted.

Thimerosal side-effects include:

Aphthous, stomatitis, catarrhal gingivitis, nausea, liquid stools, pain, liver disorder, injury to the cardiovascular system and haematopoietic system, deafness, ataxia, headache, paresthesia of the tongue, lips, fingers and toes, other non-specific dysfunctions, metallic taste, slight gastrointestinal disturbances, excessive flatus, diarrhoea, chorea, athetosis, tremors, convulsions, pain and numbness in the extremities, nephritis, salivation, loosening of the teeth, blue line on the gums, anxiety, mental depression, insomnia, hallucinations or central nervous system effects.

Exposure may also cause irritation of the eyes, mucous membranes and upper respiratory tract. Acute poisoning may cause gastrointestinal irritation, renal failure, fine tremors of extended hands, loss of side vision, slight loss of coordination in the eyes, speech, writing and gait, inability to stand or carry out voluntary movements, occasional muscle atrophy and flexure contractures, generalized myoclonic movements, difficulty under-standing ordinary speech, irritability and bad temper progressing to mania, stupor, coma, mental retardation in children, skin irritation, blisters or dermatitis. Exposure may be fatal. [77]

Formaldehyde

Another ingredient commonly found in vaccines is the preservative formaldehyde. Here are the published side-effects:

Eye; nasal; throat and pulmonary irritation; acidosis; acute sense of smell; alters tissue proteins; anemia; antibodies formation; apathy;

---

[76] www.thedoctorwithin.com

[77] www.mercola.com, search under 'autism'

blindness; blood in urine; blurred vision; body aches; bronchial spasms; bronchitis; burns nasal and throat; cardiac impairment; palpitations and arrhythmias; central nervous system depression; changes in higher cognitive functions; chemical sensitivity; chest pains and tightness; chronic vaginitis; colds; coma; conjunctivitis; constipation; convulsions; corneal erosion; cough; death; destruction of red blood cells; depression; dermatitis; diarrhoea; difficulty concentrating; disorientation; dizziness; ear aches; eczema; emotional upsets; ethmoid polyps; fatigue; fecula bleeding; foetal asphyxiation (and they say they don't know what could cause SIDS?)

Flu-like or cold like illness; frequent urination with pain; gastritis; gastrointestinal inflammation; headaches; haemolytic anaemia; hacmolytic haematuria; hoarseness; hyperactive airway disease; hyperactivity; hypomenstrual syndrome; immune system sensitiser; impaired (short) attention span; impaired capacity to attain attention; inability or difficulty swallowing; inability to recall words and names; inconsistent IQ profiles; inflammatory diseases of the reproductive organs; intestinal pain; intrinsic asthma; irritability; jaundice; joint pain; aches and swelling; kidney pain; laryngeal spasm; loss of memory; loss of sense of smell; loss of taste; malaise; menstrual and testicular pain; menstrual irregularities; metallic taste; muscle spasms and cramps; nasal congestions; crusting and mucosae inflammation; nausea; nosebleeds; numbness and tingling of the forearms and finger tips; pale, clammy skin; partial laryngeal paralysis; pneumonia; post nasal drip; pulmonary edema; reduced body temperature; retarded speech pattern; ringing or tingling in the ear; schizophrenic-type symptoms; sensitivity to sound; shock; short term memory loss; shortness of breath; skin lesions; sneezing; sore throat; spacey feeling; speaking difficulty; sterility; swollen glands; tearing; thirst; tracheitis; tracheobronchitis; vertigo; vomiting blood; vomiting; wheezing.

If your child is autistic and was vaccinated, these two vaccine ingredients alone cause exactly the type of damage from which your child is suffering

Autism – the nutritional approach

That autistic children respond well to megavitamin therapy has been known for decades. Nevertheless, many drug treatments given to autistic children and adults revolve around keeping them quiet and out of trouble. Dr Catherine Spears, a paediatric neurologist, and Dr Allan Cott of New York found treatment with B6 and zinc to be highly affective. Spears reported that *all* her autistic patients responded to the treatments, which included a change of dietary regimen. Parents, teachers and professionals all noted differences and improvements in behaviour and speech. Dr Henry Turkel reports:

"Wendy was 3 years old when her parents realised she was not developing normally. At 48 months, her mental age was 21 months. She achieved an IQ of 44 and was classified as retarded. When 4 years old, then testing with an IQ of 49, she began megavitamin therapy. Her attention span went from 10 to 15 seconds to ten minutes. Within three months, she began to speak in complete sentences. After six months of treatment, her IQ score had jumped to 72. By the age of 8, her IQ score was 85, classifying her as no longer retarded, with low-average ability – a 40 point shift in four years."[78]

B6, zinc and magnesium

Dr Bernard Rimland took these successes and ran his own study. His sixteen patients showed marked improvements with B6, magnesium and vitamin C supplementation. Twelve demonstrated regressions when the nutritional elements were replaced with placebos. Supplementing with magnesium at half the levels of B6 proved even more effective. After a battle, his findings were published in the *American Journal of Psychiatry*.[79] Following Rimland's success, five further studies were conducted, all showing positive results with the zinc, magnesium and B6 combination.

In cases where retardation is accompanied with facial swelling, frequent colds and middle ear infections, pyroluria should be suspected. Tissue swells with deficiencies in zinc and B6, preventing the auditory tubes from draining adequately into the throat. Tests for low Immunoglobulin (IgA) will also indicate susceptibility to infection.

---

[78] **Turkel, H et al**, "Intellectual improvement of a retarded patient treated with the 'U' series", *J. Orthomo. Psychiatr.*, 13(4), pp.272-276
[79] **Rimland, B et al**, "The effect of high doses of Vitamin B6 on autistic children: a double-blind, crossover study", *Am. J. Psychiatr.* 135, 1978, pp.472-475

'Leaky gut'

Often children appear to develop normally through to age 3 and then, after repeated ear infections, which are treated with antibiotics, seem to cease normal development. Bernard Rimland found that many of the children exhibiting these problems may have leaky gut syndrome, where food proteins have entered the bloodstream through a permeable intestinal wall as a result of damage to the intestinal lining. Treatment with antibiotics, which can further damage the gut, can allow more food proteins to enter the bloodstream, thus creating more allergic reactions. Rimland investigated the link between allergies and autism by testing the effects of removing wheat, milk or sugar from the diets of hundreds of autistic children. About 50% improved from the removal of any one of these.[80] Proteins, such as gluten and casein, can be obnoxious to an early, developing immune system in a child, which can develop antibodies against the invading 'toxins'. These immune system components can cause any of several burgeoning disorders, such as MS, arthritis and type-1 diabetes (see appropriate sections).

Cow's milk – here we go again

Dr Joseph Mercola reports: *"Findings from two animal studies indicate autism and schizophrenia may be linked to a person's inability properly to break down a protein found in cow's milk. The digestive problem might actually lead to the disorders' symptoms, whose basis has long been debated. This research was done by a physiologist at the University of Florida, Dr. J Robert Cade.*

When not broken down, the milk protein produces exorphins, morphine-like compounds that are then taken up by areas of the brain known to be involved in autism and schizophrenia, where they cause cells to dysfunction. The animal findings suggest an intestinal flaw, such as a malfunctioning enzyme, is to blame. Preliminary findings from that study - which showed 95 percent of 81 autistic and schizophrenic children studied had 100 times the normal levels of the milk protein in their blood and urine - have been presented at two international meetings in the past year but have not yet been published.

---

[80] **Rimland, B, et al**, "Comparative effects of treatment on child behaviour", *Inst. For Child Behaviour Research*, Pub 34b, January 1988

The researchers also noted that all milk products must be excluded from the diet. This includes such things as ice cream, yogurt and whey. Even natural flavourings in food must be avoided unless the processor can guarantee beyond a shadow of a doubt that caseinate, the main protein in milk, is not included. We now have proof positive that these proteins are getting into the blood and proof positive they're getting into areas of the brain involved with the symptoms of autism and schizophrenia." [81]

Other problems

Reuters reported on the 13th June 2001: *"Dr. Ted Kniker has been investigating the theory that poorly degraded food proteins leak from the gut into the blood, presenting a drug-like effect that changes brain activity. In the first part of his study, Kniker, of the San Antonio Autistic Treatment Center in Texas, found that 5 out of 28 children and adults with autism showed improvements in their symptoms after elimination of dairy products and wheat glutens from their diets.*

In the second part of the study, the researchers eliminated several other foods, including buckwheat, soy products, tomato, pork and grapes from the patients' diets. Symptoms changed dramatically in 39.3% of patients during the second phase of the 3-month intervention period. Eight out of 28 patients showed clear improvements, as measured by a variety of quantitative scoring methods, including the Autistic Treatment Evaluation Checklist.

Kniker argues that autism is not usually a defect in brain development, but is more likely to be a brain dysfunction that is secondary to extraneous factors, such as dietary factors, immune dysfunctions, infections or toxins."[82]

Take action♥

Those parents wishing to seek alternative help for their children with autism, a great place to start is the Institute of Optimum Nutrition, a British organisation based in south-west London (Tel:

---

[81] www.mercola.com
[82] *Reuters*, 13th June 2001

+44 (0)208 877 9993). ION will be able to advise you or your co-operative doctor on a megavitamin regimen that will maximise nutritional supplementation while at the same time helping to remove heavy metals and restore health to your child. There is great news for those suffering from this condition. An autistic patient may also benefit from the following:

- **DIET: COMMENCE THE *FOOD FOR THOUGHT* DIETARY REGIMEN**
- **RESTORE NUTRIENT BALANCE: THE BASIC SUPPLEMENT PROGRAM**, increasing zinc, B6 and magnesium intakes, as directed
- **DETOXIFICATION:** Magnesium oxide bowel cleanse
- **TIP:** Have an intradermal allergy test and restrict sensitive food items, such as wheat, dairy, egg whites, etc. as appropriate
- **TIP:** Discuss gradual removal of mercury amalgam fillings with a co-operative dentist[83]
- **TIP:** Measures combating autism, especially vaccine-induced autism, must be applied patiently, *consistently*, over the long-term

Further Resources
Wake up to Health in the 21st Century by Steven Ransom
Health Wars by Phillip Day
The Mind Game by Phillip Day
Toxic Bite by Bill Kellner-Read

---

[83] **Kellner-Read, Bill**, *Toxic Bite*, Credence Publications, 2002

Cancer

Profile

Cancer, the second leading killer in most western industrialised nations, is a disease which has crept from an incidence rate of around 1 in 500 in 1900 to between 1 in 2 to 3 today. Over 625,000 people are expected to die from cancer in America in 2003, and yet, in spite of supposedly the brightest and the best walking the corridors of our leading cancer research institutions, armed with the latest technology and limitless budgets, the incidence rates for cancer continue to rise.

Breast cancer serves as a poignant yardstick. This type of malignancy is now the leading cause of death in women between the ages of 35 and 54. In 1971, a woman's lifetime risk of contracting breast cancer was 1 in 14. Today it is 1 in 8.[84] *Rachel's Environment and Health Weekly*, No. 571 reports:

"More American women have died of breast cancer in the past two decades than all the Americans killed in World War 1, World War 2, the Korean War and Vietnam War combined."

Perhaps the most amazing thing is, most physicians in the world today have absolutely no idea what cancer is, or even how it is contracted. Some believe cancer is age-related. Others believe the cause is parasites. Others yet examine the environmental causal link.

Definition

Cancer can be described as a healing process that has not terminated upon completion of its task. Damage occurs to the body via a number of modalities (e.g. physical blows, viruses, bacteria/fungal/yeast proliferation, radiation, toxins, hormonal imbalances, etc.), and the body attempts to heal the damage. If the healing process replicates damaged cells and does not terminate properly due to malnutrition and certain other causations, the end

---

[84] **Epstein, Samuel S & David Steinman**, *The Breast Cancer Prevention Program*, Macmillan, USA, 1997 ISBN 0025361929

result will be an ongoing proliferation of mutated healing trophoblastic material - a tumour.

The current of injury

Dr Arthur Guyton's *Textbook of Medical Physiology* talks about the healing process in the context of what happens after a heart attack. He writes:

"Many different cardiac abnormalities, especially those that damage the heart muscle itself, often cause part of the heart to remain partially or totally depolarised all the time. When this occurs, current flows between the pathologically depolarised and the normally polarised areas. This is called the current of injury. Note especially that the injured part of the heart is negative, because it is the part that is depolarised while the remainder is positive." [85]

Canadian cancer researcher Ron Gdanski comments also on the current of injury: *"...A current of injury is used to polarise the depolarised tissue. The injured part is negative. The current of injury flows from the healthy or 'polarised' to the injured or negative or depolarised area. The current of injury is actually an increased region of measurable ionic activity that exists over the injury, but does not flow elsewhere. The current of injury stays on until the injury is repaired."* [86]

The current of injury has been studied extensively and has been manipulated to grow tissue, as Dr Robert Becker describes in his *The Body Electric*. At the heart of Gdanski's research is the revelation that *"...injury disrupts the ionic field of cell-wall membranes, turns on the current of injury, and repair of injury turns it off unless an infection* [or ongoing damage to the body] *disrupts the healing process."* [87]

Years before, Professor John Beard and US biochemist Ernst T Krebs Jr. wrote about how this healing process organises the

---

[85] **Guyton, Arthur**, *Text Book of Medical Physiology*, W B Saunders Co.
[86] **Gdanski, Ron**, *Cancer: Cause, Cure and Cover-up*, Nadex Publishing, Canada: 2000
[87] Ibid. p.171

regeneration of ordered tissue in the same way that cells replicate as a child grows. They discovered the role embryonic stem cells play in the formation of trophoblastic cells which are employed by the body in pregnancy. But it is in their additional role as 'healers' that the importance and potential cancer hazards of stem cells become known. These fibroblasts or neoblasts, as they are known, are primarily employed to repair trauma sites. These cells can transform themselves into any body-part: bone material, blood, tissue or hair depending on the particular morphogenetic stimulus they receive.

When our bodies are damaged in any way, estrogen stimulates the production of these cells for healing the troubled area in the same way they form trophoblast for pregnancy. Usually the cessation of the current of injury terminates this healing process once it is complete. Pancreatic enzymes assist in the stripping down of the protective, cellular coating of healing cells, allowing the immune system, together with other nutrients, such as vitamin B17, to kill the cells. In the event that this process does not terminate satisfactorily, cancer tumours are the result of the ongoing 'rogue' healing process. Notice that the location of resultant cancer or trophoblastic mass is specific to the original area of damage. This too becomes important as we proceed.

For many years, cancer tumours were viewed by specialists as being 'foreign' to the body. In fact, the opposite can be said to be true, according to Beard and Krebs. They were curious as to why cancer existed at all if the immune system was there to repel any foreign invasion. They concluded that the immune system must not be viewing cancer as a foreign threat if the cancer commenced its existence as a healing process natural and familiar to the body.

So here we have three parts to the picture that have to be in place for cancer to initiate:

- Cancer commences with an injury, howsoever caused
- Cancer is the result of normal cellular healing processes that continue in a rogue process due to the fact that the cells being replicated are damaged and do not knit together properly. Thus the repaired tissue is not polarised and so the current of injury does not 'switch off'

- Due to our diets, which generally contain processed foods, cooked to destruction, lacking essential vitamins, minerals, enzymes and other nutritional co-factors, our immune system is depressed and ineffectual at halting this cellular rogue healing

How parasites cause cancer

Aside from toxins, malnutrition and other more obvious causes for cancer, one key area that is bound up with the cancer enigma is that of parasites.

An impressive body of scientific literature has built steadily over the years demonstrating the damage fungi and yeasts, such as *Candida albicans*, can wreak in the body. If we return to examine Professor John Beard's assertion that cancer is a healing process that has not terminated upon completion of its task, then the case against rogue critters in the body is hugely compelling.

Ron Gdanski tells us: *"Cancers initiate in membrane walls of storage vessels and ducts, such as the lungs, colon, breast, prostate, etc. due to injury. If cells that multiply to repair the injury are infected with bacteria or fungi, the microbes within the cell produce cell-wall proteins and enzymes that mutate the new cell walls. These mutated cells are rejected like a skin graft that does not take. For each normal cell that multiplies, we end up with two cancer cells and one less normal cell. That's how cancer consumes tissue.*

Cancer is the continuous multiplication, microbial mutation, and bodily rejection of cells produced normally by the body to repair an injury." [88]

Gdanski is a passionate and extremely articulate advocate of the school of thought that implicates the rabid consumption of sugars and refined, high-glycaemic carbohydrate foods that unbalance the crucial internal environment of our bodies causing usually beneficial microbes, such as *Candida*, to begin their monstrous breakouts. All of my research corroborates the startling assertion that processed sugar and high-glycaemic foods that break down into glucose in the

---

[88] Gdanski, Ron, op. cit.

body are one of the primary causes. How they do this is another astonishing fact in itself.

Yeasts like *Candida* are single-cell fungi which multiply prolifically when fed organically bound carbon, one essential element that characterises all dead and living matter. Fungi and yeasts are like the hyenas of the veld. They are scavengers. Abundant carbon compounds like sugars are their favourite. The more sugary foods we eat, the more these life-forms feast within us. The symptoms vary from the embarrassing to the annoying to the downright fatal:

Symptoms of parasitic infection

Poor immune function, lack of sex drive, candidiasis, toe-nail fungus, chronic bloating and gas, rectal itching, mouth sores (white patches on the tongue or inside the cheeks), tingling, sexually transmitted diseases (STDs), numbness or burning sensations, chronic fatigue (ME), allergies, food sensitivities, chemical sensitivities, thrush, chronic vaginal yeast infections and discharges (usually thick, white), rashes and itching around male genitalia, bladder infections, intestinal cramps, cravings for sugar-rich foods and sweets, cravings for foods rich in yeast and carbohydrates.

The connection between parasites and cancer

Yeasts are well known to ferment sugar into alcohol in the absence of oxygen. Breweries depend on it! If we fail to exercise or eat oxygen-rich, organic fruits and vegetables, we are inviting the dangerous and unwelcome proliferation of parasites like *Candida* by providing them with an oxygen-poor, fermentation-rich breeding ground in which to thrive. *The Columbia Encyclopaedia* states:

"Their bodies [fungi] consist of slender, cottony filaments called hyphae; a mass of hyphae is called a mycelium. The mycelium carries on all the processes necessary for the life of the organism, including in most species, that of sexual reproduction."

Candida and other trouble-makers have a powerful ability to hurt our bodies, their thread-like mycelia (roots) penetrating and invading the walls of human cells to take root and feed. They discharge their mycotoxin waste products into the cells they infect, which in turn switches on the current of injury that characterises the healing process. If this multiplication of infected cells proceeds in the right oxygen-poor environment, we get rejected, mutated cells which do not knit together correctly, which in turn means the current of injury does not shut down satisfactorily. These rogue (cancer) cells have wall membranes which contain chitin, a protein found abundantly in the skins of fungi, such as mushrooms. This on-going rogue healing process is of course fuelled by the sugary diet of the patient which, in a continuing acidic, anaerobic environment, produces alcohol waste products through fermentation, which in turn fuels the cancer fermentation process further.

Here we have the dynamic connection between parasites/ yeasts/fungi and cancer. Blood clots, stagnant lymph fluids, injuries that won't heal and benign tumours are all prime spots where blood sugars collect and become trapped to provide fodder for opportunistic critters. As they thrive and multiply, fuelled by sugary diets, they damage a whole spread of cells by penetrating their cells walls with their root-like mycelia, depositing their mycotoxins. This in turn triggers the current of injury and the multiplication of stem cells, which replicate these infected cells into tumours, and so on. Notice that because the rogue cells are rejected by the body, the current of injury doesn't switch off because the healing isn't complete, since the new cells are not properly polarised. The result is an on-going proliferation of these cancerous cells.

As these fungi and yeasts thrive, along with the tumours they provoke, they secrete enzymes of their own to depress the immune system of the host and rob surrounding cells of their oxygen, thus expanding the ideal fermentation environment, enabling them to invade and corrupt more cells. Gdanski and others confirm that a single cell mutation alone won't trigger cancer: *"A colony of fermenting cells must be formed before a tumour can develop. A quantity of trapped blood in a storage vessel or duct feeds fungi and bacteria, and provides the initial toxins that alter the environment and metabolism of adjacent cells allowing cancer to start."*

Gdanski further believes that cancer orthodoxy's dogged assertions that defective genes are the cause of cancer are woefully wide of the mark, since they fail to explain:

- *Why the natural process for repair of damaged skin, or the natural growth process itself, starts replication that ends up as cancer*
- *Why the essential difference between normal cells and cancer cells is how well or poorly they knit together to form new membranes*
- *Why we do not have cancer of the heart or arteries*
- *Why up to 96% of cancers occur in cells adjacent to storage vessels and ducts, such as lung, breast, colon and prostate*
- *Why cancer tumours develop in fast-growing youngsters*
- *How spontaneous remissions often occur with a change in lifestyle*
- *Why tumour membrane tissue (chitin) resembles the material that forms the outer membrane of mushrooms (a fungus)*[89]

The scientific literature is tantalisingly replete with information on the sugar-yeast-cancer connection. In my book *Health Wars*, we have an entire chapter dedicated to the dozens of serious health problems excess sugars cause in the body, all studied and annotated by medical science. Interestingly, the few drugs that have worked well with cancer all have one key fact in common: they are anti-fungals and anti-mycotoxic. Nobel laureate Otto Warburg's assertion that cancer only thrives in an environment that has had at least a 35% oxygen reduction also corroborates the precise environment parasites require to thrive. Provocative also is the fact that ALL cancer patients have a parasite problem.

B17 metabolic therapy
The most effective anti-cancer strategy

During the past sixty years, doctors around the world have worked tirelessly, and often under tremendous intimidation from their own medical establishment, to build a nutritional arsenal to

---

[89] Ibid.

both prevent and cure cancer. During my years of research into cancer, I have seen various forms of the following regimen applied by the most successful cancer physicians. The conviction underpinning vitamin B17 metabolic therapy states that:

- Conventional drug and radiation treatments are not only NOT extending life in the major, epithelial cancers, they often kill the patient after wrecking the immune system
- First, the doctor must stop the damage being done to the patient, which has resulted in the cancer (smoking, chemicals, sugar-rich foods, drugs, chemo, etc.)
- Second, the bowel system and associated organs must be cleansed in order to expel toxins and debris efficiently. The patient must be fed a special high-fibre, raw diet, along with certain herbs, aimed at killing yeast, fungi and harmful bacteria, while promoting probiotics (friendlies). This diet must also alkalise the patient's internal environment, thus rendering it hostile to fermentation processes upon which cancer depends to thrive
- Third, the patient is simultaneously fed superfoods and supplements that promote high enzyme activity in the body to chew off the protein coating of trophoblastic (cancer) cells
- Fourth, key nutrients are introduced into the body, such as vitamins B17, C complex and A-emulsion which have a known and proven anti-tumoural, anti-fungal, anti-mycotoxic effect.

Vitamin B17 – nature's miracle food

One of the most studied nutrients of recent times, vitamin B17 is covered extensively in my book, *Cancer: Why We're Still Dying to Know the Truth* as well as *B17 Metabolic Therapy – a technical manual.* This nutrient is contained in foods known as nitrilosides, variously comprising the seeds of the common fruits (excluding European citrus), pasture foods, and many vegetables and pulses. However, it is within the seeds of the humble apricot that the highest concentrations of this nutrient have thus far been found, bound together with enzymes and minerals in their whole-food forms.

Apricot kernels are a favourite of a number of agrarian peoples, such as the Hunzas, Abkhasians and Karakorum, who have no record of cancer in their isolated state. Other peoples around the world consume different sources of vitamin B17 and have similar records of success. According to scientists who have studied and published on the nutrient, B17 must work in conjunction with enzymes, vitamins C, A & E to achieve a targeted anti-cancer mission in the body. It cannot, and does not work alone.

Vitamin B17 is a stable, chemically inert and non-toxic molecule when taken as food or as a refined pharmaceutical in appropriate quantities (Laetrile/amygdalin). However scientists discovered the compound reacts to the enzyme beta-glucosidase, located in huge quantities at the site of cancerous tumours, but not to any degree anywhere else in the body. In this reaction, beta-glucosidase manufactures two potent poisons at the cancer cell site: hydrogen cyanide and benzaldehyde (an analgesic/painkiller), stabilised with two molecules of glucose. These two poisons, produced in minute quantities at the cancer cell site, combine synergistically to produce a super-poison many times more deadly than either substance in isolation. The cancer cell meets its chemical death at the hands of vitamin B17's selective toxicity.

Scientists studying B17 were aware that indigenous peoples consuming large quantities of nitrilosidic foods were not experiencing any harmful side-effects from this reaction. On the contrary, their lives were characterised by abundant good health and great longevity. Later they found that healthy tissue broke down excess levels of B17 into two nutritious by-products, one of which, sodium thiocyanate, reacts with the precursor hydroxycobalamin in the liver to form the other well known nutrient with the cyanide radical: vitamin B12 (cyanocobalamin).

Take action ♥
So let's put it all together and see what we have. Now follows a more expanded bullet-point breakdown of what B17 metabolic therapy is, and the various components doctors use to achieve specific goals within your body.

Preventing cancer

1. **DIET: COMMENCE THE *FOOD FOR THOUGHT* DIETARY REGIMEN**
2. **DIET:** Ensure the majority of your food is whole, organic, high fibre and eaten raw. Remove grains where possible from the diet
3. **DIET:** Small meals, consumed often
4. **DIET:** Reduce meat and eliminate dairy intake
5. **DIET:** Cut out ingestion of sucrose and refined, high-glycaemic carbohydrate foods
6. **DIET:** Drink 4 pints/2 litres of clean, fresh water each day
7. **DIET:** Balance any hormonal irregularities – cut out unfermented soy products (soy milk, soy 'meats', etc.)
8. **DETOXIFICATION:** Remove all toxins and damage triggers from your environment and lifestyle (harmful personal and household products, chemicals, smoking, drugs, SUGAR)
9. **DETOXIFICATION:** Detoxify your body and kill fungi, yeasts and parasites
10. **RESTORING NUTRIENT BALANCE: COMMENCE THE BASIC SUPPLEMENT PROGRAM**
11. **RESTORING NUTRIENT BALANCE:** Nutritional supplementation, including minerals, vitamins, including C complex, B-groups, including B17 (usually taken as apricot kernels), essential fats (the correct omega 3:6 ratio)
12. **PREVENTION:** Avoid, where possible, drugs, radiation scans and intrusive 'diagnostic' testing
13. **PREVENTION:** Regular exercise and rest
14. **PREVENTION:** Be happy and stress-free

Combating cancer – B17 metabolic therapy

1. **SUPERVISION:** Seek a qualified health practitioner who uses the nutritional approach to cancer
2. **DIET: COMMENCE THE ANTI-*CANDIDA* DIETARY REGIMEN** and alkalise your body's internal environment. Cancer thrives on an anacrobic environment which lacks oxygen and becomes a haven for fermentation and the

proliferation of bacteria, fungi and yeasts. Alkali solutions prevent these problems because they attract large amounts of oxygen

3. **DIET:** The main part of your diet will be fresh, organic vegetables, pulses, legumes, nuts and seeds eaten raw. A little broiled fish is OK

4. **DIET:** Small meals, consumed five to six times a day to even out blood sugar

5. **DIET:** Drink at least four pints of clean, still mineral water each day (not out of plastic bottles and avoid distilled water). Avoid all alcoholic drinks, including beer (which contains sugar, yeast, grains and alcohol)

6. **DETOXIFICATION:** Eliminate ALL processed foods, meats, dairy products, sugar, grains, etc. These are often contaminated with chemicals and fungi

7. **DETOXIFICATION:** Absolutely cut out sucrose, aspartame, saccharin and high-glycaemic carbohydrate foods (foods that break down rapidly into glucose, such as bread, pastas, potatoes, rice, bakery products). Also cut out high-glycaemic fruits such as grapes, raspberries, strawberries, mangoes, etc. Apples and pears in moderation (including their seeds) are OK

8. **DETOXIFICATION:** Remove all toxic personal care and household products and damage triggers from your environment and lifestyle. Don't smoke and avoid second-hand smoke

9. **DETOXIFICATION:** Conduct a two-week bowel cleanse with magnesium oxide. Cancer patients should also consider colon hydrotherapy afterwards for extra internal cleanliness

10. **ANTI-PARASITE:** Take fresh sticks of cinnamon (not the processed supermarket dust), and grind them down in a coffee grinder. Take a teaspoon of this ground cinnamon powder, mixed in a glass of warm water, two/three times a day

11. **ANTI-PARASITE:** Take wormwood capsules, one four times a day

12. **ANTI-PARASITE:** Enteric-coated capsules of the following oils are all effective antifungals: oregano, thyme, peppermint, rosemary, garlic

13. **ANTI-PARASITE:** Colloidal silver, as directed

14. **ANTI-PARASITE:** Brew Essiac tea properly (see **A Guide to Nutritional Supplements**) and drink 2oz or more of it 4 times a day

15. **ANTI-PARASITE:** Take a parasite purge formula (this should contain items such as black walnut, clove, ginger root, anise seed, pau d'arco, peppermint and fennel)

16. **ANTI-PARASITE:** L-arginine (as directed) to assist in the removal of ammonia waste products

17. **ANTI-PARASITE:** Take 3-5 grams of water soluble fibre such as psyllium husks or guar gum to help flush out the bowel as the killing proceeds apace. **THE ANTI-*CANDIDA* DIETARY REGIMEN** will also provide you with haystacks full of bowel-scraping fibre to help broom your innards clean

18. **ANTI-CANCER:** Take an enzyme supplement away from food. This should contain, but not be limited to, bromelain (from pineapples), papain (papayas), thymus, trypsin, chymotrypsin, lipase, amylase, etc.

19. **ANTI-CANCER:** Apricot kernels, 7 g per day, spread throughout the day, for the first few days, increasing as directed to a maximum of 28 g per day (ideal for a 200 lb male, or 140 lb female). Those with low bodyweight, (including children and pets), should reduce intakes accordingly (see **A Guide to Nutritional Supplements**)

20. **ANTI-CANCER:** 5-10 g vitamin C complex (ascorbates plus bioflavonoids) per day. 5 grams amounts to approximately one heaped teaspoon of C complex powder. Take one teaspoon in a bland juice, such as pear, every morning and another at night

21. **COMMENCE THE BASIC SUPPLEMENT PROGRAM,** ensuring:

22. Selenium, 200 mcg per day

23. A priobiotic supplement to install beneficial flora

24. **BOOSTING IMMUNITY:** Astragalus and echinacea for the immune system, as directed

25. **PREVENTION:** Balance any hormonal irregularities with natural progesterone cream – cut out unfermented soy products (soy 'milk', soy 'meat', etc.)

26. **PREVENTION:** Indulge in regular and vigorous exercise (unless health problems prevent this) to exercise and pump

the lymphatic system, rid the body of waste products and draw oxygen into the body

27. **PREVENTION:** Avoid behavioural and lifestyle problems that promote stress
28. **PREVENTION:** Get plenty of regular rest
29. **PREVENTION:** Avoid radiation scans and intrusive 'diagnostic' testing
30. **PREVENTION:** The patient may consider absolutely avoiding conventional radiation, chemotherapy and other toxic treatments unless life-threatening tumours require shrinking in a hurry
31. **TIP:** Consider surgery only if tumours are life-threatening
32. **TIP:** Find out as much as you can about cancer. Confront it, don't hide from it
33. **TIP:** Use spiritual contemplation and prayer to focus your mind into taking action consistently
34. **TIP:** Never give up, no matter how badly off you think you are. Go for it, one day at a time. Remember, *"The secret of a long life is to keep breathing."*

Herxheimer's reaction

During the detoxification and parasite-killing process, the body may become clogged with catabolic debris, swords, shields, ammunition, dead beasties and their resultant mycotoxins, including ammonia. You may feel ill as your symptoms apparently worsen. This is known as Herxheimer's reaction, after the venerable German dermatologist of the same name. It is temporary and will be experienced in proportion to the vehemence with which you apply your attack strategies. Symptoms may be alleviated by commencing the anti-*Candida* diet a full two weeks prior to starting on the anti-fungal/yeast supplements.

Maintenance – The open road ahead

Once clear of cancer, avoid the minefields to prevent re-occurrence of illness. THIS IS VITAL. No going back to your wicked old ways. Remember: what you eat determines the condition of your body's immune system, and poor immunity is written on the gravestone of many a promising lad and lass. Solving malnutrition, dehydration and fungal/parasite problems in the body can lead to tremendous health benefits, not to mention burying many of the other vexing diseases which are afflicting us.

Do the right thing by your body.

Further resources:
Cancer: Why We're Still... by Phillip Day
Health Wars by Phillip Day
Great News on Cancer... by Steven Ransom
B17 Metabolic Therapy, a technical manual compiled by Phillip Day

Candidiasis
Candida albicans, yeasts, fungi, parasites, bacteria, etc.

Profiles

Candida albicans
Little critters are a fact of life with all organic life-forms. The human body is no exception. Our bowel, for instance, plays host to over three pounds' weight of up to 400 species of bacteria and other organisms that help break down food for nutrient absorption and create the necessary waste products to be eliminated from the body. These micro-organisms, in a properly healthy body, exist in harmony with one another inside the host human. It's when we change our internal environment through diet and lifestyle choices that serious problems start.

Candida albicans, a usually benign and beneficial yeast, is one of the main trouble-makers. When fed a constant diet of its favourite totty, glucose, and housed in its ideal environment of acidic, oxygen-repelling, fermentation-rich tissues and ductal structures, it multiplies prolifically and feeds and grows, damaging healthy cells and producing toxins that compromise the body's own immune defences.

Parasites
All people, especially those with cancer, play host to one form of parasite or another. Parasites are life-forms that are uninvited lodgers in our acidic bodies who do not pay rent. They can range from tiny amoebae detectable only with a microscope to tapeworms many feet in length.

We inadvertently pick up parasites through our day-to-day activities and especially through eating undercooked or contaminated food. Try an experiment and put some cat food out in an isolated part of your yard for a few sunny days and then go back and examine it (don't let any pets interfere and keep away from grass and earth). You will invariably find it crawling with infestation.

Blood flukes can enter our systems through infected drinking water and take up residence in the bladder, intestines, liver, lungs, rectum and spleen, laying their eggs and breeding in humans for up to 20 years. Trichina worm larvae found in undercooked pork migrate from the intestines through the blood and lymphatic system, eventually lodging in muscles and ducts. Threadworm larvae enter skin from the soil and pass through the bloodstream to the lungs, sometimes causing pneumonia.

Eliminating parasites is effectively a three-phase program. Killing them, flushing them out and then supplementing our relieved bodies with healthy nutrients to maintain optimum health.

Fungi and yeasts

Fungi and yeasts also inhabit our bodies. Canadian researcher Ron Gdanski describes them to us: *"There are about 500,000 fungal species on Earth. Biologically, they are closely related to both the plant and animal kingdoms…. Fungi are not plants because they lack the vascular tissues (phloem and xylem) that form true roots, stems and leaves of higher plants. Fungi also lack chlorophyll for photosynthesis and must therefore live as parasites. Their function on Earth is to break down dead and dying matter for renewal.* ***Fungi also attack living tissue and survive by producing toxins and enzymes to defeat the host's immune system."* [90]

Yeasts like *Candida* are single-cell fungi, which multiply prolifically when fed organically bound carbon, one essential element that characterises all dead and living matter. Fungi and yeasts are like the hyenas of the veld. They are scavengers. Abundant carbon compounds like sugars are their favourite. The more sugary foods we eat, the more these life-forms feast within us. Yeasts are well known to ferment sugar into alcohol in the absence of oxygen. Breweries depend on it! If we fail to exercise or eat oxygen-rich, organic fruits and vegetables, we are inviting the dangerous and unwelcome proliferation of fungi – by providing an oxygen-poor, fermentation-rich breeding ground in which they can boom. We literally become our own brewery to the delight of our squiggly little lodgers deep inside. *The Columbia Encyclopaedia* states:

[90] Gdanski, Ron, op. cit. p.29

"Their bodies [fungi] consist of slender, cottony filaments called hyphae; a mass of hyphae is called a mycelium. The mycelium carries on all the processes necessary for the life of the organism, including in most species, that of sexual reproduction."

The connection between parasites and cancer

Cancer is a healing process that has not terminated upon completion of its task.[91] *Candida* and other trouble-makers have a powerful ability to hurt our bodies, their thread-like mycelia penetrating and invading the walls of human cells to take root and feed. This damage initiates a healing process of these infected cells which can proceed uncontrolled into a cancer tumour. This cancer is fuelled further by the sugary diet of the patient which, in an acidic, anaerobic environment, produces alcohol waste products through fermentation, which in turn fuels the cancer further.

As fungi and yeasts, and their progeny – tumours – thrive, they secrete enzymes of their own to depress the immune system of the cells around them and rob them of their oxygen, thus maintaining their ideal fermentation environment, enabling them to invade and corrupt more cells.

Here we have the dynamic connection between parasites/yeasts/ fungi and cancer. In our section on cancer in this book, you will learn how cancer occurs commonly in areas of the body hosting tubes, ducts and storage areas where blood sugars can become trapped and bereft of oxygen, for this is where the critters can feed most gluttonously. Blood clots, stagnant lymph fluids, injuries that won't heal and benign tumours are also prime spots where blood sugars collect and provide fodder for opportunistic parasites. These then thrive and damage cells, which trigger the healing process, which replicates these mutated cells into tumours, etc.

Killing overgrowths of *Candida* and other parasites is not the only task necessary for a full and complete remission from diseases like cancer, heart complaints, multiple sclerosis and AIDS, as this

---

[91] Day, Phillip, *Cancer: Why We're Still Dying to Know the Truth*, op. cit.

95

book demonstrates. A reorganisation of your body into a well nourished, oxygen-rich, active and toxin-free environment is essential to ensure that you cut off the food supply to these insidious and selfish beasties, and boost immune function and cleansing to restore your body to its rightful health.

Candidiasis

Trouble caused by *Candida* is known as 'candidiasis' or 'the yeast syndrome'. The problems parasites, fungi and yeasts cause in the body are only now being understood and appreciated. Before, most doctors would not suspect this type of problem unless presented with the obvious symptoms of thrush, jock itch, athlete's foot or toenail fungal infections. But, like a leviathan, fungal problems have risen from obscurity within our consciousness to become a major health hazard today. What's caused it? Excess antibiotic intake and those sugary, yeasty, alcoholic lifestyles.

Symptoms of parasitic infection

Poor immune function, lack of sex drive, toe-nail fungus, chronic bloating and gas, rectal itching, mouth sores (white patches on the tongue or inside the cheeks), tingling, sexually transmitted diseases (STDs), numbness or burning sensations, chronic fatigue (ME), allergies, food sensitivities, chemical sensitivities, thrush, chronic vaginal yeast infections and discharges (usually thick, white), rashes and itching around male genitalia, bladder infections, intestinal cramps, cravings for sugar-rich foods and sweets, cravings for foods rich in yeast and carbohydrates.

Those suffering from candidiasis may have a history of use of antibiotics, prednisone or other cortisone-type drugs. They are bothered by tobacco smoke and perfumes. They can feel spacy or 'not quite there', variously suffering menstrual irregularities, endometriosis, spots in front of eyes, diarrhoea, constipation, chaotic bowel movements, muscle aches and prostatitis.

Associated complaints

Irritable bowel syndrome, eczema, psoriasis, depression, irritability, pre-menstrual syndrome (PMS), cancer, multiple sclerosis, heart disease, arthritis, osteoporosis, chronic fatigue syndrome (ME), leaky gut syndrome, esophageal reflux, lupus, gout, Crohn's disease, hyperactivity, infertility, herpes, chlamydia, Alzheimer's, scleroderma, Raynaud's disease, kidney stones, Cushing's disease.

Causes

Parasites, yeast, fungi and bacteria invariably proliferate in moist, warm zones, especially when beneficial gut flora, which usually control the uglies, are killed by prolonged exposure to any of the following:

- Antibiotics and other drugs
- Malnutrition
- Constant cooked food devoid of enzymes
- Constant acid ash food consumption[92]
- Cigarette smoking
- Fluoridated water consumption
- Antacids
- Excess sugar and high glycaemic carbohydrate intake

The antibiotic assault

Steven Ransom in his *Wake up to Health in the 21st Century*, conducts a full-on assault against the wilful prescription of antibiotics, arguing that often they do more harm than good, especially to children, who tend to have them routinely prescribed for common ailments, such as middle ear infections (*otitis media*):

"During the first two years of their lives, American children will spend an astounding 90 days taking antibiotics. This may be causally related to the current increase in chronic respiratory diseases, such as wheezing and asthma, in young children. A research group from Boston reported recently that 32 percent of

---

[92] See **Day, Phillip**, *Food For Thought*, Credence Publications, 2002 – the official recipe companion to all Credence health titles

such children wheeze, 26 percent use bronchodilators, and 12 percent have asthma before the age of five." [93] [94]

Michael Schmidt states in his book, *Beyond Antibiotics*:

"[Antibiotics] cause the destruction of normal bowel flora. Like pesticides, antibiotics kill good bugs along with the bad ones. Wide-spectrum antibiotics are notorious for this. The human intestine has a delicate ecology in which certain bugs help digest food, produce certain vitamins, and maintain a balance of organisms that prevents harmful bacteria and yeasts from multiplying. Wide-spectrum antibiotics derange the normal ecology of the intestine. This can cause parasitic infection, vitamin deficiencies, loss of minerals through diarrhoea, inflammation of the gut, mal-absorption syndromes and development of food allergies due to defects in intestinal function." [95]

Take action♥

Clinics can do a stool analysis in which *Candida* and other problems will be apparent if they are the cause of your problems. Measures adopted against *Candida*, fungi, yeasts and other parasites are designed to starve the parasites into submission. **THE ANTI-CANDIDA DIETARY REGIMEN** forms the backbone of this and should be adhered to strictly. Components below are designed to kill parasites and flush them from the system. The magnesium oxide bowel cleanse will take three truck-loads out in one go, but beneficial flora such as *Lactobacillus acidophilus/bifidum* need to be reinstated afterwards to keep the balance.

- **DIET: COMMENCE THE ANTI-*CANDIDA* DIETARY REGIMEN**
- **DIET:** AVOID ALL SUGAR AND YEAST
- **DIET:** Avoid all products that readily break down into glucose or have a yeast component: e.g. bread, pasta,

---

[93] **Ransom, Steven,** *Wake up to Health in the 21st Century*, Credence Publications, 2003
[94] "Time to Stop the Misuse of Antibiotics", *Mothering Magazine* online at http://www.mothering.com/10-0-0/html/10-4-0/10-4-healingear104.shtml
[95] **Schmidt, Michael**, *Beyond Antibiotics*, North Atlantic Books, 1992

pastries, sweets, pies, alcohol, beers and some fruits and vegetables (see diet above)

- **DIET:** Drink at least four pints of clean, still mineral water a day (not out of plastic bottles and please avoid distilled water)
- **PREVENTION:** Don't smoke and avoid second-hand smoke
- **PREVENTION:** Avoid behavioural and dietary problems that have caused the condition
- **DETOXIFICATION:** Conduct a two-week bowel cleanse with magnesium oxide
- **DETOXIFICATION:** Cancer patients should also consider colon hydrotherapy for extra internal cleanliness
- **RESTORING NUTRIENT BALANCE: COMMENCE THE BASIC SUPPLEMENT PROGRAM**, including:
- **ANTI-*CANDIDA*/FUNGAL SUPPLEMENTATION**
- A priobiotic supplement to install beneficial flora
- Vitamin C complex (ascorbates plus bioflavonoids), 5 g per day. This amounts to one heaped teaspoon of C-complex powder. Take a half teaspoon in a bland juice, such as pear, every morning and another half teaspoon at night
- Vitamin A emulsion, as directed
- 1 tbsp of ground flaxseed (linseed) meal or oil daily
- **BOOSTING IMMUNITY:** Astragalus and echinacea (herbs), two capsules, three times a day
- **BOOSTING IMMUNITY:** Indulge in regular and vigorous exercise (unless health problems prevent this) to exercise and pump the lymphatic system, rid the body of waste products and draw oxygen into the body
- **BOOSTING IMMUNITY:** Get plenty of rest!
- **TIP:** Be consistent!
- **TIP:** Do not fall prey to sugar cravings. Who really wants to splurge and feed inside you? Starve 'em.

Herxheimer's reaction

During the parasite-killing process, the body may become clogged with catabolic debris, dead beasties and their resultant toxaemia, including ammonia. You may feel ill as your symptoms apparently worsen. This is known as Herxheimer's reaction, after the venerable German dermatologist of the same name. It is temporary and will be experienced in proportion to the vehemence with which you apply your attack strategies. Symptoms may be alleviated by commencing the anti-*Candida* diet a full two weeks prior to starting on the anti-fungal/yeast supplements.

Maintenance – The open road ahead

Once clear of the problem(s), avoid the minefields to prevent re-infestation. Remember: what you eat determines the condition of your body's immune system, and poor immunity is written on the gravestone of many a promising lad and lass. Solving the fungal/parasite problem in the body can lead to tremendous health benefits, not to mention advances in finding the answers to many of the vexing diseases which still afflict us.

Chronic Fatigue Syndrome

Profile

For years, the medical establishment would not recognise chronic fatigue syndrome (CFS), even though doctors were reporting cases showing up at the surgery with disconcerting regularity. Known variously down through the years as Iceland disease, post-infectious neuromyasthenia, chronic Epstein-Barr virus syndrome, etc., CFS has had a rocky ride getting itself taken seriously by all but those suffering from its debilitating symptoms. Many doctors for years wrote it off as Yuppie flu, or, in plain English, malingering.

Symptoms

Flu-like symptoms, constant sore throat, listlessness, fatigue, allergies, muscle pain, sleep disorder, stiffness, visual blurring, swollen lymph nodes, multiple chemical sensitivity, fibromyalgia, migratory joint pain, depression and emotional disturbances.

Commentary

CFS is a classic immune system challenge. Those suffering from its various symptoms have likened it to driving with the handbrake on. As mentioned, Epstein-Barr virus (EBV), a member of the herpes group, has been blamed, as have others, like Cytomegalovirus, Brucella, Human herpes virus-6, etc. CFS sufferers often discuss with others how tired and debilitated they are, and how hopeless their condition is, which is one of the first clues to what is going on.

Nine out of ten people who approach me with complaints of CFS actually do not think they will recover. This is what I refer to as 'tossing yourself under the bus'. Emotional negativity and depression are a key feature in *Candida albicans* and fungal infestations (gastrointestinal overgrowths), since fungi and yeasts release toxins that manipulate their host's environment to their advantage, often having a direct impact on mood and motivation.

Poor diets and stressful, 21st century lifestyles are at the heart of CFS – fizzy sugar drinks, foods saturated in sugar and coffee abuse in particular - which depress the immune system, giving rise to a number of spin-off conditions: hypoglycaemia, hypothyroidism, food allergies (sensitivities), *Candida* overgrowths, etc. A multi-factorial approach to CFS almost always brings relief from symptoms, *but only if the patient is prepared to take action!* Part of the problem with CFS has always been that the patient, all too often, cannot bring themselves a) to appreciate that recovery is waiting for them and b) to do what it takes *consistently* (there's that word again) to work their way out of the problem.

Take action♥

Working your way out of CFS *will take time*, and the more consistent you are about taking action, the quicker your recovery will be. The regime is all about what you stop doing as well as what you take. It always helps to have professional supervision to ensure compliance with the measures below:

- **DIET:** For the first three months, **COMMENCE THE ANTI-*CANDIDA* DIETARY REGIMEN** and anti-fungal supplementation, taking special care to avoid the foods in the exclusion section. After three months, or as directed by a physician, change to **THE *FOOD FOR THOUGHT* LIFESTYLE REGIMEN**, a slightly more liberal regime
- **RESTORE NUTRIENT BALANCE: COMMENCE THE BASIC SUPPLEMENT PROGRAM**
- **DETOXIFICATION:** Conduct a magnesium oxide bowel cleanse
- **DETOXIFICATION:** Ensure that harmful lifestyle actions, such as taking drugs, smoking, and excessive drinking are halted immediately
- **TIP:** Exercise regularly. Join a gym and make it fun
- **TIP:** Rest, rest, rest and get into a good book or do something that takes you emotionally out of your day-to-day grind
- **TIP:** Give up reading newspapers and watching the news
- **TIP:** Are you on medication which might be depressing your mood and creating side-effects?

- **TIP:** Avoid stressful situations. Ideally, take a holiday where you can relax and have fun while eating good, wholesome foods with people you enjoy being with
- **TIP:** Compel yourself to stand back from your situation and evaluate it for what it is. Have you been jamming the needles to the red and smoking the rubber to the cord? Are you exhausted, stressed out and not having a good life?
- **TIP:** Working your way out of CFS, in my view, is actually about working your way out of the stress and diet cycles you have compelled upon yourself over the years
- **TIP:** It's a beautiful life. Embrace it

Common Cold

Profile

The common cold is known and loathed by all. But, as with other apparent 'disorders', the cold is really just an elimination procedure being undertaken by the body. Those of us who get colds regularly need to examine whether we are challenging our immune systems with certain foods our bodies are having a problem with, e.g. cow's milk, sugar, gluten from wheat, barley, rye, etc. Certainly 'snotty nosed' kids, who suffer from what I call 'Niagara Nose', generally have a problem with cow's milk, as I explain in a chapter in *Health Wars* dedicated to this subject. Food intolerances, such as those with cow's milk, may also present themselves in kids, not only as colds, but as rashes, diarrhoea, behavioural problems, the 'Terrible Twos' syndrome, etc. (see **Allergies**).

Symptoms

Dry scratchy throat, general feelings of listlessness, headache, upper respiratory tract congestion, sneezing, etc. Thick mucus will be ejected through nose and mouth which contains dead organisms, toxins, white blood cells, and other debris the body is trying to expel. Colds generally last from three days to a week. Longer terms of illness may indicate a deeper problem with immune function, which might involve the patient being too stressed, not enough rest, inadequate nutrition, etc.

Commentary

Those of us whose immune systems are robust and whose bodies are clean and detoxified don't suffer from colds. Frequency of colds are a good indicator of whether yours is a happy body or whether it is constantly getting gummed up with toxins, immune system reactions and other debilitating causes. One of the chief culprits of a depressed immune system is a constant intake of refined sugar, which depletes vitamin C reserves in the body. Sugary, fizzy drinks are a real problem for children and should be phased out and eliminated permanently.

Traditional treatments

Go into any pharmacy today, and you'll be confronted with rack upon rack of patented products that all claim to do something for the common cold. Actually all most do is suppress symptoms rather than eliminate the root cause of why your body found it necessary to clean itself out to begin with. In Steven Ransom's book, *Wake up to Health in the 21st Century*, the author highlights many examples of cons being perpetrated by companies pushing the latest flu and cold cures on an unsuspecting public. Best avoid them all and address the root problem instead.

Take action♥

Turning off the toxin tap to avoid colds will involve changing diet in the way we have examined with previous disorders, and employing techniques to boost the immune system, assisting the body in eliminating the problem rather than suppressing the immune system's ability to do its job properly (which is all most over-the-counter cold medicines accomplish anyway). Here are some pointers for prevention as well as remedy:

- **DIET: COMMENCE THE *FOOD FOR THOUGHT* LIFESTYLE REGIMEN**, paying special attention to items to eliminate
- **RESTORING NUTRIENT BALANCE: COMMENCE THE BASIC SUPPLEMENT PROGRAM**, ensuring, if suffering:
- Vitamin C complex (ascorbates plus bioflavonoids), 500-1,000 mg taken every two hours. If diarrhoea results, back dosage down to threshold level
- Vitamin A emulsion, 20,000 – 25,000 IU per day during the usual four-day period of the cold
- Zinc (elemental), 25 mg per day for a four-day period of the cold
- Vitamin B6, 100 mg per day
- **IMMUNE FUNCTION:** Echinacea, 1 g, three times per day
- **IMMUNE FUNCTION:** Astragalus, 1 g, three times per day

- **TIP:** Drink at least four pints (2 litres) of clean, fresh water per day
- **TIP:** Get plenty of rest. Do NOT exercise during the cold period. Potent immune factors are released during deep rest
- **TIP:** Avoid stress! Very important....

Criminal Violence
Anti-social behaviour, rages, Jekyll/Hyde behaviour

Profile
There are many reasons why people become violent or do bad things: lack of money, drug abuse, alcoholism, idealism, etc. However, a growing number of studies are showing that the *predisposition to crime and violence* is often fuelled by glucose intolerance, heavy metal poisoning and junk diets. As a result of refined diets and an excess of sugar and other high glycaemic foods, the offender experiences chaotic blood sugar levels, glucose intolerance and 'reactive' hypoglycaemia - the rebound low experienced after sugar levels have plunged following the resultant over-production of insulin.

Bernard Gesch of Natural Justice, a UK-based charity, is championing the move towards improving nutrition in prisons, as well as society. A former probation officer, Gesch is adamant that the most central strategy towards discontinuing a culture's flirtation with social violence must be to feed its people properly:

"What we're trying to do is introduce something new into the criminal justice system, that is, the existence of the human brain."

Gesch believes that exposure to neurotoxins, such as lead, cadmium, beryllium, mercury, arsenic, aspartame and food additives, together with nutritional deficiencies and a constant intake of low-nutrient-density, sugary junk foods are all it takes to get the riot police out:

"There are many chemicals around us that are known to affect behaviour. Our environment is increasingly polluted. Our food supply has fundamentally changed. In the same way that we don't notice ageing, how would we notice the effects of gradual changes in our diet and environment?"

The cycle of violence
Consider that all behaviour is controlled by the brain, which is completely dependent on nutrition. Consider that a disrupted or

chaotic supply of glucose, the only fuel the brain accepts, has a marked effect on behaviour, and that junk food is directly responsible. Consider also that anti-nutrients, such as lead, aspartame and cadmium, directly affect brain function. And then recognise that when criminals are 'brought to justice' and imprisoned, the same low nutrient-density food, drugs, cigarettes and pollution accompany the inmate and continue the deleterious effects. Then he is released into the same society to ingest the same junk food, take the same drugs and stimulants and experience the same hopeless behaviour patterns.

In the UK, Gesch's South Cumbria Alternative Sentencing Options Scheme (SCASO) required young offenders to undergo 'nutritional rehabilitation' as part of their processing. Tests recorded the levels of vitamins and minerals as well as toxins, blood sugar and an overall assessment of the inmate's dietary habits. _Every subject tested had abnormal glucose intolerance on a five-hour glucose tolerance test_. Zinc deficiency was also extremely prevalent.[96]

Finnish researcher Virkkunen studied 69 repeat offenders for reactive hypoglycaemia. With no exceptions, _all had glucose intolerance._ A later study showed abnormal insulin activity among all violent re-offenders who participated.[97]

In the US, behavioural expert Professor Stephen Schoenthaler placed 3,000 inmates on a low saturated fat, high-fibre diet which restricted sugary, refined foods. The results were extraordinary. Schoenthaler reported a

> ➤ 21% reduction in anti-social behaviour
> ➤ 25% reduction in assaults
> ➤ 75% reduction in the use of restraints
> ➤ 100% reduction in suicides[98]

---

[96] **Holford, P**, "Crime – Nourishment or Punishment?" *Optimum Nutrition*, Vol. 8.2 (ref 82): 1995

[97] **Virkkunen, M**, *Neuropsychobiology*, 3,35-40 & 8,30-34: 1982

[98] **Schoenthaler, S J**, "The Northern California diet-behaviour program: An empirical evaluation of 3,000 incarcerated juveniles in Stanislaus County Juvenile Hall", *Int. J. Biosocial Res.*, 5(2),99-106: 1983

Another study confirmed that amending the diet indeed has startling consequences in behaviour modification. The project reported a 44% reduction in anti-social behaviour with the most significant reductions occurring with repeat, serious offenders.[99]

Toxic metals

A combination of the previously noted dietary problems, coupled with measurable increases in lead and cadmium in the subjects tested, demonstrated pronounced delinquency, impaired intellectual performance and a predisposition to commit violence. These pollution problems have been repeatedly measured in studies around the world.[100] Perhaps more startling is the fact that the amount of lead and cadmium required to affect behaviour is around 1% of that needed to produce physical symptoms of poisoning, so the link between the two effects has been more difficult to pinpoint.

Perhaps the most damning aspect of social violence comes from the fact that, in spite of the heap of science demonstrating quite unequivocally that good nutrition has this quieting effect, and that even adding orange juice to the diets of inmates has been known to produce a staggering 47% reduction in antisocial behaviour among juvenile offenders,[101] still nothing is done, either by government, the prison services, the food industry or the medical establishment centrally to correct the problem. Can violence be described as an economic necessity? After all, prisons are quite the boom industry in America, while newspapers and the entertainment industry rely on a steady diet of violence, rape and anti-social behaviour to fill their columns and screens for the gossip-hungry and violence-titillated public. To all 'public servants' and politicians out there, desiring to make their mark and do something to leave society in a better state

---

[99] Ibid.

[100] **Freeman, R, Gamys, VP, & LE Smythe**, "Lead burden of Sydney schoolchildren", University of New South Wales, January 1979; **Needleman, HL, Davidson, I, Sewell, LE, et al**, "Sub-clinical lead exposure in Philadelphia schoolchildren: Identification by dentine lead analysis", *New Eng. J. Med.*, 290, 245-248: 1974; **Thompson, GO, et al**, "Blood lead levels and children's behaviour: Results from the Edinburgh lead study", *J. Child. Psycho. Psychiatr.*, 30(4), 515: 1989; **Pihl, RO and F Ervin**, "Lead and cadmium in violent criminals", *Psychol. Rep.*, 6(3), 839: 1990

[101] **Schoenthaler, SJ**, "Diet and delinquency: A multi-state replication", *Int. J. of Bio. Res.*, 5(2), 73: 1983

than that in which they found it, the jury is in – now what will you do?

Food allergies and violence

Is the reader any longer surprised that the very problems stirring up hyperactivity and a dive in intellectual performance among our youth are precisely those which blight our streets and nations today? Junk diets, food allergies, such as milk and gluten intolerance, digestive problems, disturbed sleep, and reactions to food additives are ever part of the root cause. Menzies discovered that of 25 children with tension fatigue complications, 84% had abnormal EEG and 72% had digestive problems specific to the diets they were consuming.[102] Gesch summarises:

"75% of our referrals were for violent offences, many of whom were multiple offenders.... Of those kept on the combined social and nutritional regime, none re-offended with [violence] by the end of the 18-month pilot study." [103]

The cost of this amazing supplement 'treatment'? Between £4-£10 a month. The cost of keeping a juvenile in detention? Over £2,000 a month.

Once again, a fundamental reappraisal of society's basic relationship with its food and environment is the key to overcoming the social mayhem experienced in so many parts of the world today. The majority of the conditions which give rise to violent behaviour can be treated simply and effectively with nutritional and lifestyle changes. This will of course adequately explain why the Hunzas and certain other 'isolated' groups around the world have no track record of violence or anti-social behaviour in their cultures due to their nutrient-dense diets, clean environment and socially responsible attitudes. As Harvard professor Ernest Hooten once remarked: *"Let*

---

[102] **Menzies, IC**, "Disturbed children: The role of food and chemical sensitivities", *Nutr. Health*, 3, 39-45: 1984
[103] **Gesch, B**, "Natural justice: A pilot study in evaluating and responding to criminal behaviour as an environmental phenomenon: The South Cumbria (England) Alternative Sentencing Options (SCASCO) project", *Int. J. Biosocial Med. Res.*, 12(1), 41-68

us go to the 'ignorant savage', consider his way of eating, and be wise." [104]

Take action ♥
The following is recommended for those experiencing violent epsidoes or Jekyl and Hyde behaviour:

- **DIET: COMMENCE THE *FOOD FOR THOUGHT* DIETARY LIFESTYLE REGIMEN**
- **DIET:** Take special heed of the **Foods to avoid** and the No's
- **RESTORING NUTRIENT BALANCE: COMMENCE THE BASIC SUPPLEMENT PROGRAM**
- A consistent program of exercise
- Rest

Further resources
The Mind Game by Phillip Day

---

[104] **Hooten, Ernest A**, *Apes, Men and Morons*, Putnam, New York: 1937

Depression, Suicidal Tendencies

Profile

In her opening address, the World Health Organisation's Director General Dr Gro Harlem stated: *"...initial estimates suggest that about 450 million people alive today suffer from mental or neurological disorders.... Major depression is now the leading cause of disability globally."* [105]

There is of course no question that depression blights the lives of millions around the globe. A million people commit suicide every year, with between 10 to 20 million suicides attempted annually.[106] Suicide in the US for males between the ages of 35-49 is the number three cause of death, outstripping even diabetes, iatrogenic death (physician-induced) and motor vehicle accidents.

Canada has a particularly bad problem with depression and suicides, with a person killing themselves every two hours. Hospital records for 1998/1999 show that females were hospitalised for attempted suicide at one and a half times the rate of males. Around 9% of those hospitalised for a suicide attempt had previously been discharged more than once following an attempt on their own life in that same year.[107] Physicians wrote out 3 million prescriptions for Paxil (paroxetine) alone, one of the most common anti-depressant medications. Sales for Paxil in 2000 exceeded those in 1999 by 19%.[108]

Depression symptoms

Feelings of doom, the inability to take action, listlessness, and that thick lead blanket of despair wreck the lives, not only of the sufferer, but their family, friends and co-workers too.

---

[105] WHO World Health Report 2001, www.who.int/whr/2001/main/en/chapter2/002g.htm
[106] Ibid.
[107] Canada Health Reviews: www.statcan.ca/Daily/English/020124/d020124b.htm
[108] *National Post*, 29th March 2001, Vol.9, No.129

Histadelia

On the physical front, nutrient deficiencies, glucose intolerance and allergy are extremely common in those suffering from depression. One major cause is an excess of the neurotransmitter hormone histamine – a condition known as histadelia. Dr Carl Pfeiffer asks: *"Do you sneeze in bright sunlight? Cry, salivate and feel nauseous easily? Hear your pulse in your head on the pillow at night? Have frequent backaches, stomach and muscle cramps? Do you have regular headaches and seasonal allergies? Have abnormal fears, compulsions and rituals? Do you burn up food rapidly and sometimes entertain suicidal thoughts? ...If a majority of these apply to you, you may benefit from a low-protein, high complex carbohydrate diet (fruits and vegetables), 500 mg of calcium, am and pm, 500 mg methionine am and pm and a basic supplement program. Avoid supplements containing folic acid as these can raise histamine levels."* [109]

Some of our most loved stars, such as Marilyn Monroe and Judy Garland, were likely histadelics. Drawing from over 30 years' experience, Pfeiffer estimates that at least 20% of schizophrenics are histadelics and these are often the problem patients in psychiatric hospitals, since they do not respond to the usual drug treatments, electroshock or insulin coma 'therapy'.

Blood histamine levels can be analysed. Often, the compulsive obsessions, blank mind, easy crying and confusion may highlight an underlying chemical addiction to cane sugar, alcohol or drugs. Histadelics experience high saliva discharge and rarely have cavities. Often they are seen wiping saliva from the corners of their mouth. Excess histamine presents rapid oxidation in their body, and their high metabolic rate and subsequent attractive body shape are sometimes potential indicators for the underlying condition. Marilyn Monroe was often heard to remark to photographers: *"You always take pictures of my body, but my most perfect feature is my teeth – I have no cavities."*

A high sex drive characterises the histadelic, who achieves orgasm and sustains it easily. Drug addicts and alcoholics also tend

[109] Pfeiffer, Carl & Patrick Holford, op. cit. p.103

to be histadelic. Heroin and methadone, for instance, are both powerful histamine-releasing agents. A severe insomnia also characterises the condition, and sufferers often use heavy doses of sedatives in order to get to sleep. The sedatives themselves often become an addiction problem, further compounding the plight suffered by those with depression.

Depression – the nutritional link

Traditional psychiatric treatments are mostly useless for the histadelic depressive. Electroshock, examined in detail in *The Mind Game*, is a barbarous initiative, which mostly traumatises the patient further. Lithium in lower doses of 600-900 mg is partially effective, but does not have greater efficacy at higher dosages. Anti-depressant drugs are simply mood ameliorators and can be addictive. Nor do histadelics respond to B3 mega-doses usually recommended for schizophrenics. B9 (folic acid) definitely worsens the condition.

What has been shown to work are treatments which modify how the body releases and detoxifies histamine. Calcium supplementation releases the body's stores of histamine and the amino acid methionine detoxifies histamine through methylation, the body's usual method of breaking down the neurotransmitter. Laboratories can test for histamine levels in the blood and this is often one of the first best steps a practitioner can take to determine if histamine is a player in their patient's depression.

Maes et al also found that serum levels of zinc in 48 unipolar depressed subjects (16 minor, 14 simple major and 18 melancholic subjects) were significantly lower than those in the 32 control volunteers.[110]

Helping those with suicidal tendencies

The major problem with those suffering from chronic depression is suicide. Today, such family members are often consigned to psychiatric care, which, as we have seen in *The Mind Game*, creates problems of its own for the patient. Research group Truehope states:

---

[110] **Maes, M, et al**, "Hypozincemia in Depression", *J. Affect. Disord.*, 31, 1994, pp.135-140

"One of the particularly tragic outcomes of a mood disorder is suicide. Over 90% of suicide victims have a significant psychiatric illness at the time of their death. These are often undiagnosed, untreated, or both. Mood disorders and substance abuse are the two most common. Around 15-20% of depressed patients end their lives by committing suicide." [111]

In times gone by, caring family members gathered around and gave the depressed relative the assurance and attention to talk things through. Often drug addiction or substance abuse were key factors. Today, with the fracturing of the family unit, the denigration of religion, and the separation of many families from each other with the hectic pace of 21st century life, psychoanalysis has simply taken over the task of counselling that used to be carried out by caring relatives or the neighbourhood minister. I feel strongly that this has had a deleterious effect on our society, in view of the medications prescribed which appear to have a quieting effect, but underneath are propagating a roiling of the emotions.

I further believe that a neighbourhood pastor/minister, or the equivalents in the other religions, have a pivotal role to play in maintaining the mental stability of their parishioners. It simply has not worked the psychiatric way, with psychiatrists themselves, as we discuss in *The Mind Game*, often committing suicide more often than the public they are supposed to be treating.

Combining nutritional good sense with counselling

In our current times, more than ever, it is essential for the depressed to have an understanding friend or relative with them constantly. Ideally this should be someone the depressed person looks up to, and from whom they can take guidance. Measures should be taken to remove influences that can have a depressing effect on the patient. These include newspapers, TV news, video and computer games, heavy metal, rap, pop and other 'culture' music

[111] Truehope Ltd., *Defining a New Model for the Care of the Mentally Ill*, www.truehope.com; **Robins, E**, *The Final Months: A Study of the Lives of 134 Persons*, Oxford University Press, NY: 1981; **Conwell, Y, et al**, "Relationships of Age and Axis 1 Diagnoses in Victims of Completed Suicide: A Psychological Autopsy Study", *American Journal of Psychiatry*, 153, pp.1001-1008

preaching negative conditioning messages. Instead, positive influences, serene surroundings, such as countryside outings and an active, outdoors lifestyle with plenty of exercise, far removed especially from those settings which have surrounded the patient during their bouts of depression, are ideal for setting the tone for recovery.

Negativity is an emotional, spiritual force which has a compounding effect on the body. Religious writings, such as the Bible, concentrate on eradicating negativity from a person's life and replace it with a model that offers an explanation of where that person fits in the overall scheme of things. Since Nietzsche apparently killed God, man has become his own deity. This little god has not been doing very well in administering his own creation, over which he seems to exercise so little control. We're born. We live. We die. Then what? It's enough to drive anyone to depression.

And then we see the constant onslaught of bad news. During my lectures, I invite the audience to go home and comb through a daily national newspaper with marker pens and put a big red 'X' next to every article that is bad news. Then I ask them to do the same for the TV listings. Then go back through the newspaper and put a big blue 'X' next to every single article that is absolutely NONE OF THEIR BUSINESS. This will give a stark indication of how much junk we take into our brains for absolutely no achievable gain.

What we focus on becomes our reality. Ecuador does not feature in most people's lives in the west, because very few people go there and we don't focus on it. Yet out street, our workplace, our family, our cars – these are part of our focus and so describe our physical context. *When we understand that we become what we focus on, then we need to change the focus.* It isn't hard to see how someone fixated on splatter films and Satanism is going to have a negative focus in that direction – with all the concomitant effects this will stir up.

Take action ♥

On the physical side, the following may be of benefit to the depressive:

- **DIET: COMMENCE THE *FOOD FOR THOUGHT* LIFESTYLE REGIMEN**
- **RESTORE NUTRIENT BALANCE: COMMENCE THE BASIC SUPPLEMENT PROGRAM**, ensuring:
- Vitamin B6, 50 mg, am and pm
- Zinc (gluconate), 25 mg, am and pm
- Calcium, 500 mg, am and pm
- Magnesium, 200 mg, am and pm
- Manganese, 10 mg, am and pm
- Methionine, 500 mg, am and pm
- **TIP:** Histadelics should avoid supplements containing folic acid as these can raise histamine levels
- **TIP:** Avoid negative conditioning, including newspapers, TV (especially soap operas) and acquaintances with a negative attitude
- **EXERCISE:** A regular program should be set up with a personal trainer, if possible, to keep you in the traces
- Plenty of rest
- No stress

Diabetes

Profile

The world is in the grip of a diabetes epidemic. Estimates that as many as 1 in 10 Americans might have the condition have shocked many, and yet, apart from offering the connection between the disease and our body's impaired ability to process sugars, medical science still seems to be clawing around in the dark as to what is behind the plague. Well, I have some great news for you. But first, let's define what the problems are:

Type-1 – Insulin-dependent diabetes mellitus (IDDM) – Occurs most often in infants and adolescents. This is the rarer (10% of all diabetics) but more dangerous form, where some, or all of the beta cells in the pancreas, which produce insulin, seem to have been destroyed by the immune system. The condition also appears to be accompanied by the inability of these valuable islet cells to regenerate.

Type-2 – Non-insulin-dependent diabetes mellitus (NIDDM) – Known as adult-onset diabetes, as the condition usually appears in patients over forty years of age. Type-2 is one of the fastest growing diseases in the western world, and is usually what someone refers to when they say they are 'diabetic'. The condition occurs when the body's cells become resistant to the pancreatic hormone insulin, which regulates blood sugar levels, resulting in dramatically lowered sugar-absorption by the cells, and thus excess sugars remain in the blood, unable to be oxidised to produce energy.

Gestational Diabetes – During pregnancy, women experience increased estrogen and cortisol hormone secretions, which raise blood sugar levels. This in turn prompts the pancreas to generate more insulin to regulate this extra glucose. In 3-5% of women, the increased insulin appears to have marginal effect on how the cells of their body absorb sugars and the result is a form of type-2 (glucose intolerance) diabetes.[112]

---

[112] **Vambergue, A, et al**, "Pathophysiology of gestational diabetes", *J. Gynecol. Obstet Biol Reprod (Paris)*, 31(6), Suppl: 3-10, October 2002

Symptoms

In type-1, insulin-producing beta cells do not die simultaneously, so early diagnosis of the condition is important in order to take appropriate action to save the remainder. Thirst, dramatic loss or gaining of weight and the excessive production of urine. Increased blood pressure, increased appetite, nausea, hyperglycaemia, or an over-accumulation of glucose in the blood (unregulated by insulin). Type-1 can lead to foot ulcers, blindness (diabetic eye disease, or retinopathy), nerve damage (diabetic neuropathy), heart disease, gangrene of limb(s) (peripheral vascular disease), requiring amputation, kidney failure and coma.

Commentary

Medicine states that the exact mechanism for how all the types of diabetes occur in the body is still theoretical, however a tremendous amount is already known about the different types of the disease in general. So let's start putting some pieces together:

Type-1: Mostly recognised as an 'auto-immune' disorder where the immune system has destroyed the beta cells which produce the glucose-regulating hormone, insulin. Question: what has triggered such a specific attack? The wisdom of the day states that the body's immune system has decided to attack the beta cells, believing the latter are invading microbes, such as bacteria or viruses. This does not explain 'why the beta cells' in particular?

With insulin production completely disrupted, the cells of the body cannot be fed the glucose they need to provide energy. An extreme tiredness sets in with the patient. Blood sugar levels go through the roof, since there is no insulin to regulate them. The kidneys get in on the act, vainly attempting to filter out the excess sugars, resulting in frequent bathroom trips and a raging thirsty requirement for water to flush out the sugary gunk. Kidney failure is a common result of type-1, for reasons we shall examine.

Type-2: The problems with type-2 diabetes begin with how our bodies process foods that break down into glucose. Refined sugar, or sucrose, hydrolyses into glucose and fructose after consumption. Fructose is metabolised directly to produce energy. Abrupt intakes of glucose into the bloodstream however provoke a massive secretion of insulin, responsible for regulating blood sugar levels and storing excess glucose as fat. The result of this over-production of insulin is a sudden drop in blood sugar, which, as I discuss in *The Mind Game*, often brings on mood changes and behavioural upsets.

Now we have low blood sugar, we can get that wobbly sensation and become growly and as mean as a snake. What are our bodies craving? Sugar! So, in go the doughnuts, Twinkies, Ding-Dongs, Mars bars and Bear Claws; up go the blood sugar levels again; out squirts all that insulin to regulate the glucose, and down come those blood sugar levels again with a thump. This spiky, chaotic pattern of blood sugar in the body will eventually cause our cells to become resistant to all that insulin, resulting in the condition of type-2 diabetes.

Sucrose and massive insulin secretions have long been known to be a leading causative factor in type-2 diabetes. The condition usually occurs in adults, who have had years of food abuse to render their cells insulin-resistant. Type-2 can be controlled and even eliminated with a combination of diet and exercise. People with the condition not only lose their sensitivity to insulin, which regulates the build-up of blood sugar, but this repeated overload of insulin and glucose can lead to an increase in systolic blood pressure, fainting and diabetic coma.

Excessive consumption of refined, high-glycaemic carbohydrates, including items like white bread, white flour, chocolate, sweets, pastries, white rice, breakfast cereals, as well as alcohol drinks, especially wine and beer, will all yield excessive sugars into the bloodstream with the predictable, aforementioned, excess insulin effects.

Another problem is physical and emotional stress. This triggers what is known as Fight or Flight Syndrome. When we become agitated, stressed or physically threatened, the body prepares for combat or flight by generating powerful shots of adrenalin. This provokes the releasing of stored glucose (glycogen) into the bloodstream for energy to fuel explosive physical action. This in turn causes a surge of insulin to regulate blood sugar levels. Notice how, in previous eras, the Fight/Flight response would resolve itself *with explosive physical action* (either Fight or Flight!), which in turn would burn off the sugars.

What about today? When we are stressed with money, relationships, hardships or work pressures, or simply getting our kicks watching the FA Cup or playing video games, this Fight/Flight response still occurs and may endure for days or weeks. Consequently, the amount of insulin produced by the pancreas in today's stressful, sugar-laden environment is substantially higher. This excess energy does not tend to discharge itself through physical action, since we are remarkably inactive today. The results of this insulin response can also be diabetes.

Dr Joseph Mercola clarifies type-2: *"The overall concept of [prescribing] insulin for type-2 diabetes is absurd and makes absolutely no sense if one understands the way the body is designed to work. However, since nearly all traditional physicians don't comprehend basic human physiology with respect to diet and health, it is not surprising that they could come up with the prescription for disaster of giving someone who is already overloaded with insulin more of what caused the problem.*

The main reason most adult-onset (type-2) diabetics have diabetes is that they have too much insulin. This is usually a result of having too many grains. The solution in nearly all of these individuals is to consume a no-grain diet and to exercise one hour per day."[113]

The role critters play in type-1

There is some tremendously compelling research pointing the finger squarely at fungi as the cause of diabetes in general. Remember, simply eating sugar alone cannot cause diabetes, since millions eat sugar and don't have the condition. Being overweight alone cannot be the cause for diabetes, since millions in the world are overweight and do not suffer the condition. Contrariwise, there are lots of thinnies among us who have diabetes. There has to be another factor, and that's where fungi come in. Doug Kaufmann and David Holland MD remark:

"Why on earth would fungi launch such a specific mission as an attack on the beta cells to begin with? What do they stand to gain? The answer is: food! With the beta cells out of the way, insulin

---

[113] www.mercola.com

production drops to zero. Blood sugar skyrockets, creating the ultimate splurge opportunity for fungi.

That said, it's open to debate just how well type-1 diabetes works for the fungi that initiate it. If the fungus-infected beta cell is destroyed by the diabetic's immune system, then all of the parties immediately involved lose out. Although fungi that arrive after the beta cells are destroyed stand to benefit a great deal, it could be that their forerunners have run your basic suicide mission."[114]

In examining the smoking gun at the ground zero of diabetes type-1 activity, we find dead beta cells, tantalising traces of recent immune activity, but no dead critters. This isn't the end of the story however, since scientists can easily overlook dead fungal matter, which will be removed by the bloodstream and disposed of through the kidneys anyway. If you hear a crash in the kitchen, storm in and find a broken milk bottle on the floor, with the cat in the corner covered in milk, do you automatically assume the cat is responsible? Did you see your little boy hiding behind the door?

That the immune system has destroyed the beta cells is quite well established. But why? What if the beta cells were infected with fungi which were attempting to sabotage the body's sugar-regulating mechanisms? Science has shown well that fungi have the disconcerting ability to manipulate their environment in order to secure their food sources. Let's look at some scientific evidence:

In 1973, Escher et al found that cured mutton is loaded with mycotoxins from fungi. Eight years later, Helgason and Jonasson reported a highly disproportionate number of Icelandic women who ate cured mutton immediately prior to pregnancy who gave birth to babies with diabetes type-1. The year before in 1980, Pojo showed how alloxan, a fungal toxin, directly damaged beta cells which produce insulin. Hayes caused diabetes in lab animals by injecting them with streptozotocin, another fungal toxin. Coleman found that a 10% brewer's yeast diet caused diabetes in his lab animals. Varsano discovered that cancer patients given the chemo Asparaginase

[114] **Kaufmann, D & D Holland**, *Infectious Diabetes*, Mediatrition, Texas, 2003, p.51

consistently developed diabetes.[115] L-asparaginase is a mycotoxin developed from the soil fungus *Cylindrocarpon obtusisporum*.

Aspergillus niger is a fungus often found contaminating peanuts and corn which is known to cause ear infections. The fungus also produces oxalic acid in large quantities, which is known to stop the conversion of sugars into energy.[116]

Many fungus mycotoxins are used as antibiotics, even as Pencillin still is. *Streptomyces achromogenes* is a soil fungus which excretes streptozotocin, an antibiotic. Notice that the US Department of Health and Human Services lists this mycotoxin as a carcinogen, which can also cause kidney and *pancreatic* tumours in lab rats.[117] Not such great medicine after all.

How exposed are we to fungi?

The world eats grains like they are going out of fashion. Much of this grain material is stored for some time, promoting the growth of mould, yeasts and fungi. Farmers entering corn silos are at some risk from *Aspergillus ochraceus*, for instance, a fungus whose mycotoxin, ochratoxin, is given off as a gas. Inhaling ochratoxin can have serious consequences. The kidneys attempt to detoxify this toxin can cause the nephron tissues within the kidneys to become infected, unleashing the hounds of the immune system. The result is often acute tubular necrosis (ATN), the precursor to kidney failure.

Gliotoxin, an airborne poison given off by *Aspergillus, Candida, Gliocladium and Penicillin* moulds, is also extremely toxic to cells and nerves in small concentrations, as we shall see when we study multiple sclerosis later.[118] Fumonisin toxins are also implicated in

[115] **Constantini, AV**, *Fungalbionics Series: Etiology and Prevention of Atherosclerosis*, Johann Friedrich Oberlin Verlag, Freiburg, Germany 1998/9

[116] **Wallace, A**, *Principles and Methods of Toxicology*, Raven Press, New York: 1989, p.694; **Kibbler, CC**, "Fungal infections of the respiratory tract", *Principles and Practice of Clinical Mycology*, John Wiley and Sons Ltd, England: 1996

[117] Streptozotocin, CAS No. 18883-66-4. *Ninth Report on Carcinogens*. US Department of Health and Human Services, revised January 2001

[118] **Forsby et al**, "Cellular neurotoxicology", *Neurochem.su.se*, 25th November 2002; Council for Agricultural Science and Technology: "Mycotoxins: Risks in plant, animal and human systems", Task Force report No. 139, January 2003

corn products and can cause nerve damage.[119] Patulin, a fungal mycotoxin, is also commonly found in apple juice.

As previously discussed, populations around the world are all indulging in the common behaviour of eating sugar-rich foods, as well as consuming foods which break down into glucose (remember too that alcohol is a mycotoxin! It is the product of yeast acting on sugars). The western diet has resulted in the many fungal complaints commonly seen (thrush, vaginal yeast infections, toe-nail fungus, rashes, jock itch, athlete's foot, etc.), but also the more serious infestations which will result in cancer, heart disease, diabetes, stroke, multiple sclerosis, and others we shall examine. While critters may not be at the root of every one of these problems, THEY ARE MAJOR PLAYERS AND CO-CONSPIRATORS. Science is only now determining just to what extent. Incredibly, doctors are not required to report diseases caused by fungi. Many of them don't even entertain them as a cause for many complaints, simply because they were not taught to do so. Food agencies, such as USDA and Britain's FSA, hardly test the food chain for these hidden contaminants.

Take action♥
Here's what you can do with your food and lifestyle:

- Consult a doctor who is familiar with, or has some grounding in mycotoxicology (critters and their poisons)
- **START THE ANTI-*CANDIDA* DIETARY REGIMEN**, cutting out grains completely
- **AVOID ALL SUGAR AND YEAST**
- **RESTORE NUTRIENT BALANCE: COMMENCE THE BASIC SUPPLEMENT PROGRAM**, ensuring:
- **ANTI-*CANDIDA*/FUNGAL SUPPLEMENTATION**
- Vanadium or chromium picolinate, 200 mcg a day, taken every other day, two weeks on, two weeks off. Note: do not continue this supplement over a protracted period of time
- 4 g Vitamin C complex (ascorbates plus bioflavonoids)

---

[119] **Etzel, R**, "Mycotoxins", *Journal of the American Medical Association*, 287(4): 425-427, 23rd January 2002

- Vitamin B3 (in the form of inositol hexaniacinate – the no-flush version of B3), 2-3 g per day
- Vitamin B6, 100 mg per day
- Increase garlic and onion in the diet
- **EXERCISE AN HOUR A DAY IN A GYM.** This is a vital component of the program and must be taken very seriously. Secure the services of a personal trainer who will devise a proper program for diabetics. Exercise improves glucose tolerance by increasing the sensitivity of cells to insulin. Exercise massively increases oxygen intake and renders your internal environment extremely hostile to parasites
- **NOTE: At no time should diabetics discontinue any prescribed medication without sanction from their physician**

Doctors

Profile

Hard though it may be to accept at first, western healthcare has indeed become the third leading cause of death in most industrialised nations. In the Credence titles *Health Wars* and *Wake up to Health in the 21st Century,* author Steven Ransom and myself cover the harsh statistics plainly demonstrating that often doctors not only *don't* have the answer to what ails us, but instead do irreparable harm with those industry sanctioned 'cures' the public is bullied into accepting without question.

Of course, doctors are not bad or evil people, but they have been trained in institutions funded by the drug industry, and so their licence to practise is dependent on them conforming to the medical orthodoxy of the day. Any use of treatments unsanctioned by the establishment can bring swift and summary retribution, depending on the regime involved.

Banking on fear

Then there's the sickness racket, stirred up by the unholy alliance of Big Pharma, Big Business and Big Media. Steven Ransom writes:

"Using the mainstream media as their chosen vehicle for change, powerful vested interests within the pharmaceutical industries are deliberately instigating national and international fearsome headlines. Through these channels, the 'nightmare problem' – the epidemic – the psycho-plague, is manufactured. Take a look at these recent quotations and headlines for example:

"Even if we rapidly eliminate SARS, we remain at risk of future viral mutations, and should expect more dangerous new viruses to emerge over the next ten years." **Dr Patrick Dixon, April 2003**

PLAGUE ATTACK *The horrifying spectre of terrorists turning themselves into walking biological weapons on Britain's streets was raised by doctors. Fanatics could be given smallpox and walk amongst us infecting people, yet we only have a vccine for one in three.* **Express Newspapers, 6th March 2003**

SMALLPOX KILLS! *Smallpox kills about 30% of those infected with the disease. There is no cure, but there is a vaccine. If given before exposure, the vaccine will prevent the disease from appearing. But is there enough for everyone?* **BBC NEWS, 13ᵗʰ Jan 2003**

FEARS OF KILLER FLU EPIDEMIC: The world is on the brink of a flu epidemic which could claim millions of lives. The mutant virus has already killed one man in Hong Kong. We need to find out as much as we can about this deadly new virus. **Express Newspapers, 21ˢᵗ February 2003**

TUBERCULOSIS! NEW SPECTRE OF THE WHITE DEATH - We had it beaten, but TB is back and deadlier than ever.... Anyone who refuses inoculation is a danger both to society and to himself. **Daily Mail, 30ᵗʰ March 2001**

MEASLES! *Public health officials have stressed the severity of the situation. The Government is now urging parents to take heed of this warning and allow their children to be immunised with the MMR jab before an epidemic sweeps the nation.* **Readers Digest, Jan 2001**

Steven Ransom: *"The crisis has now been firmly embedded into the minds of the populace. "We must have a solution!" we cry. Lo and behold! A corporate solution is speedily proffered, usually in the form of vaccination, antibiotics and associated conventional 'ministrations'. The epidemic needing 'swift state intervention' has been nothing more than a Trojan Horse for creating immense profit for various pharmaceutical industries and as we shall discover, for implementing such abhorrent measures as population control. Throughout this whole process, we are being taught what to think about global health and disease, but not how."* [120]

Failing to heal

Traditional medicine has failed very conspicuously to halt the metabolic syndromes, such as heart disease, cancer and diabetes. It serves us to study the fundamental flaw in the basic methodology

---

[120] **Ransom, Steven**, *Wake up to Health in the 21ˢᵗ Century*, Credence Publications 2003

followed by allopathic[121] medicine today that is at the root of this devastation. The flaw is simply this: our medical peers are treating our bodies with toxic drugs, radical surgeries and poisonous radiation treatments to combat diseases that are, in almost all cases, either metabolic (nutritional) deficiency syndromes or diseases already caused by poisons (diseases of toxicity).

Doctors often do not appreciate the four major statements below that condemn their current treatment approaches to metabolic diseases:

1. Metabolic diseases are the big killers (cancer, heart disease, etc.)
2. A metabolic disease is a disease that is wedded to your utilisation of food
3. No metabolic disease can be reversed by anything other than the missing metabolic preventative(s), which are always food factors
4. Doctors receive no formal training in nutrition

If we become what we absorb, and the body is the battlefield for the doctor, why *doesn't* our medical establishment train our doctors in that most basic of body sciences? The long answer is, it's due to a complex web of greed, big business and ignorance. The short answer is, fruits and veggies don't make Porsche payments.

Teaching on nutrition

John Robbins cites statistics on western medical and nutritional curricula in his *Reclaiming our Health*:

➢ Number of accredited medical schools in the United States – 127
➢ Number with no required courses in nutrition - 95
➢ Average US physician's course work in nutrition during four years of medical school - 2.5 hours
➢ Percentage of first-year medical school students who consider nutrition to be important to their future careers - 74%

---

[121] allopathic – drug/technology based medicine, as practised by industrialised societies today

> ➤ Percentage who, after two years of medical school, still consider nutrition important - 13%
> ➤ Percentage of US physicians who are overweight - 55%
> ➤ Percentage of US physicians who eat the recommended daily servings of fruits and vegetables - 20% [122]

Dr M R C Greenwood, President of the American Society for Clinical Nutrition (ASCN), was responsible for the following article:

Doctors Need More Nutrition Training: *Nutrition experts say American physicians are under-trained when it comes to issues of nutrition and health. Less than 6% of medical school graduates receive adequate nutrition training. "Until physicians are better trained to provide high levels of information on nutrition, Americans are missing countless opportunities to take advantage of the growing body of scientific research on the role of diet in preventing and treating disease."[123]*

Nutrition expert Dr Michael Klaper is the Director of the Institute of Nutritional Education and Research at Pompano Beach, Florida. He says:

"What's really tragic about this is that we were so busy learning how to fix broken arms, deliver babies and do all of those 'doctor' things in medical school that we considered nutrition to be boring. But after we get into practice, we spend most of the day treating people with diseases that have huge nutritional concerns that have long been essentially ignored. I frequently get calls from doctors across the country saying that their patients are asking questions about nutrition and its role in their conditions and they don't know what to tell them."[124]

Steve Ransom writes in his *Great News on Cancer:* *"It appears that medical students begin with the best of intentions, but the pharmaceutically-oriented curriculum gradually reshapes their understanding. Another good barometer for measuring the*

---

[122] **Robbins, John**, *Reclaiming our Health*, Stillpoint Publ. 1987
[123] *American Journal of Clinical Nutrition*, Issue 68, 1998
[124] www.campaignfortruth.com/nutrition.htm

importance the conventional medical community attaches to nutrition is by sampling hospital food. Budgetary restrictions aside, in a recent letter to the New England Journal of Medicine, a group of researchers contends that hospital food is not healthy. Led by Dr Adam Singer of the State University of New York at Stony Brook, the researchers compiled nutritional breakdowns of meals offered to patients with no dietary restrictions in 57 university hospitals. Fifty-three of the menus failed to meet all the US Public Health Service's dietary guidelines."[125]

A colourful account of what might appear on the patient's food tray is included here:

"If you want to know what an average physician thinks about a balanced diet, look at any hospital food fed to patients, doctors, staff and visitors. Iceberg lettuce with a glob of cottage cheese and a wedge of canned pineapple. Slices of overdone and warmed-over beef that have suffered for hours in some electronic purgatory, coated with a gravy made of water, library paste, and bouillon cubes. Peas, corn and carrots, boiled. The pie is a sickening slab of beige goo, flavoured with artificial maple sugar, in a crust of reconstituted cardboard, topped with sweetened shaving cream squirted from an aerosol bomb." [126]

Dr Andrew Saul comments on western attitudes to diet and nutrition:

"I have seen the foolishness of conventional disease care wisdom. I have seen hospitals feed white bread to patients with bowel cancer and 'Jello' to leukaemia patients. I have seen schools feed bright red 'Slush Puppies' to 7-year-olds for lunch and I have seen children vomit up a desk-top full of red crud afterwards. And I have seen those same children later line up at the school nursery for hyperactivity drugs.

---

[125] **Dembling, Sophia**, *Health & Fitness News Service*, http://detnews.com/index.htm, 14th May 1997

[126] "What supplements don't have": www.mothernature.com

I have seen hospital patients allowed to go two weeks without a bowel movement. I have seen patients told that they have six months to live when they might live sixty months. I have seen people recover from serious illness, only to have their physician berate them for having used natural healing methods to do so.

I have seen infants spit up formula while their mothers were advised not to breast-feed. I've seen better ingredients in dog food than in the average school or hospital lunch. And I have seen enough."[127]

Summary

In my books, I examine this problem of doctors in more depth. But for our purposes here, let us firstly appreciate that doctors, while often best-intentioned, are working under difficult circumstances in which their treatment options are determined, more often than not, by economic rather than scientific considerations. One key area of their training, namely, the understanding and application of nutritional strategies against disease, has been completely neglected, resulting instead in the patient being given expensive and largely useless chemical remedies with predictable, often serious side-effects.

Those suffering from an illness must make up their minds about the type of approach they feel is best for them. Whilst I do not condemn all drug medicine as useless and deadly, I see an urgent need for patients themselves to become educated on the options and often simple, natural strategies which have been shown to be effective. Too often, the patient is bamboozled, cajoled, coerced and subjected to medical terrorism in an attempt to get them to agree to drug intervention, often with disastrous results, as we'll see in the next section. And yet, in the twenty years I have been studying and reporting on health issues, I have seen, thousands of times, a return to a simple, nutritious diet and straightforward lifestyle changes bring untold rewards of strength, health, vitality, happiness and an extension of life to those who used them consistently.

---

[127] **Saul, Andrew**, *Doctor Yourself* at: www.doctoryourself.com

Drugs and Medicine

Commentary

The first president of the United States, George Washington, was bled to death in 1797 by some of the most well-educated medical practitioners of his day. No doubt, had you been at the august president's deathbed raising a fuss as they incised his wrists, these learned professionals would have angrily turned on you: *"We know what we're doing. We're DOCTORS!"* It must be noted that the men who killed George Washington were extremely intelligent. They were among the most experienced practitioners of their day – they were highly educated. And they were wrong.

King Charles II of England's doctors were also wrong. When His Majesty fell into a swoon in 1685 (possibly suffering a stroke), he was attended by fourteen of the nation's most well-educated and skilled physicians. His treatment is recorded thus:

"...the king was bled to the extent of a pint from a vein in his right arm. Next his shoulder was cut into and the incised area was supped to suck out an additional eight ounces of blood. An emetic and a purgative were administered followed by a second purgative followed by an enema containing antimony, sacred bitters, rock salt, mallow leaves, violets, beetroot, camomile flowers, fennel seed, linseed, cinnamon, cardamom seed, saphron, cochineal and aloes. The king's scalp was shaved and a blister raised. A sneezing powder of hellebore was administered. A plaster of Burgundy pitch and pigeon dung was applied to the feet. Medicaments included melon seeds, manna, slippery elm, black cherry water, lime flowers, lily of the valley, peony, lavender and dissolved pearls. As he grew worse, forty drops of extract of human skull were administered followed by a rallying dose of Raleigh's antidote. Finally bezoar stone was given. [128]

---

[128] **Buckman, Dr Robert & Karl Sabbagh**, *Magic or Medicine?* Pan Books, 1993   Dr Buckman explains that a bezoar was held by legend to be the crystallized tears of a deer which had been bitten by a snake. In fact most bezoars used in therapy were gallstones found in the stomachs of goats. See also **Silverman, WA**, *Controlled Clinical Trials*, "The Optimistic Bias Favouring Medical Attention", Elsevier Science, New York, 1991

Curiously His Majesty's strength seemed to wane after all these heroic interventions and as the end of his life seemed imminent, his doctors tried a last ditch attempt by forcing more Raleigh's mixture, pearl julep and ammonia down the dying king's throat. Further treatment was rendered more difficult by the king's death."[129]

Nothing much has changed, except perhaps for the pigeon dung. Many drugs routinely prescribed to the public today cause side-effects and diseases of their own. Patients should exercise extreme caution whenever they are prescribed. Antibiotics can wreak havoc with the body's immune system and gut flora. Psychiatric drugs (including anti-depressants) have a known propensity themselves for causing mental disturbances, violence, lethargy, depression, suicide and many physical reactions. Chemotherapy drugs are known to cause cancer. The benzodiazepines are highly addictive, hooking tens of thousands of people in Britain alone in their relentless grip. In America alone, millions of children are routinely prescribed Ritalin and Prozac for bogus disorders such as ADD/ADHD, often with tragic results. In *The Mind Game*, I have a chapter set aside which examines the school shooting phenomenon in that country and the real causes, which the media and the medical establishment refuse to acknowledge.

Symptoms

People experiencing unusual symptoms often ignore the fact that it could be the medication they are taking which may be the problem. In the United States alone, a staggering 106,000 people die, on average, each year because of *correct* drug prescribing. Yet around 7,000 perish through medication errors.[130] These figures show you the problem of death by *correct* drugs in the starkest light.

Am I telling you to stop taking your medicine? Not at all. But drugs treat symptoms, almost never addressing the underlying cause. That's why, if you have a headache and you take Advil, you are

---

[129] Noted by H W Haggard and quoted in **Silverman, W A,** *Human Experimentation,* Oxford Medical Publications, Oxford, 1985
[130] *Journal of the American Medical Association,* Vol. 284, 26th July 2000

merely treating the pain, not correcting the underlying reason you got the headache in the first place.

In certain circumstances, discontinuing your medication without proper supervision can be dangerous. For instance, if you are taking the blood-thinner Warfarin (actually a rat poison) because you have thick, clumpy blood sluggishly coursing through your body, the Warfarin may be the only thing stopping you from having a stroke or the many heart complications arising from your condition. Discontinuing it would be ill-advised. Notice though that the Warfarin is not solving the problem of why you have the condition in the first place, it's merely putting you in a holding pattern. Arthritis medication isn't solving the problem of why you have the condition in the first place, it's merely treating the symptoms, etc.

Steven Ransom, in his *Wake up to Health in the 21st Century*, spells out the two different approaches to disease in what is known as orthodox and alternative medicine:

THE EMPIRICIST - COOPERATING WITH NATURE
The Empiricist (alternative) approach in medicine looks at the human body as an integrated whole and how it interacts with its environment. Symptoms are viewed as the body's reaction to some aspect of its environment - stress, food, pollutants, climate and certain 'medicines' etc. Treatments are based on all of the patient's symptoms, which are not necessarily common to other persons suffering from the same so-called 'disease'. The empiricist does not categorize groups of conditions, but sees each individual as a unique case relating to his environment in his own unique way. Most importantly, the empiricist sees the healing force as being within the body and the physician's role is to assist the body back to its natural state by cooperating with its efforts to heal itself.

THE RATIONALIST - NATURE IS WEAK
The Rationalists (orthodox medicine) need to explain illness in order to be able to develop a body of scientific knowledge and specific treatments. Rationalists look for greater precision and their reasoning leads them to search for common denominators and groups of symptoms that are found identical in all patients having

the same assumed disease. Writing on his travels to 1st century AD Egypt, Herodotus noted:

"Medicine is practised among the Egyptians on a plan of separation. Each physician treats a single disorder, and no more. Thus the country swarms with medical practitioners, some undertaking to cure diseases of the eye, others of the head, others again of the teeth, others of the intestines, and some of those which are not local." [131]

'HEROIC INTERVENTION'

The Rationalists see the disease as the primary concern and assume that it is the doctor who possesses the ability to effect the healing inasmuch as nature is inherently weak and has 'gone wrong'. The physician is responsible for the healing, and the 'disease' has to be driven from the body using heroic intervention. The Rationalists seek to destroy disease, which necessitates that they deny the innate healing powers of the body. Major interventions including bloodletting, and strong elements, such as sulphur and mercury concoctions, were originally used in an attempt to root out or eradicate the disease. Unavoidable to this approach was the subsequent weakening of the body.

In many of our Credence titles, we examine the phenomenon of drugs and the problems they cause in the context of different illnesses studied. Our society has come to worship medicine. We are a public often times desperate to participate in an elaborate religious healing ritual, one in which danger, personal cost to the patient and a potent fear actually appear to be the vital ingredients.

Psychologist and medical researcher Richard Totman studies the effects of faith and suggestion at the heart of our drug-based medical religion today. He has this to say:

"Take anything that is either nasty, expensive or difficult to obtain, wrap it up in mystery and you have a cure."

---

[131] **Herodotus**, 'The Persian Wars', as reported in 'The Origins of Medicine' at http://www.giveshare.org/Health/medicinehistory/chapter4.html

Have we become the congregation of a medical religion in whose surgery and hospital temples we attempt to seek a kind of redemption? Certainly we take an almost ghoulish delight in telling others what is wrong with us and what our doctors are trying to do to put it right. I remember my daily train journey into London involved enduring the non-stop medical anecdotes of a family friend - what Kevin was suffering from today; what Mary's latest pills were doing for her, and so on. These conversations are an extremely common social ritual, as is apparently the need to endure some kind of ghastly sacrifice at the altar of ill-health and emerge bloodied but victorious, thanks to our faith in doctors and their wonderful, life-saving chemicals.

Do some of us subconsciously make ourselves sick in order to enter this healing/redemption ritual? Judging by the following testimonies from doctors themselves, such a 'blasphemous' notion does not appear too wide of the mark.

"I was brought up, as I suppose every physician is, to use placebo[132], bread pills, water injections and other devices... I used to give them by the bushels..."
Professor Richard Cabot, Harvard Medical School, 1903

"Whatever the rights and wrongs, placebo prescribing is widely practised and, if we admit it to ourselves, so is the habit of prescribing for largely social reasons."
Dr K Palmer, British general practitioner, 1998

Drug-taking as a ritual

Not much has changed in 95 years, it seems. Many studies have been conducted examining the effects of placebos. The fact that pharmacologically inert substances such as bread pills have a measurable clinical effect on illness is proof positive that our healing religion is alive and even kicking into a higher gear today.

To illustrate this point, in a television episode of the series *Trust Me (I'm a Doctor)*, shown on British TV on 11th November 1997, Dr

---

[132] **placebo** – a harmless, pharmacologically inactive medicine given to a patient which effects 'a cure'

Phil Hammond asks a group to test the strength of a fictional drug he named Ketofenfobraphen. Hammond describes the impressive-sounding drug to the group as *'a powerful new painkiller that works by selectively blocking the effects of prostaglandin 2 alpha'.*

"It's been licensed in the USA and Japan for a year," Hammond enthusiastically tells his volunteers, *"and sales have gone through the roof. In fact, I'd recommend you to buy shares in the company. Its beauty is that it works quickly – usually within ten minutes – although it can occasionally give you a dry mouth and make you feel dizzy. Mind you, it's expensive – seven tablets for £14.99 and they do not taste very nice – but it's the best drug in its class and I use it all the time for my knee. And when the British Lions were on tour in South Africa, they insisted on having some flown out especially..."* etc. etc.

Note that in giving out the details of Ketofenfobraphen, Dr Hammond is careful to mention each aspect which will affect the outcome of the healing ritual: The drug is a 'wonder drug'. It is officially sanctioned (licensed). It produces side-effects (dry mouth and dizziness). It is horribly expensive and has an unpleasant taste. And lastly, a group most of us look up to (the British Lions) think it's the business (the all-important, independent professional endorsement).

The volunteers were randomly split into two groups after being told they would receive either Ketofenfobraphen or a placebo. In reality both groups were given different coloured placebos. Ten minutes after taking the tablets, they were blindfolded and asked to submerge a hand in ice and pull it out only when it got uncomfortably painful. Hammond reports that after five minutes, twice as many volunteers who thought they had been given the painkiller still had their hands in ice:

"When I asked if anyone had suffered side-effects as a result of taking the 'powerful painkillers', one woman said she had felt faint and dizzy soon after swallowing the pills."[133]

[133] **Hammond, Phil**, *Trust Me (I'm a Doctor)*, Metro Books, 1999 p.91

Officially sanctioned quackery

We hear cries of 'quackery!' levelled by the medical establishment against treatments unsanctioned by them and yet official quackery on a vast scale, involving highly toxic and deadly drugs, surrounds us in breathtaking abundance. Got a pain? Have a drug. Got a headache? Have a drug. Got a bad attitude? Have a drug. When the only tool you have is a hammer, very soon everything starts looking like a nail. The pharmaceutical industry cynically ignores unprofitable prevention in favour of successfully snowing us that biotechnology is the future for mankind's health. I beg to differ. I think, if we do not get prudence and quick, biotechnology will be the ruin of us.

As Ralph Nader and many others have found out, 'orthodox' medical quackery has created sickness and death on a scale that is hard for us to accept at first, but the true picture is beginning to emerge along with the scandals and hard statistics which show us where the real problem lies.

Have we become like the shade-tree mechanic who spends so much time tinkering with his car that it no longer runs the way it used to? Professor Chris Bulstrode, an orthopaedic surgeon turned medical teacher, puts the compelling case for *less* doctors and medicine, not more:

"More doctors just means more illness. If we want a healthier and happier country, we should get rid of a lot of doctors. I cannot have been the only person who was absolutely incensed to discover that when the Berlin Wall came down, the military strength of the Eastern Block was an order of magnitude less than we had been led to believe. I want to try all the western generals for lying to the public about how strong the Russians were. These generals have done three things over the last thirty years. They have frightened the hell out of the Russians, they have frightened the hell out of us, and they have stolen a huge amount of money from the budget that could have been used elsewhere. As I was thinking about this, I realized that this is exactly what we as doctors do in health care."

Take action♥

If you think you have a problem with a drug you are taking, or are unsure about the side-effects of a particular concoction, your doctor is duty-bound to provide you with this information. If you find yourself drawn towards any medicines, especially those that can be purchased over-the-counter in drug stores, ask yourself whether you intend merely to correct the symptom, or turn the tap off the underlying cause to what ails you. Remember that in most cases, your body will heal itself if given the raw materials and enough time to do so. That is not to say that doctors should not be consulted. But best to consult those who have been trained in nutrition and prevention, for they are the ones with the more complete picture of your condition.

Do not discontinue any medication without consulting a physician. Doctors are on-hand to advise, not dictate. Ultimately, you must take responsibility for your own health and welfare. However, while deciding about what to do with any medication you are currently taking, why not take the prudent step anyway of giving your body what it really needs? If you can discontinue any medication, do so, boosting your body's immunity and vitality all the while with good, wholesome nourishment:

- **COMMENCE THE *FOOD FOR THOUGHT* LIFESTYLE REGIMEN**
- Pay particular attention to the **Foods to avoid** section
- **COMMENCE THE BASIC SUPPLEMENT PROGRAM**

Epilepsy, Fits & Convulsions

Profile

Vaccine damage and aspartame poisoning are known to cause convulsions and epileptic-like seizures. Two elements that are frequently deficient in those suffering from convulsions and epilepsy are magnesium and manganese. To date, four studies have shown a correlation between low levels of manganese and epilepsy.[134] Once supplementation starts, the subject appears to suffer less. Manganese supplementation is ideally carried out within the framework of the basic supplement program (see **A Guide to Nutritional Supplements**) and a change to **THE *FOOD FOR THOUGHT* LIFESTYLE REGIMEN**.

Manganese is available in many foods normal to a healthy diet, but junk foods are noticeably deficient in this vital mental mineral. Magnesium injections have been known instantly to suppress convulsions. Vitamin B6 and zinc are also key nutrients that can be employed to treat fits and convulsions.

Those suffering from these problems are advised to have an intradermal allergy test to see if foods are playing a role. Also a hair mineral analysis should be carried out to discover if there are any deficiencies or excess metals. Once these are corrected, the fits usually cease.

Take action♥

- **DIET: COMMENCE THE *FOOD FOR THOUGHT* LIFESTYLE REGIMEN.**
- **RESTORE NUTRIENT BALANCE: COMMENCE THE BASIC SUPPLEMENT PROGRAM,** ensuring:

---

[134] **Dupont, Cl, & Y Tanaka**, "Blood manganese levels in children with convulsive disorder", *Biochem. Med.* 33(2):246-55, 1985; **Papavasilou, PS, et al**, "Seizure disorders and trace metals: manganese tissue levels in treated epileptics", *Neurology*, 29:1466, 1979; **Sohler, A and CC Pfeiffer**, "A direct method for the determination of manganese in whole blood: Patients with seizure activity have low blood levels", *J. Orthomol. Psychiatr.*, 8(4):275-280, 1979; **Tanaka, Y**, "Low manganese level may trigger epilepsy", *Journal of the American Medical Association*, 238:1805, 1977

- Vitamin E, 800 IU per day
- Zinc, 35 mg, am and pm
- Vitamin B6, 100 mg, am and pm
- Manganese, 10 mg, am and pm

Glaucoma

Profile
Glaucoma is a condition in which the pressure of fluid in the eyeball increases, leading to blurred vision, damaged optic nerves and eventually a loss of vision. Fluid called aqueus humour is produced in the posterior chamber of the eyeball (behind the pupil) and then passes through the pupil into the anterior chamber, before draining out through outflow channels above and below the eyeball. When the fluid created in the posterior chamber builds up at a faster rate than it can drain through the iris into the anterior chamber (in front of the pupil) and out through the outflow channels, a condition of glaucoma becomes known. Generally, intraocular pressure (in the anterior chamber) exceeding 20-22 mm will tend to indicate the problem.

Glaucoma has become increasingly common and is linked with the explosion of diabetes across the world. In America, approximately two million people suffer the condition. Nearly two percent of people over forty have the disorder in the US, and by age seventy, over ten percent of the population suffer the condition – one of the major causes of blindness in adults in the western world today.

Glaucoma has three recognised types: **open-angle (chronic)**, **closed-angle (acute)**, and **secondary**. In open-angled glaucoma, fluid does not drain rapidly enough from the anterior chamber, creating a build-up of pressure, leading eventually to optic nerve damage and a progressive loss of vision. This disorder occurs usually in both eyes and is the more gradual and progressive of the three types.

Closed-angle glaucoma is when the outflow channels abruptly become constricted or blocked, causing a sudden rise in pressure. Sometimes, conditions which cause the pupil to dilate will squeeze off the outflow channels in those with the condition, leading to acute attacks.

Secondary glaucoma occurs when another condition results in damage to the eye (infection, tumour, inflammation, uveitis, eye injury, eye surgery, etc.) which causes the effects described in glaucoma. Corticosteroid drugs, such as prednisone, have a notorious propensity for weakening collagen structures (see below) and should be avoided by all glaucoma patients. In these cases, the primary condition should be treated as a priority.

Symptoms

Open-angle (chronic) glaucoma: Increased pressure in both eyes often produces no symptoms, but as the condition develops, distortion of peripheral vision may occur, including seeing haloes around electric lights. Mild headaches. Adaptation to the dark becomes more difficult. Tunnel vision begins to develop (an inability to view objects in the peripheral arc, only straight ahead), and blind spots may occur in the vision field.

Closed-angle (acute) glaucoma: Symptoms occur suddenly, in 'attacks', which are usually forewarned with symptoms similar to open-angle glaucoma (above). An extended attack occurs after a few hours of the vague symptoms, and may include severe headache, nausea, vomiting, and a throbbing pain in the eye (usually one side only). The pupil appears moderately dilated and fixed and does not react appropriately when light is shone on it. The eyelid swells and reddens, and the affected eye becomes red and watery. The patient will complain of blurred vision. Each successive attack may cause a further, progressive loss of vision.

Traditional treatments

Usually the condition is diagnosed by an ophthalmologist or optometrist who recognises the tell-tale signs. Typically, eye-drops will be prescribed, as well as beta-blockers, and other medications which variously restrict the production of aqueous humour or improve outflow. However no medication claims to cure the disorder. The Merck Manual admits modern medicine does not know the precise cause of glaucoma. It appears to 'run in the family'. Surgery (drainage or filtering operations) may also be used to modify the outflow channels and eye structure (including cutting part of the iris) to relieve pressure in the most acute cases.

Commentary

Glaucoma is primarily found in those suffering from malnutrition, specifically in the way the tough, elastic, fibrous material collagen has not formed correctly in the supporting structures of the patient's eyes.[135] Collagen, as we have seen in other disorders like heart disease and scurvy, is directly dependent upon adequate intakes of vitamins C, E and supporting amino acids, such as lysine and proline, in order to form correctly (see **Heart Disease**). In the absence of sustained levels of these nutrients, an early form of scurvy develops, as the collagen disintegrates, manifesting itself in many different conditions around the body treated by different specialists. Perhaps the fractioned method of today's medicine is why an overview of the patient's general state of health and nutrition is often *not* taken into consideration and the more obvious nutritional causations missed.[136]

Take action♥

A progressive nutritional program aimed at a) reducing intraocular pressure and b) building up the collagen matrix in the body is the way to go. Allergies and food intolerances also increase fluid pressure and so these need to be identified and treated in the appropriate manner.

Please note that acute glaucoma is a serious matter and an ophthalmologist should be consulted immediately. Serious and permanent damage to eyesight may result in a matter of days if emergency steps are not taken to treat the condition.

The regimen below is designed to treat collagen matrix problems in the body, as well as fortify the immune system and provide proper nutrition over an extended period of time. It should be rigorously adhered to. You will note that this regime bears a similarity to the

---

[135] **Weiss, J and M Jayson**, *Collagen in Health and Disease*, Churchill, Livingstone, New York: 1982, pp.388-403

[136] **Tengroth, B and T Ammitzboll**, "Changes in the content and composition of collagen in the glaucomatous eye: Basis for a new hypothesis for the genesis of chronic, open-angle glaucoma", *Acta Ophthalmol* 62 (1984): pp.999-1008; **Rohen, J**, "Why is intraocular pressure elevated in chronic, simple glaucoma?" *Ophthalmology* 90 (1983): pp.758-765

heart disease protocol, as the latter is also a collagen problem in the majority of cases.

- **DIET: COMMENCE THE *FOOD FOR THOUGHT* LIFESTYLE REGIMEN**, ensuring a robust intake of fresh, organic fruits and vegetables. Also oily fish (salmon, herring, mackerel, etc.) and other foods containing the essential fats. Take special note of the **Foods to avoid** section
- **RESTORING NUTRIENT BALANCE: COMMENCE THE BASIC SUPPLEMENT PROGRAM**, ensuring:
- Vitamin C complex, 4 – 10 g per day in divided doses, as directed (ideally C should be prescribed to the threshold level before bowels become loose)
- Vitamin E, 800 IU per day
- Bioflavonoids (mixed), 1 – 1.5 g per day
- Chromium, 200-400 mcg per day
- Lysine and proline, as directed
- Magnesium, 200-600 mg per day
- Flaxseed oil, 1 tbsp per day
- Gingko biloba, as directed
- **EXERCISE:** At least an hour, four times a week. Just aerobic, no weight-training until advised
- **TIPS:** Those suspecting they have the condition should commence the above dietary regimen as soon as possible in order to stave off the effects of the condition in its later development
- Avoid all refined foods, especially sugar, alcohol and items to which the patient may be sensitive

Heart Disease

Profile
The leading cause of death in the western world today is heart disease. Over 3,000 Americans die EVERY DAY from heart disease in its various forms. So, if we are interested in living to be 100, heart disease must be one of the first hurdles we must overcome. Is that possible?

If you were able to remove heart disease from the general population, our world today would be radically different from what we see. How many relatives would still be with us? How much more money would there be available for proper research to conquer other, less well-known problems?

We are about to find out that heart disease can end today based entirely on existing scientific knowledge. That is why I become increasingly tired of the whining British National Health Service and its government over cash shortages in Britain and how financially strapped the hospitals and health services are today. None of this would be happening if the population and its health services WOULD EXERCISE PREVENTION INSTEAD OF CURE. For who, in reality, is responsible for the soaring costs of healthcare today, if not we, the population, through not taking proper care of ourselves? That's our responsibility, by the way, not the government's.

Types of heart disease
All forms of heart disease will be dealt with in this chapter as the approaches to them are essentially the same. Let's first take a look at the major problems:

Cardiomyopathy: Any disease affecting the heart muscle's ability to pump juice. The heart works through electrical/muscular contraction. When this becomes impaired, the decreased efficiency of the heart to circulate blood begins to cause warning signs. Shortness of breath, arrhythmia (see below), fatigue, a chronic, unproductive cough and blue extremities are common indications.

Congestive heart failure: Failure or impairment of the pumping action of the ventricle of the heart, resulting in a back pressure of blood, engorging the veins in the neck creating fluid retention in the tissues, or edema. Shortness of breath, even when lying prone, swelling of the legs, etc.

Myocardial infarction: The classic heart attack, where part of the heart muscle, usually the left ventricle, dies, following an interruption of the blood supply. The patient experiences a 'heart attack' – an abrupt, severe chest pain, which may spread to the arms and throat.

Arrhythmia: Any disturbance or abnormality in the regular beating of the heart. These include specific variations, such as ectopic beats, atrial fibrillations, ventricular tachycardias and severe ventricular arrhythmias. Arrhythmias may result from a whole host of different heart conditions. More ominously, the *Oxford Concise Medical Dictionary* warns: *"Arrhythmias may... occur without apparent cause."* [137]

Atherosclerosis: Fatty lipoprotein plaque build-up in the arteries, which prevents proper blood flow, leading to heart failure and other conditions.

Arteriosclerosis: Hardening or thickening of small artery walls. The term is often used interchangeably with atherosclerosis (incorrectly).

Thrombosis: A condition in which liquid blood solidifies or thickens in an artery, preventing blood flow. This may happen in the brain artery, impairing blood flow to the brain, resulting in a stroke. Thrombosis in any artery disrupts blood flow to the tissue it supplies. Coronary thrombosis often results in myocardial infarction, or 'heart attack'.

Angina pectoris: What I term 'the slow heart attack'. Pain in the centre of the chest, spreading to the arms and jaw. Often brought

---

[137] *Oxford Concise Medical Dictionary*, Oxford University Press, Oxford, 2000

on by exercising, where the demand for blood from the heart exceeds the cardiovascular system's ability to provide it. Angina often occurs as a result of damaged or occluded arteries (athero/arteriosclerosis and other heart conditions).

Embolism: A blood clot or other solid body restricting blood flow to vital organs (including the heart and lungs) and tissues. The embolus may become detached and be carried to another part of the body, where it becomes lodged, creating localised or systemic problems.

Heart murmurs: A mitral valve prolapse occurs when this heart valve becomes misshapen or deformed, causing a leakage of fluid between the left upper chamber (atria) of the heart and the left ventricle. Such murmurs may be detected by stethoscope.

Commentary

So, here we are, examining the leading killer of humankind in the western industrial nations.... Doesn't that give you a clue to the where the problems may lie immediately?

The heart and its circulatory (cardiovascular) system are all about tubes, a pump and lots of blood. Notice the problems described above in semi-medical vernacular really come down to the fact that if you don't want to get the leading cause of death, you must have a strong and efficient heart muscle, clean, well constructed pipes (veins and arteries) and blood that is pure and not filled with the kind of debris and rubbish you might find in a Staten Island junkyard.

The human heart beats around 100,000 times every 24 hours, pumping six quarts of blood through a freeway system of over 96,000 miles of blood vessels. This staggering feat is the equivalent of the heart moving 6,300 gallons a day, or shunting 115,000,000 gallons of blood by time you reach fifty. None too shabby, eh?

Then consider that those six quarts of blood each of us have are made up of over 24 trillion cells, seven million new ones of which are produced by our body every second, to replace worn-out cells and continue the work of transporting nutrients and removing waste and toxins. This amazing pump, responsible for all the action, has the capability to run maintenance- and service-free for decades without missing a beat. And no, it doesn't come with a warranty.

Coronary heart disease, heart attacks, angina pectoris, thrombosis, myocardial infarctions – trouble by any name – can be caused by certain types of drugs, as we shall see, and also by coronary arteries that have become progressively clogged by fatty material which prevents normal blood-flow (atherosclerosis). If you take your garden hose, which is supplying water to your lawn sprinkler (in countries which allow you to have one), and bend the hose, the water flow ceases to the sprinkler. Likewise, if the arteries supplying blood to the heart become clogged with deposits, or blood clots brought on by sticky platelets, the same starving of liquid to the pump will occur.

Drs. Pauling and Rath

But it's the underlying cause of almost all heart problems that is the most provocative and misunderstood issue in medicine today. Two doctors, Linus Pauling and Matthias Rath, popularised the scientific truth that had been whispered fearfully in medical corridors for decades, but which had failed to come out because of huge vested interests in the corporate profitability of heart disease – namely that heart disease was primarily a fulminating deficiency of vitamin C complex and the amino acids lysine and proline, which help form the collagen fibres that knit the artery walls together. Dr Matthias Rath sums up his findings:

"Animals don't get heart attacks because they produce vitamin C in their bodies, which protects their blood vessel walls. In humans, unable to produce vitamin C (a condition known as hypoascorbemia), dietary vitamin deficiency weakens these walls. Cardiovascular disease is an early form of scurvy. Clinical studies document that optimum daily intakes of vitamins and other essential nutrients halt and reverse coronary heart disease naturally.

The single most important difference between the metabolism of human beings and most other living species is the dramatic difference in the body pool of vitamin C. The body reservoir of vitamin C in people is on average 10 to 100 times lower than the vitamin C levels in animals."[138]

What a revelation, eh?

Low density lipoprotein - Lp(a)
The makings of scurvy

Scurvy occurs when the collagen matrix in the body begins to break down. With heart disease, the scurvy process is much slower, sometimes taking years to develop. As Dr Rath reports, vitamin C is essential for the production of collagen and elastin, the elastic, fibrous materials which knit the walls of arteries and blood vessels together. Collagen fibres are a lot like the steel girders you see when builders are erecting a new skyscraper. Each fibre has been calculated to be far tougher and stronger than an iron wire of comparable width. Collagen cells form the structure for arteries, organs and skin, and so a chronic vitamin C deficiency causes the beginning of a collapse in the arterial walls, necessitating a healing process to commence, in the form of lipoprotein(a) fats which the body attempts to use to bond the thousands of tiny breaches in the arterial walls.

These lipoproteins are Nature's perfect Band-Aid. They are extremely sticky and form the atherosclerotic deposits associated with advanced forms of heart disease today. Cardiovascular medicine, unaware or willingly ignorant of the underlying nutritional deficiency cause of atherosclerosis, focuses its attention on vilifying the lipoproteins' LDL (low-density lipoprotein) cholesterol content as one of the primary *causes* of heart diseases, when it is in fact the healing (survival response) precursor *brought on by a chronic vitamin C deficiency.* Today the drug industry has predictably mobilised a multi-billion-dollar business of anti-cholesterol drugs, which have wrought devastating results in cardiac patients, necessitating a further $20 billion drug program to combat all the side effects.[139] Rath and Pauling discovered that

---

[138] **Rath, Matthias**, *Why Animals Don't Get Heart Attacks – But People Do!* MR Publishing, 2000, p.10
[139] Sellman, Sherrill, *Hormone Heresy*, op. cit.

> Optimum vitamin C intakes (600 mg – 3 g daily), along with supportive intakes of vitamin E (800-1,000 IU), the amino acids lysine and proline, the B vitamins, essential fatty acids (EFAs), magnesium, minerals, trace minerals and amino acids, provide healthy arteries

> A long-term vitamin C deficiency will lead to atherosclerotic deposits in the arterial walls to cover the breaches caused by the disintegrating collagen, eventually resulting in coronary heart disease and, further north, strokes in the brain

> Vitamin C depletion over a few months will lead to massive blood loss through collagen disintegration, resulting in leaky artery walls, collapsing organs and death by scurvy[140]

Vitamin C depletion (complete absence of the nutrient) in the industrial nations is almost an impossibility, even with the ghastly diets with which we feed ourselves today. However long-term vitamin C deficiency is very common and occurs in almost all the population, hence the prevalence of heart disease in all its forms.

Coronary arteries sustain the most stress since they are the primary roadways for blood being pumped by the heart. The need for ongoing repairs of the leaky artery walls produces an overcompensation of repair materials, such as cholesterol, triglycerides and low-density lipoproteins (LDL), produced in the liver, which lead to infarctions as this plaque builds up. Other areas, such as arteries in the legs, are also affected. Varicose veins often develop as a result of this ongoing healing process (see **Varicose veins**).

Collagen in our body is made up of proteins composed of amino acids, particularly lysine and proline. An optimum supply of vitamin C complex, E, proline and lysine are decisive factors for the regeneration of connective tissue in the artery wall and thus for the reversal of cardiovascular disease. These factors are almost never prescribed by allopathic medicine, which is why, in spite of the most

---

[140] Rath, Matthias, *Why Animals Don't Get Heart Attacks, but People Do*, op. cit. p.23

technical medicines and surgical procedures available, heart disease continues to be the main killer of industrialised, commercially fed, vitamin C-deficient humanity.

Let's look at the problem in action

An interesting parallel can be seen in nature with hibernating animals which, during their extended sleep period, deplete their vitamin C reserves, due to lack of incoming nutrition. As a result, fat molecules are deposited along their artery walls, which lead to a thickening of these vessels. In spring however, once these animals recover from their hibernation and begin consuming vegetation and fruits, such as berries, their vitamin C, amino acid and antioxidant intakes rise sharply, resulting in a reversal of these repair factors, leading to a re-stabilisation of their arterial walls and their normal function.

Lack of antioxidant material is also a major contributing factor. Current theories on this subject suggest that oxidative elements, known as free radicals, are brought into the body through smoking, car exhaust, pollution and smog, damaging the collagen in the artery walls, bringing on the need for further lipoprotein repairs. It is believed the damage is done because electron-hungry free radicals rob healthy cells to produce degradation in the cell and cell-death. These oxidative elements are now widely thought to be the leading cause of pre-ageing and cell degradation.

Autopsies of military personnel killed during the Korean and Vietnam wars showed that up to 75% of the victims had developed some form of atherosclerosis even at ages of 25 or younger. Yet those servicemen who had been captured by the enemy and incarcerated on rice and vegetable diets were later, upon release and a medical examination, found to have cleared the plaque during their period of captivity.

Victims of accidents are often found to have developed atherosclerotic deposits that would have become a problem for them, had they lived longer. Dr Rath comments:

"The main cause of atherosclerotic deposits is the biological weakness of the artery walls caused by chronic vitamin deficiency

[malnutrition]. *The atherosclerotic deposits are the consequence of this chronic weakness; they develop as a compensatory stabilizing cast of Nature to strengthen these weakened blood vessel walls."* [141]

Heart disease studies with nutrition

So chronic vitamin and mineral deficiencies produce a breakdown of collagen in the arterial walls, leading to increased artery wall tension, narrowing of the artery diameter, thickening of artery walls and therefore high blood pressure. The result is heart attack, strokes (impairment of arterial flow to the brain), high blood pressure, irregular heartbeat (arrhythmia) and heart failure. Interestingly, as time marches forward, the public's ability to garner adequate supplies of vitamin C from its diet through fruits and vegetables becomes progressively less as our food chain is corrupted further with processed, chemical foods and the public's penchant to move away from healthy, natural foods in favour of the more 'tasty' and better advertised artificial alternatives.

Ironically heart disease manifested itself less in medieval times during spring, summer and autumn since the predominantly vegetarian diet of the average working class citizen often provided well mineralised vegetables and fruits. Winter however was another matter. Freezing was not possible back then, and nutritional intake took a dive as diets only comprised those foods that could be adequately salted and preserved during the winter months. Strokes and heart disease were common during these months.

Back then, of course, the killer was the more extreme of the vitamin C deficiency ailments – scurvy - which resulted when sailors, for instance, dramatically halted their vitamin C intake, due to the restriction of provisions available on board their ships.

Dr James Enstrom and colleagues from the University of California Los Angeles (UCLA) dramatically proved the heart disease link with vitamin C when they studied the vitamin intake of 11,000 Americans over 10 years. Funded by the US Congress, their study demonstrated that citizens taking in at least 300 mg per day of vitamin C in their diet or through supplementation cut their risk of

---

[141] Rath, Matthias, op. cit. p.57

heart disease by up to 50% in males and 40% in females. This study alone should have made headline news. Who before could have claimed such a reduction in the number of deaths from the leading disease killer in the western world? But nothing was mentioned! The study focused primarily on vitamin C, but, as we will see, other nutrients also play a key role in the prevention or complete elimination of heart disease.[142] We must always remember too that nutrients in the body work in synergy, not in isolation, so any supplementation regime we embark upon should be a complete program, together with a suitable diet.

Dr G C Willis demonstrated that vitamin C complex could reverse atherosclerosis. Willis gave a sample of his patients 1.5 grams of vitamin C a day and gave the remainder of the group no vitamin C. After a year, the atherosclerotic deposits in the patients fed the vitamin C had decreased in 30% of the cases. In contrast, no reduction in deposits was observed in the control group, which had even grown further. In spite of the clear evidence over 40 years ago of the benefits of just vitamin C through Willis' work, no follow-up study was ever commissioned.[143]

Professor Gey, from the University of Basel in Switzerland, conducted studies in which he compared the vitamin C, vitamin A (beta carotene) and cholesterol intakes of citizens living in Northern Europe with those in the southern regions of the continent. His findings were recorded thus:

> ➢ Those living in the northern nations of Europe had the highest levels of cardiovascular disease and the lowest blood levels of vitamins
> ➢ Southern European populations had the reverse statistics of their northern counterparts and so were more healthy
> ➢ An optimum intake of vitamins C, E and A had a far greater impact on decreasing risks of cardiovascular disease than the reduction of cholesterol, now becoming increasingly viewed (correctly) as a secondary factor in

---

[142] **Enstrom, JE, Kanim, LE & MA Klein**, "Vitamin C intake and mortality among a sample of the United States population", *Epidemiology* 3: pp.194-202
[143] **Willis GC, Light AW & WS Gow**, "Serial arteriography in atherosclerosis", *Canadian Medical Association Journal* (1954) 71: pp.562-568

heart disease risk (an inevitable result of the primary deficiency of nutrients leading to the breakdown of the arterial walls).

Gey's report also highlighted the preference for the Mediterranean diet, rich in wine and olive oil, abundant in bioflavonoids (another part of the C complex) and vitamin E, as a main prevention regimen for heart disease in almost all its forms.[144]

Further studies showed that these nutrients separately produced impressive results for cardiac disease prevention:

> Vitamin C intake lowers cardiovascular risk by 50%[145] [146]
> Vitamin E intake lowers cardiovascular risk by one-third, documented in 87,000 study participants over six years[147]
> Beta carotene (vitamin A) intake lowers cardiovascular risk over 30%, documented in more than 87,000 study participants over six years
> No prescription drug has ever come close to matching these figures in preventing heart disease[148]

However, when these nutrients were combined with other synergistic agents, such as magnesium, vitamin B3 (nicotinic acid), vitamin B5 (pantothenate) and the amino acid carnitine, and levels of these maintained in the body over the long-term, near total prevention could be expected, and in those already suffering from a

[144] **Gey KF, Puska P, Jordan P & UK Moser**, "Inverse correlation between plasma vitamin E and mortality from ischemic heart disease in cross-cultural epidemiology" *American Journal of Clinical Nutrition* (1991) 53: p.326, supplement

[145] **Ginter E**, "Vitamin C deficiency cholesterol metabolism and atherosclerosis" *Journal of Orthomolecular Medicine* (1991) 6:pp.166-173; **Ginter E**, "Marginal Vitamin C deficiency, lipid metabolism and atherosclerosis" *Lipid Research* (1978) 16: pp.216-220

[146] **Harwood HJ Jr, Greene YJ & PW Stacpoole**, "Inhibition of human leucocyte 3-hydroxy-3-methylglutaryl coenzyme A reductase activity by ascorbic acid. An effect mediated by the free radical monodehydro-ascorbate" *Journal of Biological Chemistry* (1986) 261: pp.7127-7135

[147] **Beamish R**, "Vitamin E – then and now" *Canadian Journal of Cardiology* (1993) 9: pp. 29-31

[148] Rath, Matthias, op. cit. p.53

variety of cardiac ailments, a clear record of efficacy in reversing these conditions was observed. [149] [150] [151] [152]

Learning from our animals

While the World Health Organization announces that more than 12 million people each year die from the consequences of heart disease and strokes, this death rate is just not occurring in the animal kingdom. When vitamin C levels in animals were measured, procured as a result of their diets and own production of vitamin C, they were found to have between 1 g and 20 g available a day, when compared with human bodyweight. Humans on the other hand, unable to produce their own vitamin C, are now consuming less and less foods containing the essential nutrients available in fruits and vegetables, themselves now depleted of vital nutrients because of commercial and over-farming practices. Some do not even make the miserable 'Recommended Daily Allowance' (RDA) of C – 60 mg a day. This dramatic paradigm shift in nutritional intake by the human over the past 150 years, from a diet almost completely vegetarian (5-10% animal protein intake – meat was largely unavailable to many of the poorer citizens) to one dominated by animal food sources, has manifested itself in the most disastrous death toll from cardiovascular disease, which can now be identified primarily as a metabolic, nutritional deficiency disease.

High blood pressure and arrhythmia

Modern medicine does not know the actual cause of high blood pressure in many of its cases, referring to these unknowns as "essential hypertension". Drugs prescribed can be diuretics, beta-blockers, blood thinners (including the rat poison, Warfarin) and other medications. Yet studies again exist demonstrating that

---

[149] **Sokolov B, Hori M, Saelhof CC, Wrzolek T & T Imai**, "Aging, atherosclerosis and ascorbic acid metabolism" *Journal of the American Gerontology Society* (1966) 14: 1239-1260

[150] **Opie LH**, "Role of carnitine in fatty acid metabolism of normal and ischemic myocardium" *American Heart Journal* (1979) 97: pp.375-388

[151] **Avogaro P, Bon GB & M Fusello**, "Effect of pantethine on lipids, lipoproteins and apolipoproteins in man" *Current Therapeutic Research* (1983) 33: pp.488-493

[152] **Altschul R, Hoffer A & JD Stephen**, "Influence of nicotinic acid on serum cholesterol in man" *Archives of Biochemistry and Biophysics* (1955) 54: pp.558-559; **Carlson LA, Hamsten A & A Asplund**, "Pronounced lowering of serum levels of lipoprotein Lp(a) in hyperlipidemic subjects treated with nicotinic acid" *Journal of Internal Medicine (England)* (1989) 226: 271-276

vitamin C[153], coenzyme Q10[154], magnesium[155] and the amino acid arginine[156] are able to lower blood pressure very effectively without the attendant side-effects of prescription medications. Vitamin C also increases the production of prostacyclin, a small molecule hormone that relaxes the blood vessel walls and also keeps the blood viscosity at optimum levels.[157]

Arrhythmia, or inconsistent heartbeat, is also much misunderstood by conventional medicine. The term "paroxysmal arrhythmia", so often used, simply means "causes unknown". Beta-blockers, calcium antagonists and pacemakers are often prescribed in ignorance of the true underlying nutritional causes. Rath states:

"The most frequent cause of irregular heartbeat is a chronic deficiency in vitamins and other essential nutrients in millions of electrical heart muscle cells. Long-term, these deficiencies of essential nutrients directly cause, or aggravate, disturbances in the creation or conduction of the electrical impulses triggering the heartbeat. Scientific research and clinical studies have already documented the value of magnesium, calcium, carnitine, coenzyme Q10 and other co-factors in helping to normalise different forms of irregular heartbeat, thereby improving the quality of life for the patients." [158]

Other problems linked to the heart

Coffee is known to cause heart problems. Coffee stimulates the release of the hormone adrenalin, which relies on vitamin C as the catalyst for its production. Stress also produces adrenalin, drawing down and depleting supplies of vitamin C in the body, resulting in C

[153] **McCarron DA, Morris CD, Henry HJ & JL Stanton**, "Blood pressure and nutrient intake in the United States" *Science* (1984) 224: 1392-1398

[154] **Digiesti V**, "Mechanism of action of coenzyme Q10 in essential hypertension" *Current Therapeutic Research* (1992) 51: 668-672

[155] **Turlapaty PDMV & BM Altura**, "Magnesium deficiency produces spasms of coronary arteries: relationship to etiology of sudden death ischemic heart disease" *Science* (1980) 208: 198-200

[156] **Korbut R**, "Effect of L-arginine on plasminogen-activator inhibitor in hypertensive patients with hypercholesterolemia" *New England Journal of Medicine* (1993) 328 [4]: pp.287-288

[157] Rath M, *Why Animals Don't Get Heart Attacks...op. cit.* p.102

[158] Ibid. pp.123-124

deficiency problems. The Pill and other hormonal medications also have the effect of drawing down levels of C in the body, producing the attendant effects of heart disease in its various forms.

The great fatty acid boys

Fats are essential, which is why they call them 'the essential fatty acids', but they have to be the right kinds of fats! Omega-3 and omega-6 oils especially are the two important types of essential fatty acids. The suffixes '3' and '6' refer to differences in the particular oil's chemical structure. These 3 and 6 oils are vital for optimum health and play a central role in preventing and healing heart complaints. Needless to say, most of us get plenty of the commercial junk fats, which the body struggles to break down and eliminate, but few of the sixes and threes (and nines), let alone in their optimum configurations.

The main omega-3 oil is alpha-linolenic acid (ALA), prevalent in flaxseed (58%), pumpkin seeds and walnuts. Fish oils, such as contained in oily fish like salmon, cod and mackerel, contain the other important omega-3 oils, DHA (docosahexaenoic acid) and EPA (eicosapentaenoic acid). (Ensure these fish are fresh and cold-caught, NOT FARMED).

Linoleic acid or cis-linoleic acid is the main omega-6 oil and is found in many plant and vegetable oils, including safflower (73%), sunflower, corn, and sesame. The most useful type of omega-6 oil is gamma-linolenic acid (GLA), found in evening primrose oil, used to treat kids with ADD/ADHD problems. Once in the body, omega-3 and omega-6 are converted to prostaglandins, hormone-like substances that regulate many metabolic functions, particularly inflammatory processes. (For more information on the fat boys, see **A Guide to Nutritional Supplements**).

Summary

If we examine the three main areas for heart disease treatment and prevention, we arrive at diet (and supplementation), exercise and lifestyle choices (rejecting smoking, alcohol, drugs and adverse character traits, such as anger, jealousy and irritability) as a means of normalising blood pressure, adrenal hormone secretions and even androgens (male hormones), which are linked to male pattern baldness and a higher risk of heart disease.[159]

The diet, exercise and lifestyle strategies relevant to avoiding heart disease are explained in the **Take action♥** section below. The dietary and supplement regimens are designed to optimise nutrition in a way that is very similar to the nutritional intake of those peoples who do not suffer these problems. Modified nutrition and an associated vitamin and mineral supplementation assure optimum protection against heart attack and stroke.

THESE SIMPLE MEASURES ARE ALSO THE SAME FOR OTHER SERIOUS DISEASES, meaning, as we proceed, that we can develop a common lifestyle strategy that will work across the board for all the major problem areas. This strategy must be applied *consistently*. Those looking for a magic formula to repair a health condition need to know that the magic formula is *doing the right thing and doing it CONSISTENTLY*. Once again, there are things we must do, and there are things we must avoid.

Take action♥

So, here we go. If you have a heart complaint, or are recovering from a heart attack or stroke, firstly engage the services of an MD or ND trained in nutritional medicine. Important considerations are contraindications with medications which may have been prescribed to you. In *Health Wars*, there are two chapters on the heart which get into more detail on the problems with stress, existing diabolical medications for heart conditions, which come with their own serious side-effect problems, and how these affect your performance and well-being. Heart patients, under medical supervision and recommendation, may benefit from the following:

---

[159] Studies on male pattern baldness and its association with coronary heart disease (CHD) have shown that, from a test group of 22,071 male doctors aged 40 or older, studied over 11 years, those with some form of baldness faced the following increases in CHD risk when compared to men with no hair loss: 9% with frontal baldness only – 23% with mild vertex baldness – 32% with moderate vertex baldness and 36% with severe vertex baldness. These increased risks were increased further when compounded with other risk factors, such as high blood pressure or smoking (*Archives of Int. Med.* 24th January 2000; 160:165-171). These factors however can be effectively countered using the strategies explained in this book.

- **DIET: COMMENCE THE *FOOD FOR THOUGHT* LIFESTYLE REGIMEN**
- **DIET:** Note the things in this regime you need to give up!
- **RESTORING NUTRIENT BALANCE: COMMENCE THE BASIC SUPPLEMENT PROGRAM,** ensuring:
- Vitamin C complex (ascorbates plus bioflavonoids), 3–5 g per day, spread throughout the day
- Vitamin E, 800-1000 IU per day
- Vitamin A emulsion, as directed
- Lysine and proline, as directed
- Magnesium, 200-400 mg, three times per day
- Coenzyme Q10, 150-300 mg per day
- L-Carnitine, 300 mg, three times per day
- Vitamin B1, 200-250 mg per day
- Omega 3 & 6 essential fatty acid complex (EFAs), as directed
- **TIP:** Avoid stress, even if it means ditching your whiz $2 million-a-year city job to go farm Christmas trees in Moose Jaw. You can't drive a Ferrari if you're dead
- **TIP:** Avoid the contraceptive Pill and take some serious medical advice on discontinuing HRT, ERT and other hormonal medications
- **TIP:** Avoid eating heavy amounts of any commercially produced meats, especially the red variety (see *Health Wars* – **Meating the Main Problem**)
- **TIP:** Exercise wisely but regularly, according to your physician's advice

Further resources
Health Wars by Phillip Day
Food for Thought by Phillip Day

Hepatitis

Profile

The medical prefix hepa- refers to the liver and 'hepatitis' in its three recognised forms involves infection, inflammation and, in its most serious states, eventual degradation of this most vital organ. Hepatitis is of course a serious illness and all precautions and treatment options should be made available to the patient.

Hepatitis A: Mostly caused by food contamination (faecal content especially) in areas where sanitation and food preparation techniques are poor. Typically, symptoms appear after a few weeks when the patient develops a fever, sickness, followed by jaundice, which can last for up to three weeks. Hep A, while serious, is not usually life-threatening, and infection may confer future immunity.

Hepatitis B: Caused by an identified virus transmitted through contaminated blood/body fluids, via dirty hypodermic needles, blood transfusions, tattooing needles, transfer of body fluids, such as milk, sweat and semen during sexual contacts. Symptoms, which include fever, sweats, headaches, weakness and jaundice, occur from 1-6 months after infection. Most patients will gradually recover. Death rate 5-20%.

Hepatitis C: Formerly known as 'non-A, non-B hepatitis', this variant is transmitted in similar ways to Hep B. More virulent. Most cases develop as a result of contamination via intravenous drug use. Additional symptoms may also include dryness of the eyes, sore bones and extreme fatigue. Death rate higher than Hep B.

Other variant causes: Hepatitis D, E and G.

Common symptoms

Dark urine, fatigue, loss of appetite, nausea, fever, vomiting, headache, abdominal discomfort, light stools, muscle pain, drowsiness, irritability, itching, diarrhoea, joint pain.

Commentary

Drs. Murray and Pizzorno advise: *"Acute viral hepatitis can be an extremely debilitating disease requiring bed rest. It can take anywhere from two to sixteen weeks to recover. Most patients* recover completely (usually by nine weeks for type A and sixteen weeks for types B, C, D and G). However... 10% of hepatitis B and 10-40% of hepatitis C cases now develop into chronic viral hepatitis forms (hepatitis C contracted from a transfusion is associated with a 70-80% chance of developing into chronic hepatitis). The symptoms of chronic hepatitis vary. The symptoms can be virtually non-existent, or they can lead to chronic fatigue, serious liver damage, and even death due to cirrhosis of the liver or liver cancer." [160]

Take action♥

If hepatitis of any sort is suspected, a doctor should be involved immediately. Acute viral hepatitis B may be treated using shots of hyperimmune globulin (HBIG). Dietary considerations are vital to treat all types to assist the liver and dependent organs in clearing themselves. Fungal infestations are also implicated. During treatment, the patient should be rested and not work, exercise or otherwise exert themselves.

Naturally, a major portion of hepatitis infections may be averted through lifestyle choices, i.e. monogamous sex, ceasing intravenous drug usage, good quality sanitation measures, etc. The following regimen will be of benefit to the patient:

- **DIET: COMMENCE THE ANTI-*CANDIDA* DIETARY REGIMEN**. During acute phases of the illness, solid foods should be restricted and patient should consume diluted, blended vegetables, broths, green teas, etc. with a moderate intake of protein sources. As patient recovers, switch to **THE *FOOD FOR THOUGHT* LIFESTYLE REGIMEN**, after the anti-*Candida* course has been completed
- **DIET:** Pay especial attention to the **Foods to avoid** sections, both in the **ANTI-*CANDIDA* DIETARY REGIMEN** and *FOOD FOR THOUGHT* LIFESTYLE REGIMEN**

---

[160] Murray and Pizzorno, op. cit. p.512

- **ANTI-PARASITE:** All measures discussed in the **ANTI-*CANDIDA* DIETARY REGIMEN** should be strictly adhered to for a period of at least 28 days, or as directed by your physician
- **RESTORE NUTRIENT BALANCE: COMMENCE THE BASIC SUPPLEMENT PROGRAM**, ensuring:
- **ANTI-*CANDIDA*/FUNGAL SUPPLEMENTATION**
- Vitamin C complex, 2 g, four times per day. Intravenous C may also be administered at much higher doses, as directed
- Pancreatic enzyme capsules, two, taken three times a day away from food
- Silymarin (milk thistle extract), 140-210 mg, three times per day
- *Glycyrrhiza glabra* (licorice), powdered root, fluid extract or dry powdered extract, as directed

Hypo/Hyperglycaemia

Profile

The brain runs on glucose, claiming up to 30% of the body's production of the essential sugar. 'Blood sugar' levels are vital to the correct functioning of both brain and body. When this delicate balancing act is disrupted, hypoglycaemia (low blood sugar) or hyperglycaemia (high blood sugar) may result, throw both the body and mind into turmoil. It is estimated that 1 in 4 of us may suffer from some form of glucose intolerance, resulting in hypo/hyperglycaemia and, eventually, diabetes mellitus, type 2.

Symptoms

Trembling, anxiety, fatigue, wobbly if hungry, confusion, irritability, palpitations, blurred vision, cold hands and feet, low blood pressure, blackouts, angry outbursts, rambling speech, violence, depression, inappropriate or strange behaviour, forgetfulness, road rage, and an inability to concentrate.

Commentary

When the body has not been fed for some time and blood sugar fuel runs low, the body becomes hungry, inviting the person to consume more nutrients for fuel. The brain triggers the release of adrenalin and the pancreatic hormone glucagon, which in turn provoke the liver into releasing stored glucose (glycogen) in body tissues and the liver to use as fuel. The use of stimulants and the excessive intake of high-glycaemic carbohydrates (bread, sugar, pasta, etc.) disrupt this elegant fuel control system.

Tea, coffee, sucrose, chocolate, junk food, cigarettes and other 'mood enhancers' are constantly reported being available in mental institutions. These also stimulate the production of adrenalin and fool the body into releasing glucose from the liver (glycogen) before it is required. Blood sugar levels soar. Frequent intakes of these foods cause the pancreas to over-produce insulin, the hormone responsible for transporting glucose into the cells. The result is that excess amounts of insulin hormone cause blood sugar levels abruptly to dive. Symptoms of glucose intolerance set in and a vicious cycle is created as more sugar is craved to relieve the symptoms. The end result of this cycle may be low blood sugar (hypoglycaemia) or high blood sugar (hyperglycaemia), exhausted pancreas and adrenal glands, and the accompanying physical and mental symptoms described earlier. The end result will usually be diabetes, type 2 (see **Diabetes**).

The sweetest poison

When it comes to identifying the most common poison we willingly use against ourselves, an amazing feat resulting in millions of deaths worldwide every year, there really is no contest. The perpetrator is as unlikely a candidate as any you might wish to name, and its unmasking is probably all the more horrifying because this substance has burrowed its way into our civilisation like a parasite, draped in the false colours of comfort and familiarity. It has an entire industry behind it as usual, hell-bent on marketing the stuff any way it can. It's whiter than heroin, sweeter than your fiancée, more soluble than the National Debt, and more pernicious than nicotine because, like a true demon, this little beauty comes in a million disguises and always dresses like a friend.

We grew up being brainwashed with all the sayings: "Sugar and spice and all things nice", "Sweetheart", "Sugar-plum" – all painting the white stuff in a comforting, cuddly light. But seeing as we are in the mood for some truth, let's take a hard look at the 's' word. Are you nervous about shattering some highly refined illusions?

Dr William Coda Martin was the first publicly to label sucrose a poison. Martin's definition came about after he determined the classical definition of a poison was *"...any substance applied to the body, which causes or may cause disease."* [161] So what is sucrose? Obviously the first task we must carry out is identifying exactly what sugar is. Once again, we have to do our homework and pre-empt the vocabulary – so let's define our terms. There are a number of 'sugars' around. Here are the main ones:

Glucose – found with other sugars, but occurs naturally in fruits and vegetables. A number of core foods we consume are converted

---

[161] **Martin, William Coda**, *When is a Food a Food – and When a Poison?* Michigan Organic News, March 1957, p.3

by our body into glucose, or blood sugar as it is sometimes called, which is the form in which this highly efficient energy source is made available to our life-systems. Glucose is always present in our bloodstream and is a key material in the metabolic functions of all plants and animals.

Dextrose - known as 'corn sugar', is manufactured from starches.
Fructose - natural sugar found in fruits.
Lactose – milk sugar
Maltose – malt sugar
Sucrose – refined sugar manufactured from sugar cane and beet.

The last, sucrose, is the white and brown stuff that goes into the tea, coffee, soft drinks and sodas, and shows up in everything from bread, breakfast cereals, pasta, tomato ketchup to Pot Noodles, doughnuts, Dime Bars and Twinkies. There are few manufactured or processed foods today that do not contain either sucrose, aspartame or saccharin (see **Aspartame Disease**). Sugar's prevalence for 300 years has made the sweet-hearts in the sugar industry wealthy beyond most people's imaginations. Naturally, the sugar barons are willing to do or say just about anything to keep their products bathed in the safe and neighbourly light that results in the great unwashed scoffing it down by the bushel-box-load.

Sugar bombing

Today's penchant for eating truck-loads of high-energy, refined high-glycaemic carbohydrates, such as pastries, bread, pasta, sweets, etc., washed down with sugary drinks or alcoholic beverages, means that a tremendous amount of excess glucose, which isn't being burnt off as fuel (lack of exercise), has to be dealt with somehow. Initially, as much as possible is stored in the liver and body tissues in the form of glycogen. As more sugar is stuffed into our sagging bodies daily, the liver swells like a balloon to accommodate it, waiting in vain for the garbage truck to take it out of the body (detoxification/ elimination).[162] The truck almost never arrives because we do not detoxify our bodies (sugar has also been linked to constipation).[163] Finally, reaching its limit, the liver has had enough and pours the sucrose toxins it has accumulated back into the bloodstream in the

---

[162] **Goulart, F S**, *American Fitness*, "Are You Sugar Smart?" March-April 1991, pp.34-38
[163] Ibid.

form of fatty acids, which are then taken to storage bins in the inactive areas of the body, namely the belly, thighs, hips, breasts and the backs of our upper arms (triceps area).

Once the inactive storage areas are filled to capacity, the body begins distributing the metabolite acids into the active organs, such as the heart and kidneys.[164] These fats accumulate as rapidly as the sucrose continues to pour in, impairing the functioning of vital organs, causing hormonal imbalance[165], creating lethargy, abnormal blood pressure as the circulatory and lymph systems are invaded, depleting vital vitamin C reserves, threatening the cardiovascular system.[166] An overabundance of white cells occurs, leading to the retardation of tissue formation. The system is nearing collapse at this point, but still the sugar keeps a-coming....

How about the rampant alcoholic consumption, which in itself leads to chaotic blood sugar patterns and diabetes (see **Alcoholism**)? How about the cellulite, varicose veins and the rotten teeth?[167] [168] How about the kids bouncing off the walls with mineral depletion, ADD and ADHD because sucrose robs minerals, impairs brain function, resulting in increased emotional instability, concentration difficulties, hyperactivity and violence in the classroom,[169] [170] ending up no doubt with a Ritalin or Prozac prescription, black eyes from fighting, detention, lousy grades... and conceivably a school shooting or two....[171] (see **ADD/ADHD**)

---

[164] **Yudkin, Kang and Bruckdorfer**, "Effects of High Dietary Sugar", *British Journal of Medicine*, #281, 1980, p.1396

[165] **Yudkin, J**, "Metabolic Changes Induced by Sugar in Relation to Coronary Heart Disease and Diabetes", *Nutrition and Health*, Vol.5, #1-2, 1987: pp.5-8

[166] **Pamplona, Bellmunt, Portero and Prat**, "Mechanisms of Glycation in Atherogenesis", *Medical Hypotheses*, #40, 1990, pp.174-181

[167] **Cleave and Campbell**, *Diabetes, Coronary Thrombosis and the Saccharine Disease*, John Wright and Sons, Bristol, UK: 1960

[168] **Glinsman, Irausquin and Youngmee**, "Evaluation of Health Aspects of Sugars Contained in Carbohydrate Sweeteners", Report from FDA's Sugar Task Force, Center for Food Safety and Applied Nutrition, Washington DC: 1986, p.39

[169] **Schauss, Alexander**, *Diet, Crime and Delinquency*, Parker House, Berkeley, CA: 1981

[170] **Goldman, J et al**, "Behavioural Effects of Sucrose on Preschool Children", *Journal of Abnormal Child Psychology*, #14, 1986, pp.565-577

[171] *Journal of Abnormal Psychology*, #85, 1985

Glutamic acid, the key to proper brain function, is derived from a diet rich in unrefined plant dietary. Glutamic acid is broken down by B vitamins into compounds that regulate stop and go functions in the brain. B vitamins however are manufactured by symbiotic bacteria inhabiting our intestines. As the sucrose bombing continues, these bacteria are killed by the toxic sugar metabolites, resulting in a severe depletion of our B-vitamin production and the ongoing explosion of unregulated *Candida*. The lack of B vitamins in turn impairs brain function. The results in adults can traverse the awesome spectrum from sleepiness and the inability to calculate or remember, through to dizziness[172], heightened PMS symptoms[173] and possibly finishing with those famous murderous impulses, resulting in your lawyer's "Twinkie Defence" (see **Criminal Violence** and **Diabetes**).[174]

And so, as the human becomes the sugar equivalent of the Frankenstein monster, pancreatic and adrenal functions become inhibited by excess sucrose-triggering, resulting in the impairment of pancreatic enzymes such as trypsin and chymotrypsin, vital for arresting healing processes and preventing cancer growths.[175] Sugar may lead to cancer of the breast, ovaries, prostate and rectum (see **Cancer**).[176] It has been implicated in colon cancer, with an increased risk in women,[177] and is a risk factor in biliary tract

---

[172] *Journal of Advanced Medicine*, 1994 7(1): pp.51-58

[173] *The Edell Health Letter*, September 1991; 10:7(1)

[174] "On 27 November 1978, Dan White, a former San Francisco city supervisor who had recently resigned his position, entered San Francisco's city hall by climbing through a basement window and then shot and killed both mayor George Moscone and supervisor Harvey Milk. After White's subsequent trial for the murders, a new term entered the American lexicon: 'Twinkie defence'. This phrase came to represent the efforts of criminals to avoid responsibility for their actions by claiming that some external force beyond their control had caused them to act the way they had. The term arose from the successful defence mounted by White's legal team that White's eating of Twinkies and other sugar-laden junk foods had diminished his mental capacity."
http://www.snopes.com/errata/twinkie.htm. Author's note: Interesting that White's defence team argued that their client's junk-food diet was *evidence* of his depression, *not the cause of it*, as the papers subsequently reported.

[175] **Appleton, Nancy**, *Healthy Bones*, Avery Publishing Group, NY: 1991; see also **Day, Phillip**, *Cancer: Why We're Still Dying to Know the Truth*, Credence Publications, 2001

[176] *Health Express*, "Sugar and Prostate Cancer", October 1982, p.41

[177] **Bostick, Potter, Kushi, et al**, "Sugar, Meat and Fat Intake, and Non-Dietary Risk Factors for Colon Cancer Incidence in Iowa Women", *Cancer Causes and Controls* #5, 1994, pp.38-52

cancer.[178] Sugar can cause appendicitis[179], increase the risk of Crohn's Disease and ulcerative colitis[180] (see **Inflammatory Bowel Disease**), cause the rapid overgrowth of yeasts and fungi, thereby exacerbating the symptoms of multiple sclerosis.[181] Excess sugar consumption has also been linked to Parkinson's and Alzheimer's diseases.[182] Complete removal of sugar from the diet has seen stunning recoveries from cancer, diabetes, heart illnesses and many other conditions. The average American currently consumes over 100 pounds of sucrose and 40 pounds of corn syrup each year in their deadly addiction to all things sweet.

Take that fibre

Dietary fibre is vital to slow down the absorption of sugars, as well as performing all the bowel duties expected of a great meal. Drs. Murray and Pizzorno explain:

"The term 'dietary fibre' refers to the components of the plant cell wall as well as the indigestible residues from plant foods. Different types of fibre possess different actions. The water-soluble forms exert the most beneficial effects on blood sugar control. Included in this category are hemicelluloses, mucilages, gums, and pectin substances. These types of fibres are capable of: slowing the digestion and absorption of carbohydrates, thereby preventing rapid rises in blood sugar; increasing cell sensitivity to insulin, thereby preventing the excessive secretion of insulin; and improving uptake of glucose by the liver and other tissues, thereby preventing a sustained elevation of blood sugar."[183]

---

[178] **Moerman, Clara et al**, "Dietary Sugar Intake in the Etiology of Biliary Tract Cancer", *International Journal of Epidemiology*, Vol. 22, #2, 1993, pp.207-214

[179] **Cleave, T**, *The Saccharine Disease*, Keats Publishing, New Canaan, CT: 1974, p.125

[180] **Cleave, T**, *Sweet and Dangerous*, Bantam Books, New York: 1974, pp.28-43; also **Persson, B G et al**, "Diet and Inflammatory Bowel Disease", *Epidemiology*, Vol. 3, #1, January 1992, pp.47-51

[181] **Erlander, S**, *The Disease to End Disease*, "The Cause and Cure of Multiple Sclerosis", No. 3, 3rd March 1979, pp.59-63

[182] *Sweet and Dangerous*, op. cit. p.141

[183] Murray and Pizzorno, op. cit. p.556

Take action ♥

Various diseases, such as hypoglycaemia, diabetes, syndrome X, migraine headaches, PMS and many of the heart complaints may be viewed as the body's attempts to react and adjust to the modern, highly refined, nutrient-poor diet of our times. Those suffering from hypoglycaemia or diabetes (type 2) may benefit from the following:

- **DIET: COMMENCE THE *FOOD FOR THOUGHT* LIFESTYLE REGIMEN**, ensuring the patient cuts out junk foods, especially sodas and soft drinks, sucrose, high glycaemic carbohydrates, such as ALL GRAINS (pasta, bread, rice, pastries, etc.) and potatoes
- **DIET:** Give up the foods and beverages listed in the **Foods to avoid** section, especially alcoholic drinks, ESPECIALLY BEERS AND LAGERS
- **DIET:** If fungi and yeasts have become a problem, switch to the **ANTI-*CANDIDA* LIFESTYLE REGIMEN** (See section on *Candida*)
- **VITAL:** Increase water intake to four pints (2 litres) per day
- **VITAL:** Regular exercise (at least one hour per day, four times per week)
- **COMMENCE THE BASIC SUPPLEMENT PROGRAM**, ensuring **ANTI-*CANDIDA*/FUNGAL SUPPLEMENTATION**, where appropriate. Also:
- Zinc (gluconate), 25 mg, twice per day
- Vanadium or chromium picolinate, 200 mcg a day, taken every other day, two weeks on, two weeks off. Note: do not continue this supplement over a protracted period of time
- Manganese, 10 mg, twice per day

Hypothyroidism
Subclinical hypothyroidism, myxedema,
goitre, Hashimoto's disease, thyroiditis,
Grave's disease (thyrotoxicosis), cretinism....

Profile
Hypothyroidism is the term used to describe sub-normal (under-active) activity of the thyroid gland, situated in the base of the neck. The thyroid gland is responsible for secreting thyroid hormone which regulates cell metabolism in the body. The thyroid gland in turn is stimulated into action by the pituitary gland, which secretes thyroid-stimulating hormone (TSH).

Hypothyroidism is what I term the silent epidemic. It is estimated that about twenty percent of women and five percent of males have some sort of under-active thyroid in the industrialised world. In the old days, the cause of the condition was almost always down to a lack of iodine in the diet, an element used by the gland to manufacture the thyroid hormone and other secretory substances. This was invariably caused by the ingestion of too many goitrogenic, peasant foods (foods that suppress thyroid activity), such as soy beans, cabbage, turnips, pine nuts and millet. However, since the 1920's, the practise of adding iodine to table salt has largely eradicated this as a cause of hypothyroidism and goitres in the industrialised nations.

Primary hypothyroidism: Where the thyroid gland itself is the cause of under-active secretions of the hormone.
Secondary hypothyroidism: Where the pituitary gland is under-active in producing adequate thyroid stimulating hormone (TSH). Tests to determine which of the above conditions a patient has involve measuring levels of thyroid and TSH in their blood to see which gland is production-deficient.
Myxedema: a coarsening, thickening of the skin, giving it a dry, waxy texture. Occurs in those with under-active thyroid. Characterised by intolerance to cold, mental and physical dullness and weight gain.

Goitre: Swelling of the neck brought on by enlargement of the thyroid gland in its efforts to produce more thyroid hormone.

Hashimoto's disease: Currently the most prevalent cause of hypothyroidism, where the thyroid gland becomes inflamed due to the formation of autoimmune antibodies against the thyroid tissue. Results in a partial or total failure of the gland to produce its hormones, including thyroxine. The condition is more prevalent in women than men. Disease appears to 'run in the family'.

Grave's disease (thyrotoxicosis): Caused by too much thyroid production, resulting in rapid heartbeat, sweats, loss of weight, tremors and anxiety. Can be caused by a carcinoma of the thyroid.

Cretinism: A childhood condition, a type of dwarfism, presenting mental retardation and coarseness of skin and facial features brought on by lack of thyroid hormone from birth.

Symptoms

Low-active thyroid in infants may lead to cretinism. In adults the condition causes depression, weight-gain (and difficulty in losing weight), coarsening of the skin, undue sensitivity to cold, constipation, joint pain, menstrual problems and, in the case of goitre, a swollen neck around the thyroid area. Thyroid production is vital to the metabolic process of cells, and so the condition needs to be addressed to avoid complications later. Some believe that the rate of sub-clinical hypothyroidism in the general western populations may be as high as forty percent.

Men with the condition exhibit low libido (sex drive), while women present with prolonged menstrual bleeding with a shorter cycle. The condition will usually present problems in pregnancy, resulting in miscarriages, stillbirths and premature deliveries. Hair thinning or loss in females can occur. Nails become thin and brittle and often demonstrate horizontal striations. Hypothyroidism may also predispose the patient to atherosclerosis and other heart conditions.

Commentary

For an illness that is so common, many citizens have never even heard of hypothyroidism or its associated conditions, let alone know what causes it. Hypothyroidism is symptomatic of a disease of western civilisation, and is most likely caused by inadequate, processed diets and complications arising from yeast and fungal infections.

Hashimoto's disease, the most common manifestation, exhibits evidence of the immune system attacking tissue of the thyroid gland. This is believed to be because of 'molecular mimicry', a theory, under research since 1985, whereby invading foreign proteins (antigens) appear to have a very similar amino acid chain make-up to certain healthy cells in the body, thus 'fooling' the immune system into forming templates to destroy not just the invading proteins, but also the healthy cells appearing to be very similar to them. Problems with the immune system may occur when healthy proteins in a person's body (i.e. those that make up thyroid gland and associated tissues) correspond closely with trouble-making proteins that comprise bacteria, fungi, yeasts, etc. (see **Multiple Sclerosis, Rheumatoid Arthritis** and **Diabetes** (type 1)).

Hypothyroidism is also linked to fluoride poisoning and menopausal problems in females, and can still be exacerbated by the over-consumption of goitrogenic foods, the most prevalent of which today are the unfermented soy products, such as soy 'milk', 'meat', etc. Thyroid hormones require iodine and the amino acid tyrosine to synthesise them, so those suffering from under-active thyroid need to address this issue as well as the fungal picture. Those also on strict diets (especially females) are also at risk, since the body lowers its metabolic rate in response to what it perceives as an imminent food restriction (famine) problem. Exercise is ideal for counterbalancing these effects and stimulating thyroid action.

Take action♥

Always consult a physician. The following regimen will be of benefit to those suffering from hypothyroidism:

- **DIET: COMMENCE THE ANTI-*CANDIDA* DIETARY REGIMEN**, ensuring a full anti-fungal/parasite program is initiated and followed through consistently. Avoid goitrogenic foods, such as soy, millet, cabbage, etc. (see above – also **The Shadow of Soy**)

- **DIET:** Note the **foods to avoid** sections of both the **ANTI-*CANDIDA* DIETARY REGIMEN** and **THE *FOOD FOR THOUGHT* LIFESTYLE REGIMEN**
- **RESTORE NUTRIENT BALANCE: COMMENCE THE BASIC SUPPLEMENT PROGRAM**, ensuring:
- Iodine, no more than 600 mcg per day
- Thyroid stimulating supplements, as directed by your physician, who will usually prescribe a thyroxine medication
- **TIP:** If presenting with menopausal symptoms, such as sweats, flushing, etc. (see **Menopausal problems**)
- **TIP:** Exercise regularly to stimulate gland and increase metabolic function
- **NOTE:** This is a long-term program and should be adhered to strictly

Inflammatory Bowel Disease

Crohn's disease (regional ileitis, regional enteritis), ulcerative colitis, leaky gut syndrome, diverticulosis, diverticulitis, dysbiosis, esophageal reflux, spastic colon, malabsorption syndrome (coeliac disease), etc.

Profile

More and more, people over the past fifty years have been suffering from a number of complaints affecting the entire length of the digestive system, from mouth and throat ailments, down to the stomach, and all the way through that serpentine piping to haemorrhoids around your afterburner. Some of these disorders are mild; others are extremely serious and will need addressing without delay.

I am lumping a group of conditions together here as Inflammatory Bowel Disease, since the remedies for them are essentially the same. Once the reader appreciates what these conditions are and how they are caused, the answer to most of the problems becomes straightforward enough to implement.

Crohn's Disease (Regional enteritis): Pain in the lower right abdomen, malabsorption of nutrients, low-grade fever, weight-loss, flatulence. Crohn's is a condition where segments of the colon (large intestine) become inflamed, thickened and ulcerated. Traditional treatments will include corticosteroids, antibiotics, immunosuppressive drugs and dietary changes. Crohn's can cause partial blockage of the large intestine, causing pain and bouts of diarrhoea. The same condition occurring in the small intestine is known as regional enteritis, the chronic form of which may also create fistulae (unnatural joinings) between adjacent loops of the intestines or between bowel tissue and the bladder, vagina or skin.

Ulcerative colitis: Inflammation of the colon lining. Symptoms are pain, with blood and/or mucus in the faeces.

Leaky gut syndrome: Where damage to the small intestine wall can increase gut permeability to undigested food particles which enter the bloodstream and begin causing 'allergic' reactions. Dr Leo

175

Galland, Director of Medicine at the Foundation for Integrated Medicine, states:

"Leaky gut syndrome is a group of clinical disorders associated with increased intestinal permeability. They include inflammatory and infectious bowel diseases, chronic inflammatory arthritides, cryptogenic skin conditions like acne, psoriasis and dermatitis herpetiformis, many diseases triggered by food allergy or specific food intolerance, including eczema, urticaria, and irritable bowel syndrome, AIDS, chronic fatigue syndromes, chronic hepatitis, chronic pancreatitis, cystic fibrosis and pancreatic carcinoma. Hyper-permeability may play a primary, etiologic role in the evolution of each disease, or may be a secondary consequence of it which causes immune activation, hepatic dysfunction, and pancreatic insufficiency, creating a vicious cycle. Unless specifically investigated, the role of altered intestinal permeability in patients with leaky gut syndrome often goes unrecognised." [184]

Diverticulosis, diverticulitis: Sacs may appear in weak sections of the intestinal tract, caused by pressure from the inner lining (pulsion diverticula) or from pressure exerted without (traction diverticula). Diverticulosis describes the passive existence of diverticula. Diverticulitis describes the condition when these sacs become perforated, inflamed or impacted.

Dysbiosis: The human digestive system contains over four hundred species of microflora (bacteria, yeast, fungi, protozoa, etc.) weighing over three pounds. Usually, in a properly pH-adjusted, harmonious alimentary tract, they live together in peace and balance (homeostasis). When, through our choices of food and lifestyle, we upset this balance, dysbiosis occurs, a term, coined by Russian scientist Elie Metchnikoff, who maintained that toxic compounds produced by the aberrant breakdown of food by these bacteria caused many of the degenerative conditions, especially since this toxicity was carried to other parts of the body via the bloodstream and lymph (see **Arthritis, Cancer, Multiple Sclerosis, Alzheimer's, Parkinson's,** etc.)

Irritable bowel syndrome (IBS): A general condition, thought to affect over 15% of the western populations, describing generalised abdominal pain, usually accompanied by diarrhoea and

---

[184] **Galland, Leo**, 'Leaky Gut Syndrome: Breaking The Vicious Cycle' at http://www.healthy.net/asp/templates/Article.asp?Id=425

constipation, that leads to dysfunctional contractions in the intestine. Officially, according to orthodox medicine, unwilling to accept the existence of this as a separate disorder, the cause of IBS is unknown. Unofficially, it is yet another physical manifestation of humans trying to put diesel into a gasoline-driven automobile, if you get my drift. We'll give the food industry a proper panning as we proceed.

Coeliac disease (malabsorption syndrome): A condition in which the small intestine fails to digest and absorb food. Usually due to gluten/gliaden damage, which atrophies the lining of the intestine. Symptoms include stunted growth, distended abdomen and pale, frothy, foul-smelling stools.

Commentary

Causes: Gluten/gliaden damage from wheat, barley, rye and oat products; bacterial and/or mycoplasmic infections; small intestine bacterial overgrowth (SIBO), brought on by low digestive enzyme output; processed diet; too much refined sugar and grains; too little fibre; generally acidic, anaerobic internal environment, resulting in an inadequate immune system response; antibiotic abuse; general drug abuse; poor water intake. Phew!

Bacteria, yeasts and fungi are generally quite sparse in the upper intestinal tract, but when overgrowths allow them to proliferate in the duodenum and jejunum (the majority portion of the small intestine), they can compete for nutrition with the host. This is where the problems begin. Symptoms describing overgrowths of these critters are well known: abdominal pain and cramps, constipation, diarrhoea, fatigue, fever, flatulence, foul-smelling faeces, skin rashes and hives, leaky gut, indigestion, reflux, low back pain, malabsorption and weight loss. They can cause a corruption and putrefaction of the food chyme (food leaving the stomach for the intestine).

Enzymes ejected from these organisms (known as decarboxylases) work on the chyme, converting the amino acids histadine to histamine (hence 'allergic' reactions sometimes treated with 'anti-histamines'), ornithine to putrescine and lysine to cadaverine. Actions of these products, known as vasoactive amines, will stir up a host of the problems we are examining in this chapter.

These fungi and yeasts are responsible for many apparent food allergies. Proteins, such gluten from wheat and barley and casein from cow's milk, may also damage intestinal structure, bringing on some conditions.

Take action♥

This regime should be followed very strictly. Ensure regular food intakes, but small amounts, often.

- **DIET: COMMENCE THE ANTI-*CANDIDA* DIETARY REGIMEN**
- **DIET:** Follow also the **Foods to avoid** section of **THE *FOOD FOR THOUGHT* LIFESTYLE REGIMEN**
- **DIET:** AVOID ALL SUGAR AND YEAST
- **DIET:** Avoid all products that readily break down into glucose or have a yeast component: e.g. bread, pasta, pastries, sweets, pies, alcoholic beverages (esp. beers!) and some fruits and vegetables (see diet above)
- **DIET:** Drink at least four pints of clean, still mineral water a day (not out of plastic bottles and please avoid distilled water)
- **PREVENTION:** Don't smoke and avoid second-hand smoke
- **PREVENTION:** Avoid behavioural and dietary problems that have caused the condition
- **DETOXIFICATION:** Conduct a two-week bowel cleanse with magnesium oxide
- **DETOXIFICATION:** Cancer patients should also consider colon hydrotherapy for extra internal cleanliness
- **RESTORING NUTRIENT BALANCE: COMMENCE THE BASIC SUPPLEMENT PROGRAM**, including **THE ANTI-*CANDIDA*/FUNGAL SUPPLEMENT-ATION**, ensuring:
- A probiotic supplement to install beneficial flora
- Vitamin C complex (ascorbates plus bioflavonoids), 5 g per day. This amounts to one heaped teaspoon of C-complex powder per day. Take half of it in a bland juice, such as pear, every morning and the rest at night

- Take 1 tablespoon of ground flaxseed (linseed) meal or oil daily
- Pancreatic (digestive) enzyme capsules, two, three times daily away from food
- **BOOSTING IMMUNITY:** Astragalus and echinacea, (herbs), two capsules each, three times a day
- **BOOSTING IMMUNITY:** Indulge in regular and vigorous exercise (unless health problems prevent this) to exercise and pump the lymphatic system, rid the body of waste products and draw in oxygen
- **BOOSTING IMMUNITY:** Get plenty of rest
- **TIP:** Be consistent!
- **TIP:** Do not fall prey to sugar cravings. Who really wants to splurge and feed inside you?

Herxheimer's reaction

During the critter-killing process, the body may become clogged with catabolic debris, dead beasties and their resultant toxaemia, including ammonia. You may feel ill as your symptoms apparently worsen. This is known as Herxheimer's reaction, after the venerable German dermatologist of the same name. It is temporary and will be experienced in proportion to the vehemence with which you apply your attack strategies. Symptoms may be alleviated by commencing the **ANTI-*CANDIDA* DIETARY REGIMEN** a full two weeks prior to starting on the anti-fungal/yeast supplements.

Menopausal Problems
Menopausal symptoms, estrogen/progesterone imbalances, estrogen dominance, sweats, cysts, fibroids, endometriosis, etc.

Profile
A little girl is born with all the immature eggs in her ovaries, which will later develop and be released during her lifetime. Although the number of these egg 'follicles' within the ovaries may exceed 400,000 at puberty, only around 400 will actually develop and be released during the woman's lifetime.

Menopause occurs when a woman no longer ovulates and has menstrual periods. This was widely believed to be when her lifetime's supply of eggs (ova) was used up during successive menstrual cycles. Scientists now believe that this may not be the case – that menopause, as well as puberty, may commence through hormone-driven events triggered by the brain.

Western societies, with their propensity for enshrining youth, have painted the menopause in a negative light. Many non-industrialised cultures, however, see the menopause as a dignified new period in the woman's life, and accord those entering it with a new respect and devotion.

The chief problems surrounding menopausal disorders usually involve dysfunctional estrogen to progesterone levels in the body. Initially, this will provoke hot sweats, flushes, etc., but may progress to fibrocystic breast disease, endometriosis, and ultimately, an estrogen-positive breast or gynaecological cancer.

Fibrocystic breast disease: A relatively common condition where cysts or solid lumps of fibrous and glandular tissue form in the breast. These are not in themselves cancerous. The condition may be caused by constipation and estrogen dominance

Endometriosis: A disorder where endometrial cells of the uterine lining are found growing outside the uterus where they respond to hormonal stimuli during menstruation, resulting in inflammation of the lower abdominal organs and pain. The condition is common in women between 25 to 44, and can lead to infertility. The condition is thought to be caused by estrogen dominance.

Menopausal symptoms

Hormone levels fluctuate towards the onset of menopause, and symptoms experienced may include hot sweats, flushing, headaches, mood swings, urinary tract infections, cold hands and feet and atrophic vaginitis. Interestingly, those cultures living in non-toxic environments eating low-fat, high-fibre, non-processed diets rarely experience these symptoms. Most of the problems women endure are primarily due to fluctuating levels of estrogens and progesterone (usually too much estrogen, not enough progesterone) as the body prepares itself for the next phase of the woman's life.

Commentary

During the woman's active, periodic cycle, the egg follicle, one of many such ovarian sacs containing its immature egg in a nurturing fluid, secretes estrogen as the egg grows up to its release time. Upon release of the egg, estrogen output from the follicle and other glands remains constant and then decreases during menstruation. In addition to continuing to produce estrogen, the egg-releasing follicle also manufactures progesterone during the second half of the cycle, providing the necessary safe hormonal balance for the estrogens estradiol, estrone and estriol, working away synergistically with their very intricately controlled hormonal ballet to prepare the female for her coming pregnancy.

One of the amazing features of a woman's inner workings is the way the follicle transforms itself, after releasing its egg, into an endocrine gland, known as the *corpus luteum*, which becomes the primary production plant for progesterone during the vital second half of the menstrual cycle. Remember this fact, as it becomes important in a moment.

Contrary to popular belief, it is progesterone, not estrogen, which is responsible for preparing the uterus for pregnancy, heightening the sexual energy usually experienced by the woman during the time of ovulation, and maintaining the pregnancy after conception by

181

preventing any further release of eggs from the ovaries. In the event that no fertilised egg implants itself in the uterus, the uterus lining, engorged with blood in preparation for an imminent pregnancy, sheds itself in the blood of menstruation, and the cycle then repeats itself, with another signal from the brain and glands, telling the body to begin ripening another egg for the next cycle.

So estrogen and progesterone are responsible for orchestrating regular menstruation in the female, and the primary production site of progesterone is the *corpus luteum* (egg follicle) once it has released its egg and taken the woman into the second half of her menstrual cycle. Around 40 years of age, this interaction between the two hormones usually alters, many doctors and scientists now believe, due to changes in the brain's interaction with the glandular output of the hypothalamus and pituitary glands, *not the ovaries*.[185] At the onset of menopause, estrogen levels drop to 40-60%, low enough to prevent the follicles from maturing and releasing further eggs. Gradually, as the female enters this new period of her life, known as menopause, menstruation becomes more erratic and sporadic before finally ceasing altogether.

Perhaps less well known, even among doctors, is the fact that during menopause, a woman's ovaries are far from 'shrivelled and useless', as is often pointed out to women, although there is some contraction in the 'theca' area of the ovaries where the eggs mature and are released. On the contrary, the inner part of the ovaries, the stoma, becomes active in a way not previously experienced in the female, enabling her to enter a new phase in her life, healthy and with new purpose.

Hormones, of course, continue to be secreted, the brain playing the role of conductor between the ovaries and other gland sites, such as the pineal, adrenal as well as the skin, hair follicles, uterus and body fat to produce the required chemical messengers. The uterus too, far from being 'useless' and 'unwanted' once the female ceases

---

[185] Experiments with mice, where ovaries from young mice are implanted in older animals, have shown that the latter are incapable of reproduction. Contrariwise, old ovaries from animals no longer capable of reproducing, when implanted into younger mice, have enabled the latter to give birth after mating, giving rise to the belief that the brain and endocrine system have the majority part to play in triggering puberty, ovulation and menopause.

menstruation, becomes the main production centre for prostacyclin, a hormone now believed to protect the woman from heart disease, thrombosis and unscheduled blood clotting.[186] In the event that doctors carry out a hysterectomy and remove the uterus, prostacyclin is no longer produced by the female, pushing her into a potential risk group indicating thrombosis, coronary spasms and other complications. Scientists at present cannot synthesise prostacyclin hormone in the laboratory, thus leaving the female without this valuable protector for the remainder of her life.[187]

HRT –miracle or error?

This brief resumé of the wondrous inner workings of a woman's reproductive system is necessary in order to understand the ghastly state of affairs that will now be explained. Menopause is presented to women by doctors as a deficiency of estrogen - a *disease* no less, requiring hormone supplementation with estrogen. Dr John R Lee, the noted authority of hormonal replacement therapy and its archest critic, explains that hormone replacement therapy (HRT) violates that most precious of balances between estrogen and progesterone, resulting in the female experiencing estrogen dominance (unopposed estrogen). To supplement females with synthetic estrogens to disrupt and increase the estrogen dominance further is to invite a litany of symptoms all too depressingly familiar with women who have been down this particular path: heightened risk of cancer of the breast and endometrium (the inner lining of the uterus), ovarian cysts, uterine fibroids, anaerobic cell respiration (depletion of oxygen in cells – a cancer precursor), disrupted thyroid activity (cold hands and feet), breast fibrocysts, excessive blood clotting leading to thrombo-embolisms, and decreased sex drive. Then the doctor recommends a hysterectomy, with further catastrophic results potentially threatening the woman during the remainder of her life.

Doctors are used to explaining to worried women that their child-bearing days are over; that their sex organs are no longer required; that, to prevent the risk of osteoporosis and the shopping list of

---

[186] Vitamin C also increases the production of prostacyclin, the small molecule hormone that relaxes the blood vessel walls and also keeps the blood viscosity at optimum levels.
[187] *Oxford Medical Dictionary*, 2000

menopausal blights to their health, HRT, a hysterectomy and complete removal of their ovaries are more often than not required. Women find themselves having to take the doctor's word for it all; they are aware that many of their friends have been down the same path and have had these procedures carried out; that female comedians joke about it, rendering a depressing familiarity that states in effect 'that all women have to deal with this – doctor knows best - might as well get it over with'. This, as we will discover before this chapter is over, is about as far from the plain truth as you can get; a horrific betrayal of trust between a woman and her physician; a deliberate shortening of options that are never explained to the patient. Sherrill Sellman sums up the awful dilemma facing millions of women every year:

"With so many side-effects and dangerous complications, a woman must think very carefully about the HRT decision. Unfortunately, most doctors will say there is no other alternative and that it is relatively safe. While certainly most doctors are well-meaning and sincerely concerned about their patients, their primary source of education and product information comes directly from the pharmaceutical companies. Since most women also lack information and understanding about their options, menopause can be perceived as a rather frightening and perilous time. Women fear that if they don't follow their doctor's advice, then they may face the remaining years of their life with the threat of great suffering and physical deterioration. Women are often in for a rude awakening when they experience firsthand just how badly their health needs have been managed." [188]

The mechanics of estrogen dominance

As previously mentioned, estrogen is a generic term to describe three main hormones that have estrus activity - that is, they stimulate cells in the inner lining (endometrium) of the uterus to bloat with blood in preparation for pregnancy. Excessive amounts of estrogens in a woman's body prior to menopause will cause the 'burn out' of her ovaries and jeopardise fertility. Excessive amounts of estrogens in a male will bring on feminisation, resulting, in extreme cases, in the enlargement of his breasts (gynecomastia). Estradiol

---

[188] Sellman, Sherrill, op. cit. pp.23-24

and estrone, two of the female's estrogen hormones, are known to stimulate stem cell growth, which can lead to trophoblast-cell proliferation in healing and pregnancies which, if not terminated by pancreatic enzymes, can result in cancer. Estriol, the third estrogen hormone, is actually cancer-inhibiting.

One of the functions of estradiol is that it stores energy obtained from food as fat in the body for future use. This is the reason estradiol is given to cattle during their 100-day fattening period. To maximise the weight-load of each animal is to maximise a farmer's profits at market-time. Excess amounts of the potentially harmful estradiol thus have been corrupting the food chain for years, not only through the population's prolific consumption of commercially fattened and slaughtered meats, but also through the water supply, when estrogen from contraceptive Pill-users survives the urine effluent treatment process and is passed back into the water supply with all its biochemical estrus capabilities surviving intact.

Excess levels of estradiol occurring in the body as a result of normal hormone production and HRT will thus cause the woman to put on weight. This is because menopausal females on HRT are suffering an estrogen dominance (unopposed by progesterone). Progesterone, in its natural form produced by the body (in marked contrast to the synthetic progestins used in HRT), works opposite to estradiol, and metabolises fat into energy, causing the female to lose weight. But doctors do not tell their patients about the amazing possibilities of natural progesterone supplementation, because natural progesterone products are largely unpatentable and thus not a profit-centre for drug companies who educate doctors on the latest drugs available. Deceitfully too, doctors often refer to synthetic progestins as 'progesterone', thus muddying the waters further.

And so the female remains estrogen-dominant during hormone replacement therapy, loading on the pounds, bombarded by increased levels of estradiol and estrone in her body, not only from HRT steroid preparations, but from the estrogens now prevalent in the food chain and xeno-estrogens in the environment (estrogen mimics). Further compounding this estrogen/progesterone imbalance is the dwindling supply of progesterone in the female body after menopause commences, since the body is no longer producing progesterone from the *corpus luteum* follicles after they have released their eggs.

Anovulatory cycles

Another factor compounding the problem of estrogen dominance is when females do not ovulate during their menstrual period. This is known as an anovulatory cycle. The problem here is that the releasing follicle does not convert to the *corpus luteum* and generate progesterone. This in turn results in a month's worth of severe estrogen dominance for the female (from day 8 to day 26 of her cycle), with all the associated problems. Anovulatory cycles have traditionally occurred in females in their 40s onwards as they approach menopause. Today however, there is an alarming trend of these egg-free menstrual periods occurring commonly in females in their early thirties, and in some cases, even before this. The implications of this are potentially hazardous for the female in question, as fifteen years of unopposed estrogen dominance can easily occur before the output of estrogens eventually reduces with the onset of menopause.

Estrogen dominance and its connection to osteoporosis

Such an estrogen dominance and sharp progesterone deficiency over a protracted period of time will also have attendant side-effects with the depletion of bone mass in the female, giving rise to the fear of osteoporosis. Osteoblasts, the cells that build and replace bone mass in humans, have progesterone receptors. No progesterone, no osteoblasts, no osteoblasts, no new bone material created. Osteoclasts on the other hand, are multinucleate cells that dissolve old bone material in preparation for the osteoblasts, which move in to replace old calcified bone with fresh material. Osteoclasts have estrogen receptors. So, if there is an estrogen dominance, osteoclasts are hard at work breaking down calcified bone material, leaving bones scored and pitted in preparation for the bone-building osteoblasts, which fail to act because of the lack of progesterone docked at their receptors.

Put the two features together and you get bone murder. Estrogen dominance results in calcified (old) bone material being broken down. Couple that with a simultaneous progesterone deficiency and you do not have this calcified bone being replaced. The net result is, of course, a progressive bone loss in the female – osteoporosis – porous bones.

40-60% of females in the western world today experience PMS symptoms, ranging from the noticeable to the severe. Many millions of women are guinea-pigs for Big Estrogen's onward march to its dividend payouts. The female public are warned about osteoporosis during menopause for good reason. Dominant estrogen bodies that are progesterone deficient will bring on a progressive bone loss for the reasons explained above. Now imagine the female's diet is also acidic with excessive meat and dairy consumption, requiring the body to bloat with water and mobilise calcium out of the bones to restore the pH balance. Then imagine the free-radical activity that results from the incomplete metabolism of refined sugars she has put into her body, resulting in the destruction of healthy cells as these unstable sugars attempt to complete themselves by robbing oxygen electrons out of healthy tissue cells. And then you get fungal and yeast problems which are progressively fuelled by excess intakes of refined carbohydrates. Now do you begin to get an idea of what disasters lie in wait for women who follow the penchants for western diets, western healthcare, resulting in western diseases? Chief among these are cancer, thrombosis and osteoporosis – all tied unimpeachably to the irresponsible expansion of the menopause-as-estrogen-deficiency mindset.

Xeno-estrogens in the environment

Our petrochemically driven society, touted in the 1950s as being the future for our species, has poisoned our bodies and environment with materials that mimic the activities of natural estrogens. From cling-film, polycarbonates and plasticised bottles used to store water and foodstuffs through to commercially used pesticides, insecticides, benzenes, DDT, organochlorines and organophosphates, these xeno-estrogens, as they are known, are stored by the body in fat tissues where they become difficult to break down and remove.

Environmental changes laid at the door of these chemicals include shrunken reproductive organs in animals affected, the loss of sex drive in birds and fish, and more disturbingly, the changing sex of fish found downstream of sewage treatment plants where these estrogen mimics have been ineffectively removed from the water supply prior to release.[189] On-going studies are now examining what the long-term effect on humans might be, given what is evidently occurring in the animal kingdom. I would have thought the effects on humans are obvious.

Naturally, any problems are trivialised and downplayed by the chemical industry which no doubt fears a major financial backlash if hard evidence of its involvement subsequently comes to light and class action suits begin to materialise. Sherrill Sellman reports that eagles in Florida were noted by ornithologists as far back as 1947 to have lost their sex drive and urge to mate. In the 1960s, farm mink fed fish from Lake Michigan failed to mate and produce offspring. In 1977, female gulls in California were nesting with fellow females.[190]

The association between sexual changes and effects of estrogens in the environment was reported by Greenpeace, which announced:

"Exposure to hormonally active organochlorines early in life, especially in utero when hormonal feedback systems are being imprinted, can result in permanent alteration of systems that control estrogen and other sex hormones. Studies show increased rates of breast cancer among women born to mothers with indications of high estrogen levels during pregnancy. Thus the transfer of accumulated organochlorines from mother to daughter may indeed contribute to breast cancer."[191]

Another major contaminant in the world today is unfermented soy, often used to produce fake milk and meats, as well as employed as a food-bulking agent. Unfermented soy, with its isoflavones, can cause problems for females approaching the menopause and has been implicated in all sorts of health problems (in spite of all the upbeat rubbish written about 'soy'). For more information on the

[189] **Archer, John**, *The Water you Drink – How Safe is it?* Pure Water Press, 1996, p.34
[190] Sellman, Sherrill, op. cit. p.56
[191] **Clorfene-Casten, Diane**, *Breast Cancer, Poisons, Profits and Prevention*, Common Courage Press, Maine, 1996, pp.33-34

bean dilemma, please see **The Shadow of Soy** article at the back of this book.

Sorting the problems

Candida, fibrocystic breast disease, endometriosis, thrush, fibromyalgia, certain allergies, osteoporosis, lupus, coronary spasm, Graves' disease, thyroiditis and Sjirgren's disease are implicated in estrogen dominance. Many occurrences of these distressing illnesses have been arrested with the introduction of natural progesterone to the suffering body, along with a low-fat, high-fibre diet and dietary supplements. Yet the emphasis by the medical establishment is always on synthetic estrogens and progestins, serum tests conducted by physicians being interpreted by them as demonstrating a patient's estrogen deficiency.

Many doctors do have serious reservations with the accuracy of such tests, since a very low level of active hormones is actually picked up by these indicators (up to 9%). The practitioner will then prescribe estrogen as he sees the need to raise the levels shown by the indicators, unaware that these dismal tests fail to detect up to 90% of active hormones in the patient's body. In fact, hormone levels cannot be pre-determined by yardsticks, because of the many variables affecting hormone levels existing within the body of the female.

Further symptoms of estrogen dominance may include migraines, hay fever, skin rashes, urinary tract infection, varicose veins, ectopic pregnancy and high blood pressure. Threats from these problems too have been averted by the regulation of natural progesterone in the body through the application of natural creams and lotions, along with dietary and lifestyle changes.

Natural progesterone

At the outbreak of World War 2, research into progesterone had discovered the properties of diosgenin contained in the Mexican wild yam. It was found that this substance could convert easily and inexpensively into the identical progesterone molecule used by the body. Dr John Lee, among many doctors, has been prescribing this natural substance with tremendous benefit for the female, even noting the average bone density of his patients increasing by 15% during the treatment. Lee unequivocally states that natural progesterone can alleviate many of the symptoms associated with menopause and associated complications, even allowing the patient to decrease their levels of estrogens along with diet and lifestyle changes to complete the transition.

Sellman too gives her seal of approval in encouraging women to consider the natural alternatives to chemical treatments for menopause: *"Supplementation with natural progesterone corrects the real problem – progesterone deficiency. It is not known to have any side-effects, nor have any toxic levels been found to date. Natural progesterone protects against fibrocystic breast disease, helps protect against and uterine cancer, maintains the lining of the uterus, hydrates and oxygenates the skin, reverses facial hair growth and thinning of the hair, acts as a natural diuretic, helps to eliminate depression and increases a sense of well-being, encourages fat burning and the use of stored energy. Even the two most prevalent menopausal symptoms, hot flashes and vaginal dryness, quickly disappear with applications of natural progesterone."*[192]

With such a simple, natural alternative to the harsh chemical treatments so often fostered by the medical establishment today, what do women have to lose by doing their own research into this fascinating and life-changing subject? As with so many of the other subjects covered by *The ABC's of Disease*, often simple answers are so very before us and just waiting to be put into practice for a safer and more fulfilling life.

And lastly, consider the following:

➤ Percentage of US women who will have a hysterectomy in their lifetimes: 50%
➤ Most common reason for hysterectomy – fibroids
➤ Second most common reason for hysterectomy in the US – endometriosis
➤ Number of women with fibroids or endometriosis who are relieved of pain and heavy bleeding within three

---

[192] Sellman, Sherrill, op. cit. p.86

months of adopting a low-fat, high-fibre organic diet – the vast majority

➤ Percentage of American physicians who recommend dietary changes for fibroids and endometriosis – < 1% [193]

➤ Most widely prescribed drug in the US in 1992 – Premarin (*sic:* made from **pre**gnant **mar**es' ur**in**e - used as 'estrogen replacement therapy')

➤ Primary reasons prescribed – hot flushes, osteoporosis and heart disease

➤ Percentage of women who obtained complete relief from hot flushes by taking 200 mg of vitamin C and 200 mg of bioflavanoids 6 times a day - 67%

➤ Percentage of menopausal women who obtained relief from hot flushes by taking two herbal capsules three times a day for three months in a double-blind, placebo-controlled study - 100%

➤ Percentage of US physicians discussing natural approaches with their menopausal patients - 2% [194]

Take action ♥

OK. Let's put all this fabulous info into action. The regimen below is designed to sort some of the more general problems in a hurry, so you have nothing to lose and everything to gain by getting busy. **If you are suffering from a recognised menopausal complaint that is dealt with elsewhere in this book, then the regime attached to that section should be incorporated with the listings below, upon advice of a physician.**

Many women who are constipated (less than three bowel movements a week) have a 5 times higher risk of fibrocystic breast disease (cyclic, bilateral multiple cysts in the breasts). It is estimated that 20-40% of premenopausal women suffer from this complaint alone. Getting the bowels functioning again will of course be our most solemn duty:

---

[193] **West, Stanley**, *The Hysterectomy Hoax*, Doubleday, New York: 1994, p.1,23

[194] *Pharmacy Times*, April 1993; **DeMarco, Caroline**, *Take Charge of Your Body*, Winlaw, BC: 1994; **Hudson et al**, "A Pilot Study Using Botanical Medicines in the Treatment of Menopause Symptoms", Townsend Letter, 1994

- **DIET: COMMENCE THE *FOOD FOR THOUGHT* LIFESTYLE REGIMEN.** (If suffering from yeast/fungal/*Candida* infections, substitute the above regimen for **THE ANTI-*CANDIDA* DIETARY REGIMEN** plus appropriate supplementation
- **DIET:** Pay special attention to the **Foods to avoid** section, ESPECIALLY COFFEE!!!!
- **TIP:** Ensure that the diet is primarily vegetarian, with large intakes of dietary fibre. All foods and meats containing industrial estrogens (including soy) should be discontinued. The ingestion of birth control pills also should be halted. The diet should be dominant with fruits, vegetables, legumes, pulses, nuts, seeds and plenty of fresh, clean, unfluoridated water
- **DETOXIFICATION:** Commence a two-week magnesium oxide bowel flush
- **RESTORE NUTRIENT BALANCE: COMMENCE THE BASIC SUPPLEMENT PROGRAM**, ensuring:
- A probiotic supplement to replace healthy gut flora
- Vitamin C complex (ascorbates plus bioflavonoids) 2.5 g, twice per day
- Flaxseed oil, 1 tbsp per day
- Vitamin B6, 50 mg, three times per day (regulate intake of this nutrient until regular dream recall is achieved)
- Vitamin E, 800 IU per day, until symptoms improve, then 400 IU (as per **THE BASIC SUPPLEMENT PROGRAM**)
- Natural progesterone cream, such as Endau (Neways), to be applied topically, as directed
- **EXERCISE** regularly, preferably in an organised fashion at a gym, three/four times per week

Migraine Headaches

Profile and Symptoms

Many people today suffer from the curse of migraine headaches. These differ from usual tension headaches, inasmuch as they are characterised by a throbbing pain, sometimes on one side only, sometimes preceded by 'auras' or 'prodromes' - warnings occurring 10-30 minutes in advance that take the form of blurring, bright spots in the field of vision, loss of vision in a specific arc of the periphery, anxiety, haloes around light bulbs, psychological piques and numbness or tingling down one side of the body.

Migraine headaches occur when blood vessels in the lining of the brain constrict and then dilate, activating pain sensors in and around the *meninges* (lining) when these muscles and blood vessels are stretched. The brain itself is not involved since it has no sensory nerves. Any auras preceding an attack will usually clear as the headache develops. The patient will often be prostrated, and experience nausea, vomiting and photophobia (sensitivity to light).

Causes

Migraines are thought to be caused by the body's reaction to a number of stimuli that might trigger immune system complications. As we progress through this book, the reader is probably gaining an appreciation of just how many disorders can be traced back to problems a patient experiences with the industrial environment, i.e. foods, chemicals, radiation, pollution, drugs, etc. Several clinical studies have shown that about 70% of patients with chronic daily headaches suffer from drug-induced headaches too.[195] Many of us take daily medications for this or that with scant regard for side-effects which build over the short- to medium-term. The following are just some of the causes for migraines:

- Food sensitivities to items such as cow's milk, wheat, barley, etc. (gluten products), chocolate, eggs, shellfish, chocolate, benzoic acid, cheese and food additives and colourings

---

[195] **Mathew, NT**, "Chronic refractory headache", *Neurology* 43 (suppl.3) (1993): pp.S26-S33

- Beer, wine, alcoholic beverages
- Chemicals
- Caffeine withdrawal
- Stress
- Low serotonin levels
- Hormonal changes in females
- Toxins produced by fungi, yeast and bacteria
- Exhaustion
- Weather changes
- Pollen and dust sensitivities

Commentary

There are three main types of migraines:

Common: These comprise around 80% of migraines, can be frontal or bilateral, usually last from 1 to 3 days. Auras preceding these attacks are unusual.

Classic: 10% of migraine sufferers experience classic migraines. Half an hour before the attack, they experience auras. The attack will be mostly unilateral, lasting from 2-6 hours and accompanied by nausea and vomiting.

Complicated: 10% of sufferers will experience complicated migraines, which are characterised by a preceding aura of variable effects. The patient may suffer from speech abnormalities, a type of palsy and other neurological complications.

A tremendous amount of scientific research has been done on headaches, and migraines in particular. The problem is, the drug solutions invariably offered (pain killers and other modalities) only treat the symptoms and not the underlying causes.

Physicians have found that removing certain foods result in improvement in the majority of cases, since certain trigger foods contain histamine, or provoke its excessive manufacture. Food control, though, is not the complete answer. Migraines seem to involve a more general malaise that can also include improperly formed blood vessels (an early form of scurvy),[196] platelet disorders, where blood clumps and aggregates, and also a dysfunction in the

---

[196] **Olesen, J,** "The ischemic hypothesis", *Arch Neurol* 44 (1987): pp.321-2

levels of the neurotransmitter hormone serotonin, responsible for relaying chemical messages in the brain. Thus the action listed below is designed to address particular problems in the context of an overall change in diet and lifestyle. Notice too that this regimen should be adhered to over the long-term, to allow the body to recover immune system integrity once it is free of the constant assault of suspected migraine triggers.

Take action♥

- **DIET: COMMENCE THE *FOOD FOR THOUGHT* LIFESTYLE REGIMEN**, ensuring that suspected food triggers are avoided and the diet is based on a four-day rotation system. Consult a nutritionist to design a suitable program. If fungal problems are suspected, switch to **THE ANTI-*CANDIDA* DIETARY REGIMEN**, along with appropriate supplementation, as well as....
- **RESTORE NUTRIENT BALANCE: COMMENCE THE BASIC SUPPLEMENT PROGRAM**, ensuring:
- 'Ingenious', as directed
- Magnesium, 250-400 mg, three times per day
- Vitamin B6, 25 mg, three times per day
- Dried ginger, 500 mg, four times per day
- **TIP**: Clear out toxic products from the home and replace with safe alternatives. Ensure that artificial sweeteners, colourings and additives are avoided
- **TIP**: Ensure a regular intake of good, clean water (4 pints/2 litres per day)
- **EXERCISE**: Embark on a gentle aerobic exercise regimen, four times per week

Multiple Sclerosis

Profile

Multiple sclerosis (MS) is a condition arising out of the immune system apparently destroying the myelin sheathing which surrounds nerve tissue in the brain and spinal cord, which makes up the central nervous system (CNS). Lesions or patches of damage occur where the fatty myelin sheathing protecting these nerves has been damaged. Nerve function is thus severely disrupted, resulting in obvious signs of motor dysfunction presenting a whole spectrum of symptoms. No two cases of MS are exactly the same. The damage and resultant effects are as unique to each patient as their fingerprints.

The disease is almost always restricted to young and middle-aged adults, with an approximate 60%/40% spread across females and males respectively. The geographical spread of incidence is also quite telling with MS, with the disease more prevalent in northern latitudes, with 50-100 cases per 100,000, compared with 5-10 per 100,000 in the tropics. The exception to this spread is Japan, where the disease is rare. The Faeroe Islands (between Britain and Norway) had never experienced any signs of multiple sclerosis until the British Army landed there during World War 2 with all its supplies to set up a garrison.

Symptoms

Early symptoms include clumsiness, weakness, heaviness, tingling and electrical sensations, blurring of the vision, haziness, eyeball pain, sensation of drunkenness, incontinence, numbness, loss of sexual function. More severe symptoms include shaky movements of the limbs (ataxia), speech impediment problems (dysarthria), involuntary rapid eye movements and other motor coordination problems. 'Attacks' of symptoms occur usually followed by periods of remission.

MS symptoms vary in intensity and duration, depending on which of the many different manifestations of the disease the patient has.

Causes

The cause(s) of MS are officially unknown, but, as with the disease-spread information above, tantalising clues lead us to zero in on the chief areas of action. MS is on the increase, medicine bringing a vast array of drugs (steroids, etc.) to bear with very limited success on what is generally regarded in many cases as a degenerative 'auto-immune disease' – that is, that the patient's immune system has apparently been triggered to attack and destroy key cells in the body (see also **Diabetes** and **Arthritis**).

If we review the following key factors about MS, we can begin to build a profile of who's at risk... and where:

- The disease mostly occurs in young to middle-aged adults
- It marginally favours women
- It is more prevalent in the northern latitudes
- Japan is an exception
- It does not occur in non-industrialised, agrarian societies
- It appears as though the immune system has acted dysfunctionally to destroy key cells

From this short summary, we may surmise that:
- Sunlight, enzymes and vitamin D appear to play a role in avoiding MS
- There's something in the Japanese diet and lifestyle that appears to restrict the deployment of MS
- MS appears to be a disease of industrialisation, wherein foreign proteins (antigens) have challenged the immune system
- The immune system, which, by the way, does *not* act dysfunctionally (there's always a good, underlying reason why it does what it does), has been given a key motivation to attack myelin cells in addition to the invaders

Commentary

Many hypotheses have been offered to explain how MS is caused: viral infections, food intolerances, leaky gut, all of which may provoke the immune system into reacting in a 'dysfunctional' way to attack specific cells - in this case, myelin. But what precisely is the mechanism that may cause the immune system to do such an obscure thing? The answer may well be 'molecular mimicry.'

Molecular Mimicry

...Molecular mimicry is a theory, under research since 1985, whereby invading foreign proteins (antigens) appear to have a very similar amino acid chain make-up to certain healthy cells in the body, thus 'fooling' the immune system into destroying not just the invading protein, but also the healthy cells appearing to be very similar to it. Important to note: most of the evidence so far researched on MS (which, by the way, is considerable) *does* show that the immune system has wreaked the havoc on the myelin sheathing.

Problems with the immune system will occur when healthy proteins existing in a person's body (i.e. myelin basic protein) correspond very closely to trouble-making proteins that make up bacteria, fungi, yeasts, etc. One MS site explains the proposed mechanism this way:

"To understand how molecular mimicry works in the induction of autoimmunity, one must understand the basic mechanisms of an immune response to a foreign invader in the body. The immune system recognises a part of the protein portion of the invader. It does this with T cells which have receptors which bind to short segments (up to 10 amino acids) of a foreign protein. It is helped in this task by so-called antigen presenting cells such as macrophages.

A macrophage will engulf a foreign invader (e.g. a bacteria or food particle) and break it down into fragments. A special molecule in the macrophage then carries a protein fragment (peptide) to the surface of the cell and 'presents' it to the millions of circulating T cells. A T cell which has a matching receptor locks onto the presented protein fragment. The T cell then becomes activated and stimulates other portions of the immune system to begin an immune response against all proteins which contain a similar-looking amino acid string. The details of what constitutes a similar-looking string are beyond this summary, but suffice to say it has

198

been found that a variety of similar, yet somewhat different strings, can be recognised by the same T cell." [197]

Dr Roy Swank

Dr Roy Swank, Professor of Neurology at the University of Oregon Medical School, has done much research into MS. He found that diets heavy in saturated fats are implicated in those exhibiting MS symptoms. The patient's ability to neutralise oxidation (free-radical components) in their body was also seen to be severely compromised. Swank proposed a diet for MS sufferers, which is remarkably similar to the *Food For Thought* and Anti-*Candida* regimens discussed in this book. Swank found that this diet retarded the disease process and reduced the number and severity of attacks.

Also up for discussion is whether the chicken comes before the egg. Do food intolerances cause MS, or are food intolerances the result of an MS-compromised immune system? Do fungi provoke the immune system into destroying not only the fungi, but healthy myelin cells also, which may have a similar amino acid signature to the fungi?

Medicine uses immune-suppressing drugs in the belief that MS is the result of a dysfunctional immune system and therefore, by reducing the effectiveness of the immune system, one may retard the spread of the illness. This is what I term a 'scorched earth' policy, where the only cunning plan you have come up with to halt the advance of the enemy is to burn and destroy all the land in the path of his advance in the hope that you will starve him into submission. Not such a great strategy, in my humble opinion.

Critters

What we do know from testimonies and other reports on successful treatment of MS is that the disease, if caught early enough, may be halted and even reversed using a combination of lifestyle and dietary factors outlined below.

---

[197] http://www.direct-ms.org

Gerald Green is a herbalist who lives in Sussex, England. His grandfather was Nobel laureate Professor Fritz Huber, a leading German scientist who died in the mid-1930's. An elderly gentleman experienced in healthcare, Gerald submitted some of his MS case histories to me, with the permission of his patients, which showed the benefits of an anti-*Candida* regimen, along with sensible supplementation and changes in lifestyle.

Gerald Green works on the premise that ALL MS patients have a microbe problem, and that it is pointless trying to combat the disease unless you addressed the underlying causes first. He suggests patients adopt his strict anti-*Candida* diet. This diet, I had found, was cropping up in various permutations in highly successful cancer treatments all over the world, from the Gerson Therapy pioneered by the famous Dr Max G, through to clinics in Mexico and the UK across to physicians prescribing it in one form or another to their patients as far away as the Philippines and New Zealand. The diet itself may also explain why Japan escapes the full brunt of MS, unlike other industrialised nations of comparable latitude. Many Japanese citizens still adhere to their national, alkalising diet of rice, vegetables and *lots of fish*, although, it must be said, the fast-food monster has now taken its grim hold on those islands, with unfortunate, if predictable consequences for the future.

It is my conclusion that fungi are suspected of playing the key, primary role in this disease and may well contain the amino acid chains mimicked, in which case the immune system may be correctly attacking fungal infestation while its attack template is also destroying healthy cells in the body - in this case, myelin sheathing cells intrinsic to the successful operation of the central nervous system.

Clearly not everyone, who has overgrowths of yeasts/fungi/parasites, is getting MS. The disease in my view must have a certain number of factors working synergistically to bring on the problem. The following may be such a profile:

- A western, industrialised diet rich in refined, processed sugars and grains – aspartame may be an implicator
- A diet low in polyunsaturated fatty acids

- Lack of regular exercise
- Low intakes of Vitamin D and other vital nutrients
- Other, non-defined stressors predominant in young to middle-aged adults
- Leaky gut syndrome brought on by yeast/fungal damage to the gut lining, thus allowing MS-triggering food/foreign proteins to gain access to the bloodstream via a permeable intestinal lining
- The immune system creates templates for the invading proteins which inadvertently take out the healthy myelin cells also
- Drugs prescribed may weaken the immune system, giving the appearance of retarding the disease
- Halting the disease at source will therefore necessitate addressing the diet, lifestyle and fungal issues of the patient

Take action ♥

An MS sufferer will usually have other, sometimes minor symptoms, which may not *seem* connected to their disease, i.e. acid reflux, athlete's foot, jock itch, thrush, digestion problems, bowel gas, etc. Patients should also be aware of foods to which they are sensitive, which should be eliminated. Ideally a diary should be kept keeping track of problem foods and any observable effects of eliminating them from the diet. The following will be of benefit to the multiple sclerosis sufferer:

- **DIET: COMMENCE THE ANTI-*CANDIDA* DIETARY REGIMEN**, ensuring that the **Foods to avoid** and supplementation are rigorously adhered to
- **DIET:** See **Foods to avoid** section of **THE *FOOD FOR THOUGHT* LIFESTYLE REGIMEN**
- **DIET:** Avoid all animal foods, except cold-caught oily fish (no farmed fish!), which should be consumed daily (salmon, mackerel, herring, etc.). Normal protein intakes
- **RESTORING NUTRIENT BALANCE: COMMENCE THE BASIC SUPPLEMENT PROGRAM**, ensuring:

- **ANTI-*CANDIDA*/FUNGAL SUPPLEMENTATION**, including wormwood, Essiac, fennel, peppermint tea, etc. Physician may also prescribe anti-fungal, anti-mycotoxic drugs in addition to the above, as directed
- Vitamin E, 800 IU per day
- Flaxseed oil, 1 tbsp per day
- Brain/CNS supplementation (ideally 'Ingenious' – see **A Guide to Nutritional Supplements**)
- Pancreatic enzyme supplementation, two capsules taken three times daily away from food
- Selenium, 200-400 mcg per day
- Vitamin B12 supplementation, as directed by your physician
- Vitamin C complex (ascorbates plus bioflavonoids), 4-5 g, twice per day (in the event of diarrhoea indicating threshold level has been exceeded, reduce intake to just under threshold level)
- Gingko biloba, as directed
- Hawaiian Noni Juice, as directed
- **TIP:** Those with mild MS symptoms should exercise in a gym four times a week both with weights and on a stationary cycle or 'Stairmaster' with arm movement extensions. Those with more severe forms of the disease should try assisted movement exercises and massage to improve comfort and circulation
- **TIP:** This regimen is a long-term lifestyle change and, once again, must be adhered to strictly

Obesity/Weight Gain

Profile

Obesity is excessive weight gain and usually classified by a person being at least 20% heavier than the midpoint of their weight range on a standard height-weight table. Obesity is now a major problem in the industrialised nations, with America, Britain, Canada and Australia leading the pack.

As age progresses, metabolic rates lessen, which is why obesity is more prevalent in the elderly than the young. Obesity across race varies slightly, with obesity in Hispanics higher than white or black. Obesity however is much more common among Hispanic and black women than their white counterparts. According to the Merck Manual, about 60% of middle-aged black women are obese compared with 33% of white women.[198]

Socio-economic factors play an important role in the development of obesity. For example, American women from poorer groups have a higher incidence of obesity than the more wealthy. Binge eating, emotional disorders, peer pressure and stress may all play a part in developing bad eating habits (see *Health Wars* and *The Mind Game*). Rarely, hormonal irregularities and damage to the hypothalamus may result in obesity.

Symptoms and causes

Excessive fat accumulates, mostly in the subcutaneous tissues, and is usually the result of the patient consuming more calories than they are expending. Processed, refined carbohydrates are the key culprits, with bread, sugar, chocolate, pastas, breakfast cereals and pastries being eaten in inordinate amounts. The western refined diet, as we have oft remarked, is doing us in, one pepperoni pizza at a time. A change of diet and lifestyle usually solves the problem, as well as a change of environment, where the patient may modify their eating and exercise habits, without being tied in to the old patterns (see *The Mind Game* – also **Addictions**).

---

[198] The Merck Manual, Pocket Books, 1997, p.685

The chief problems with obesity are the associated health problems which develop. Merck explains:

"Accumulation of excess fat below the diaphragm and in the chest wall may put pressure on the lungs, causing difficulty in breathing and shortness of breath, even with minimal exertion. The difficulties in breathing may seriously interfere with sleep, causing momentary cessation of breathing (sleep apnea), leading to daytime sleepiness and other complications."[199]

Obesity may also cause back problems and stress on the joints. Skin disorders are particularly common. Swelling of the feet and ankles is also routine (edema) as the body attempts to rid itself of excess fluids.

Emotional conditions

The maintenance of obesity is primarily an emotional problem caused by patterning. These patterns, which we deal with in more detail in the **Addictions** section, need to be addressed and a new routine adhered to. Counselling in this regard is extremely important, but the patient must be co-operative in wanting to change their diet and lifestyle.

Fad diets rarely work since the underlying emotional patterning is almost never addressed and changed, paving the way for a return to the old eating and lifestyle habits.

Take action♥

Those wishing to make a change for the better are advised to read the **Addictions** section of this book and then consider the following:

- **DIET: COMMENCE THE *FOOD FOR THOUGHT* LIFESTYLE REGIMEN**, ensuring adherence especially to the **Foods to avoid** section
- **RESTORE NUTRIENT BALANCE: COMMENCE THE BASIC SUPPLEMENT PROGRAM**

---

[199] Ibid.

- **TIPS:** Reduce stressful environment. This might well mean a change of employment and friends
- Try to change the patterns and habits of your daily routine and make the new regimes fun and enjoyable, especially the exercise part
- If suffering from **Bulimia**, please see appropriate section
- **EXERCISE:** A proper program needs to be set up by a qualified instructor to consider any ancillary health problems cause by the patient's obesity. This exercise regimen needs to be carried out consistently, along with the appropriate diet, supplementation and 4 pints (2 litres) per day of fresh, clean water. A more in-depth treatment of this is dealt with in my book *Health Wars*
- Try to associate with those who are encouraging in your efforts and non-condemnatory

Further Resources
Health Wars by Phillip Day
The Mind Game by Phillip Day

Osteoporosis

Profile

On average, one in three women and one in 12 men over 50 suffer from osteoporosis in the western cultures. The word actually means 'porous bone'. Yet in more primitive peoples, this disease is all but unknown (which should have alarm bells ringing immediately). The disease is most common in post-menopausal females, where as many as one in four may suffer from the condition.

Symptoms

Osteoporosis is described by low bone density and a deterioration of bone tissue, leading to extreme fragility and hip fractures. Spine and bones become demineralised and the bones take on a honeycombed look. Osteoporosis in its early stages is also characterised by severe backache. Decrease in height will be experienced over a period of time.

Commentary

Medicine's belief that the disease is formed by a lack of calcium and corresponding shortage of vitamin D to help calcium absorption is woefully wide of the mark. The traditional approach is to change the patient's diet to include dairy products, calcium and vitamin D supplementation, which often makes things worse. HRT is often prescribed, with often disastrous results, especially in the realm of causing cancer and other serious problems.

Americans especially consume huge quantities of dairy, with approximately 1$ in every $7 spent on food purchasing some form of dairy product. The problem is, Americans have one of the highest incidences of osteoporosis in the world. Clearly there is something else going on.

Drs. Murray and Pizzorno, authors of the *Encyclopaedia of Natural Medicine*, remark: *"Osteoporosis involves both the mineral (inorganic) and non-mineral (organic matrix, composed primarily of protein) components of the bone. This is the first clue that there is more to osteoporosis than a lack of dietary calcium. In fact, lack of dietary calcium in the adult results in a separate condition known as osteomalacia, or softening of the bone. The two conditions are different, in that in osteomalacia, there is only a deficiency of calcium in the bone. In contrast, in osteoporosis, there is a lack of both calcium and other minerals, as well as a decrease in the non-mineral, organic matrix of the bone. Little attention has been given to the important role this organic matrix plays in maintaining bone structure."* [200]

So what causes osteoporosis?
The importance of acid/akali

Dr Ted Morter Jr. has spent a lifetime analysing the effects different foods have on our internal environment. Morter states that the body responds perfectly to every stimulus that is applied to it, and each of these body responses is geared towards one aim and one aim only - survival. Sometimes this response is termed 'disease', if it goes against our ideal of what 'health' should be. Morter confirms the fact that the human body likes to dwell in a slight alkali (around pH 7.4).

When we acidify our internal environment with certain types of food, the body is forced to neutralise or 'buffer' this acid using a number of ingenious systems, mostly comprising alkalising minerals, such as sodium, calcium, potassium, magnesium and iron. Urine pH is a good indicator of what is happening inside the body and varies according to how much excess protein is consumed and must be buffered. Note that blood pH must ALWAYS be between 7.35 and 7.45 or else life ends abruptly within a matter of hours. [201]

The protein levels most of us eat today are many times greater than the body actually needs (between 20-40 g a day are the estimated requirements), and the excess we consume can quite literally kill us. Some of us are slogging down up to 10 times the

---

[200] Murray, M & J Pizzorno, op. cit. p.706-7

[201] Natural (physiological) acid produced through normal cell respiration is easily expelled in the breath via the lungs. Our blood pH is normally 7.35 when it is carting this acid, in the form of carbon dioxide, to the lungs for elimination. Blood is pH 7.45 after it has been 'cleaned up', the CO_2 removed, and then oxygen is taken on to deliver to your heart and the rest of your body.

body's protein requirements or more in our efforts to consume a herd of wildebeest and drink a swimming pool full of milk with our grain 'cereals' laced with refined sugar every morning. How our system eventually exhausts itself and collapses with all the acid generated is a book all on its own. But for our purposes here, the key to osteoporosis is in understanding the effects of acid and excess protein consumption and how the body tries to deal with them. When the digestive system is hit with a storm of acid derived from excessive protein food metabolism, this acid is potentially lethal and our hard-working bodies need to sort the problem in a hurry.

Firstly the brain mobilises mineral buffers to raise the acidic pH of our internal environment towards neutral in an effort to counteract the acid.[202] After scarfing down burgers, chicken, eggs, pasta, cheese, seafood, grains – all accompanied by the inevitable acid-producing coffee, tea, sodas and alcohol - the mineral buffers use alkalising minerals such as sodium, potassium, calcium, magnesium and iron along with water to combine with the acid generated by these food ashes to raise their pH, before escorting them out of the body via the kidneys. Notice the body loses these alkalising minerals when they are eliminated along with the acid.

If we are eating mineral-deficient, processed foods and are not consuming plenty of fresh water, the body may run short of these alkalising minerals and so starts to strip them from our bones. The result of these withdrawals is 'porous bone', or osteoporosis. This disease can be correctly termed 'a survival response'.

Osteoporosis in the elderly

Diets of the elderly are especially guilty of causing osteoporosis, since old folks often rely on labour-light, processed 'ready meals' instead of an alkalising diet rich in fruits, vegetables, haricots, etc. The favourites of the elderly - milk, meat, bread and cereal grains, sugars, breads, coffee, etc. - are all prime generators of acid, thus putting the body - and the skeleton - under tremendous pressure to come up with the minerals and water required to buffer the acid. All that milk being consumed by Americans, which we touched on

---

[202] The pH (potential of hydrogen) scale runs between 0 for pure acid and 14 for pure alkali. 7 is neutral

earlier, can actually precipitate osteoporosis, since milk is a prime acid generator, especially if it has been pasteurised and skimmed.

Menopausal osteoporosis
Estrogen dominance

Ladies experiencing menopausal symptoms, which may include hot flushes, sweats, mood changes, cysts, fibroids, endometriosis, etc. are also at risk from osteoporosis, but for a different reason than above. They are experiencing estrogen dominance over a progesterone deficiency, which, over a protracted period of time, may also cause a depletion of bone mass in the female, giving rise to osteoporosis (see **Menopausal Problems**).

Bone is living tissue that is always replacing itself. Osteoblasts, the cells that build and replace bone mass in humans, have progesterone receptors. No progesterone, no osteoblasts. No osteoblasts, no new bone material created. Osteoclasts on the other hand, are multinucleate cells that dissolve old bone material in preparation for the osteoblasts, which move in to replace old calcified bone with fresh material. Osteoclasts have estrogen receptors. So, if there is an estrogen dominance, osteoclasts are hard at work breaking down calcified bone material, leaving bones scored and pitted in preparation for the bone-building osteoblasts, which fail to act because of the lack of progesterone docked at their receptors.

Put the two features together and you get bone murder. Estrogen dominance results in calcified (old) bone material being broken down. Couple that with a simultaneous progesterone deficiency and you do not have this calcified bone being replaced. The net result is, of course, a progressive bone loss in the female – osteoporosis – porous bone.

40-60% of females in the western world today experience PMS symptoms, ranging from the noticeable to the severe. Many millions of women are guinea-pigs for the estrogen industry's onward march towards its dividend payouts. But imagine also a female's diet being acidified with excessive meat and dairy consumption, causing the body to bloat with water and mobilise calcium and other minerals out of the bones to restore the blood's pH balance. Then imagine the free-radical activity resulting from the incomplete metabolism of refined sugars she has put into her body, resulting in the destruction of healthy cells as free-radicals attempt to stabilise themselves by robbing oxygen electrons out of healthy tissue cells. Now you begin to get an idea of what disasters lie in wait for women who follow the penchant for western diets and western healthcare, which result in western diseases. Chief among these are cancer, thrombosis and osteoporosis – all tied to the irresponsible expansion of the menopause-as-estrogen-deficiency mindset.

Take action♥

So, once again, we are on familiar ground when it comes to getting osteoporosis sorted. It's diet, diet, diet, diet and some supplements to help everything mend.

- **DIET: COMMENCE THE *FOOD FOR THOUGHT* LIFESTYLE PROGRAM** and study what to avoid
- **RESTORE NUTRIENT BALANCE: COMMENCE THE BASIC SUPPLEMENT PROGRAM** ensuring:
- Calcium (lactates), 1,000 mg per day
- Vitamin D, 400 IU per day
- Magnesium, 600-800 mg per day
- Take a natural progesterone cream, such as Endau (Neways) and rub it on the body as directed. This supplement provides the body with the materials it needs to manufacture natural progesterone in the presence of an adequate diet
- Boron (as sodium tetrahydroborate), 3 -5 mg per day
- **TIP:** Moderate, but consistent exercise, as directed
- **TIP:** Sunlight to assist in vitamin D and calcium metabolism

Parkinson's Disease

Profile and symptoms

Parkinson's disease is a motor system disorder marked by a destruction of the cells which produce the neurotransmitter hormone dopamine. Symptoms include muscle rigidity, impaired movement, problems with balance and coordination, sexual disinterest, tremors when at rest and agitation.

Traditional treatment includes drugs, such as levodopa, selegiline, and bromocriptine, which work to replace the brain's dwindling supply of dopamine and minocycline, which may prevent dopamine cell damage by blocking the production of nitric oxide.[203] None of these drugs cure the disease or even halt its progression, but appear temporarily to make movement easier, improving the patient's mobility for a period of time. Medications do have side-effects.

Potential causes

Aspartame: Monsanto's infamous artificial sweetener has been found to trigger or worsen cases of Parkinson's. As discussed earlier, aspartame contains a number of modalities which can cause mental degeneration. The sweetener is the bane of food regulatory agencies around the world which receive a high percentage of their total adverse event reaction complaints from people experiencing symptoms of aspartame poisoning.[204]

Anti-psychotic drugs are also known to affect the basal ganglia's ability to produce dopamine. Many anti-psychotic preparations work by modifying the production of neurotransmitter hormones (the brain's chemical messengers, of which dopamine is one). A potent street opiate, N-MPTP, is also known to cause severe Parkinson's disease.

Faulty metabolism of iron in the body[205]

---

[203] Proceedings from the National Academy of Sciences, 4th December 2001, 98:14669-14674
[204] Day, Phillip, *Health Wars*, op. cit.
[205] *Nature Genetics*, February 2001, 27:209-214

Homocysteine: Raised levels of this protein metabolite are found in Parkinson's patients, who have a corresponding lack of folate in the body. One study reports:

"While previous studies have shown that levels of homocysteine are elevated in people with Parkinson's disease, the precise role of homocysteine in the development of the disease has remained unclear. This study strongly suggests that elevated homocysteine levels can indeed render neurons vulnerable to Parkinson's disease. This study establishes that a diet with low folic acid levels increases homocysteine levels and the homocysteine, in turn, renders neurons in the brain vulnerable to dysfunction and death." [206]

Exposure to pesticides and petroleum-based, hydrocarbon solvents[207]

Fungal infestations: Mycotoxins may plan a key role in generating Parkinson's, although no definitive studies have so far been done.

Take action♥

The key to a patient developing Parkinson's appears to be the excessive production of nitric oxide within the body which in turn seems to disrupt the production of dopamine. It is important to do a complete assessment of the patient's physical condition, including symptoms which might suggest other underlying problems, such as fungal/yeast infestations, food sensitivities (intolerances), lack of dream recall, heartburn, bowel problems, skin rashes, etc.

Pilot studies with Parkinson's patients using high doses of antioxidants, such as 3-5 g of C complex and over 3,000 IU of E showed that progress of the disease could be dramatically slowed.[208] Those suffering from Parkinson's disease may benefit from the following:

- **DIET: COMMENCE THE *FOOD FOR THOUGHT* LIFESTYLE REGIMEN**, ensuring a diet rich in fish

---

[206] *Journal of Neurochemistry*, January 2002; 80:101-110

[207] Annual Meeting of the American Academy of Neurology in San Diego, CA, USA, 9th May 2000; Neurology, September 2000; 55:667-673.

[208] **Fahn, S**, "A pilot trial of high-dose alpha-tocopherol and ascorbate in early Parkinson's disease", *Annals of Neurology*, 32 (1992): S128-32

oils (salmon, mackerel, herring, halibut, etc.), fresh vegetables and fruit. If patient is exhibiting fungal infestations, then switch to **THE ANTI-*CANDIDA* DIETARY REGIMEN**, along with the **ANTI-*CANDIDA* SUPPLEMENTATION PROGRAM**

- **RESTORE NUTRIENT BALANCE: COMMENCE THE BASIC SUPPLEMENT PROGRAM**, ensuring:
- Vitamin E, 800 IU per day. (Higher doses may be prescribed by a physician)[209]
- Deanol – 100 mg per day
- DMAE – 500 mg per day
- 'Ingenious' (Neways), which includes 'smart' nutrients, such as 5-HTP, pyroglutamate, glutamine, phosphatidyl choline and pantothenic acid (B5)
- **TIPS:** Cease eating junk foods, sugar and artificial sweeteners immediately
- Cease using personal care and household products with potentially harmful ingredients and switch to safe alternatives (see **Environmental Toxins**)
- Discuss the patient's replacement of any mercury amalgam fillings with a co-operative dentist

---

[209] *Arch. Neurol.* 1997;54: pp.762-765

Periodontal Disease
Gingivitis, periodontitis, etc.

Profile
Periodontal disease is a collective term for disorders which affect the support and surrounding structures of the teeth, namely the gums, alveolar bone, and the outer layer of the tooth root. The very common gingivitis affccts the gums surrounding the teeth. The more serious periodontitis, usually following on from gingivitis, includes loose teeth, periodontal pockets (between gums and teeth) and signs of infection and the weeping of bacteria. Root fillings may also 'go bad', and produce infection, copious weeping of bacteria, and eventually the tooth should be pulled.

Periodontal disease should be viewed as a systemic problem involving poor nutrition, immunity and hormonal imbalances in females. In America, 54% of adults over fifty suffer from periodontal disease. The disorder may also indicate a serious underlying condition, such as diabetes, anaemia, vitamin deficiency disorders and collagen irregularities. Patients suffering from the toxic immune disorder AIDS often suffer gum disease problems which progress rapidly. The condition manifests itself in several different forms:

Gingivitis: One of the most common manifestations of periodontal disease is the reddened, swollen, and often bleeding gums of gingivitis, caused by the actions of bacterial plaque on the surfaces of the teeth adjacent to the inflamed tissues. Plaque, a soft, sticky film mostly comprising bacteria, if not cleared away by brushing and flossing of the teeth, hardens into tartar (calculus) within 72 hours, which has to be removed through dental cleaning. Gingivitis can also be prevalent during hormonal fluctuations in women, brought on by pregnancy, periods, puberty, menopause and the use of birth control pills. In gingivitis, the gums become red and swollen, they often bleed, and are moveable, rather than tight against the teeth.

Periodontitis: Brought on by aggravated gingivitis, a long-term accumulation of plaque and tartar between the teeth and gums will cause pockets to develop between the tooth and gum, allowing the proliferation of bacteria in an anaerobic environment, which promotes their rapid growth. Eventually, jaw bone loss will result in loose teeth. Eventually the patient will lose the affected tooth. Periodontitis progress depends on a number of factors, including the condition of the patient's immune system, frequency of dental care, brushing and flossing, and whether they have an underlying disorder which often promotes the condition, such as those with diabetes mellitus, Crohn's disease, AIDS, or a lack of red blood cells. Patients with acidosis problems may also develop periondontitis, as will those whose diet contains a high degree of acidity which promotes the growth of bacteria and plaque.

Commentary

Bacteria have long been blamed for causing periodontal disease, and yet each of us has bacteria in our mouth. The deciding factors in poor or healthy teeth revolve around, not only their lifestyle and diet, but also the condition of the patient's internal environment and immune system. Here is a checklist:

- Does the patient have poor immunity and catch infections easily?
- Do they suffer from fungal, bacterial or yeast infections, manifesting elsewhere in the body?
- Do they have poor dental hygiene, which results in the proliferation of bacteria?
- Are these bacteria secreting endo/exotoxins, collagen-destroying enzymes and bacterial antigens?
- Does the patient have an underlying systemic disorder, such as diabetes?
- Does the patient suffer from nutritional deficiency problems, bringing on disorders such as scurvy, heart disease, pellagra or schizophrenia?
- Does the patient eat a highly processed, sugary diet?
- Does the patient drink fizzy soda drinks?
- Has the patient received one or more root fillings?
- Is the patient elderly and malnourished in general?
- Is the patient exhibiting hormonal problems?
- Are they pregnant or going through the menopause?
- Has the patient complained of faulty dental work?
- Does the patient have an acidosis problem?

Smoking

One of the chief causes of periodontal disease is smoking, where acidity and free-radical damage to the structures of the mouth cause bacteria to proliferate. Smoking also consumes huge levels of available vitamin C in the body, often contributing to other immunity problems. Stubborn smokers should be taking increased levels of C complex (ascorbates plus bioflavonoids) as well as carotenes to improve their immunity. Alternatively, you should dump this nasty, destructive habit.

Take action♥

A systemic approach to periodontal disease will provide the best results. There are a few do's and don't's, which must be adhered to:

- **DIET: COMMENCE THE *FOOD FOR THOUGHT* LIFESTYLE REGIMEN**, ensuring no sugar, no sugary foods, absolutely no white bread and no teas and coffees – green teas OK
- **RESTORE NUTRIENT BALANCE: COMMENCE THE BASIC SUPPLEMENT PROGRAM**, ensuring:
- Vitamin C complex, 2 g, twice per day
- Flavonoids, such as quercetin, catechin, anthocyanidins and proanthocyanidins. These can be supplemented or provided for in a diet rich in extracts from hawthorn, bilberry and green tea
- Vitamin E, 400 IU, twice per day
- Selenium, 200 mcg, twice per day
- Coenzyme Q10, as directed
- Beta-carotene (vitamin A precursor), as directed
- **TIPS**: Keep to an alkalising diet
- Stop smoking
- Reduce alcoholic intake or stop altogether
- If suffering from hormonal irregularities or other disorders, see appropriate section(s) of this book
- Exercise regularly to boost circulation, detoxification and immunity

Phobias

*"All our research, everything in our clinical experience
over the past twenty-five years, has convinced us that
you can improve your emotional state by improving
your nutrition; by making sure that every body cell
receives optimal amounts of every essential nutrient."*
Cheraskin, Ringsdorf and Brecher, authors of *Psychodietetics*

Profile

Previously, with depression, we examined the effects of high
levels of the neurotransmitter histamine, which is used by the brain
to regulate water usage, tears, mucus, saliva and other bodily
secretions. Equally, low levels of this neurotransmitter may also
create problems that are often linked to schizophrenia. This
condition is known as histapenia.

Symptoms

Undue suspicion and paranoia of people. The ability to withstand
pain well. Hirsutism (heavy growth of hair). Hard to achieve orgasm
with sex. Canker sores. Phobias and fears. Abnormal sensory
perceptions – seeing and hearing things. Ringing in the ears.
Excessive dental fillings. An absence of headaches and allergies.

Low histamine is often accompanied by high levels of copper, two
factors in themselves which may produce abnormal behaviour. Many
studies done over the years have gauged the correlation between
excess copper and behavioural abnormalities. Dr Michael Briggs
from Wellington, New Zealand, for instance, postulated that many
cases of schizophrenia could in fact merely be copper poisoning. Dr
Carl Pfeiffer studied the connection between histapenia, copper and
behavioural problems with his patients for many years. He reports
that a sub-group of around 50% of his schizophrenic patients were
high in copper. Pfeiffer also noted that low levels of zinc and
manganese were also implicated and that excess copper depresses
histamine and can be implicated in copperised pipes which bring
water into the household. Abnormal lead and mercury levels are also
well known to produce schizophrenic symptoms.

Histapenia-pellagra-estrogen link

Several studies have seen a link between pellagra, the classic vitamin B3 deficiency disease, and excess copper. Doctors Finddlay and Venter discovered that pellagra patients were also high in copper. Dr Krishnammachavi discovered this connection in India in 1974 and found that vitamin B3 appeared to regulate copper levels in the body.[210] Vitamin C deficiency also seemed to raise copper levels, which in turn produced a vicious spiral, since excess copper is known to destroy vitamin C. Thus a combined deficiency in B3 and C works to elevate copper levels in the body, which in turn destroy further supplies of vitamin C.

Histapenic modality

Excess or dominant levels of the female sex hormone estrogen in the body, which brings on the classic menopausal symptoms such as hot flushes, depression and mood swings, is also known to raise copper levels in the body, which in turn deplete Vitamin C. In the section on **Heart disease** in this book, we examine the connection between heart disease and depletion of vitamin C in the body (scurvy), brought on by the dissolving of collagen, a tough, fibrous material which clads the cardiovascular system, giving it structure and form. In the 1960s, when the first contraceptive pill, Envoid, was introduced, healthy young women began perishing from thrombosis. The contraceptive pill, with its elevated levels of estrogen, raises copper levels and depletes vitamin C. This excess of copper in turn depresses levels of histamine. Low levels of histamine produce inadequate levels of saliva, which in turn fail to protect the teeth from bacterial decay.

Take action♥

By restoring the balance of nutrients in the body, histamine can be brought to normal levels and the patient will experience relief from their symptoms. Any patient suffering from phobias, fears, hallucinations, or exhibiting many of the symptoms described earlier, can obtain a blood test to track levels of copper and histamine to determine whether they are histapenic. Histapenic patients may benefit from the following:

---

[210] **Krishnammachavi, K**, *Am. J. Clin. Nutr.*, 1974, 27:108-111

- **DIET: COMMENCE THE *FOOD FOR THOUGHT* LIFESTYLE REGIMEN**, increasing protein in diet
- **RESTORE NUTRIENT BALANCE: COMMENCE THE BASIC SUPPLEMENT PROGRAM**, ensuring:
- Niacin, 500 mg, am and pm (may cause blushing. If undesirable, use the 'no-flush' version bound with inositol)
- Folic acid (B9), 1,000 mcg each am
- B12 injection, weekly or daily supplementation
- L-tryptophan, 1,000 mg at bedtime
- Zinc and manganese daily, as directed by your physician

Pyroluria

Profile

Zinc and vitamin B6 deficiencies give rise to a common physical illness, often mistaken for a mental disease, known as pyroluria. This disease occurs when a large number of chemicals called pyrroles are manufactured by the body, which act as 'anti-nutrients' – that is, they bind to zinc and aldehyde chemicals, such as pyridoxine (B6), rendering them unavailable to the body. Pyrroles can be measured in the urine and a simple test can be used to determine whether the patient has a problem in this area.

Symptoms

Patients are withdrawn and like isolation. Have set routines and become uncomfortable when these are disrupted. Pronounced 'fruity' breath and body odour. Have no dream recall. Constant colds and infections. Irregular menstrual cycle. Impotency. Upper abdominal pain as spleen and liver become engorged periodically with catabolic red cell debris. Sometimes walk stooped to ease the pain. Miscarriages with male babies. Compulsively creative. Insomnia. White spots on fingernails. Stretch marks on skin. Morning nausea and constipation. Pale skin which does not tolerate sunlight. Hypersensitive to light. May become emotionally exhausted.

Many of us can experience one or several of the above. But a patient exhibiting a range of these symptoms should incur suspicion that they might be suffering from pyroluria. Carl Pfeiffer recalls one patient at his famous Princeton Bio-Center clinic in New Jersey:

"Since she was 11, Sara's life had been a nightmare of mental and physical suffering. Her history included chronic insomnia, episodic loss of reality, attempted suicide by hanging, amnesia, partial seizures, nausea, vomiting and loss of periods. Her knees were so painful (X-rays showed poor cartilages) and her mind so disperceptive that she walked slowly with her feet wide apart like a peasant following a hand plough drawn by tired oxen.

Psychiatrists at three different hospitals gave the dubious, 'waste-basket' labels of 'schizophrenia', 'paranoid schizophrenia' and 'schizophrenia with convulsive disorder'. At times, her left side went into spasms with foot clawed and fist doubled up. Both arm and leg had a wild, flaying motion. Restraints were needed at these times. Psychotherapy was ineffective and most tranquillisers accentuated the muscle symptoms. Sara tested positive for pyroluria and was given B6 and zinc.

Urinary kryptopyrrole was at times as high as 1,000 mcg%, the normal range being less than 15. She was diagnosed as zinc and B6 deficient and treatment was started. Over three months, her knees became normal, the depression subsided, as did the seizures, her periods returned, the nausea vanished and so did the abdominal pain. She has had no recurrence of her grave illness, finished college and now works in New York. She takes zinc and B6 daily. When under stress of any kind, she increases her intake of vitamin B6." [211]

Dream recall

Those suffering from a deficiency in vitamin B6 cannot recall their dreams. Contrary to many theories, it is this author's opinion that dream recall is normal and an essential part of cleansing and rebooting the mind in readiness for the coming day.

Science knows almost nothing about sleep, other than the physiological observations it has made about this curious part of our lives over the years. About one third of our existence is spent between the sheets, so to speak, and yet the precise reasons why we dream remain unknown.

Aside from all the soothsaying, dream interpreters and the like, many will testify that they feel more refreshed, more mentally alert and stable, more emotionally balanced, if they dream regularly. Some have reported that they feel humbled and more 'a part of something wonderful that I don't really understand'. Certainly, if dreaming can make a population more humble and part of

---

[211] Pfeiffer, Carl & Patrick Holford, op. cit. p.118

something 'wonderful', then I for one am all for it, in view of how things are in our society today.

On the nutritional side, lack of dream recall can be cured simply by supplementing vitamin B6 in increments (not exceeding 600 mg a day). Clinics can measure B6 and zinc deficiencies very easily often by analysing liver enzymes, which elevate in the absence of B6.

Skin, baldness, nails and dentistry

Pyrolurics often have pale skin due to lack of skin pigmentation. Some, who have never been able to tan, can do so after zinc and B6 supplementation. Local depigmentation (vitiligo) does not respond to B6 and zinc but may with an anti-fungal regime.[212] Baldness and lack of eyelashes and brows may often respond to zinc and B6, as can greying hair, which has been known to reverse to the original colour with zinc therapy.

Nail-biting can also be a result of zinc and B6 deficiency. Thin, brittle and weak nails strengthen in time with zinc and B6 and the nutritional supplement regimen below. Once nails are strong, nail-biting often ceases of its own accord. Small, white spots on the nail may disappear with zinc treatment, but larger discolourations sometimes have to grow out with the nail.

Crowded incisors and a narrow upper dental arch are also an indication of the pyroluric. Gums may also be red and retracted, indicating the presence of pyorrhoea where there is a zinc deficiency. Drs. Curson and Losee find both copper and cadmium to be high in the enamel of decayed teeth when compared with that of healthy teeth. Persons suffering from tooth decay will benefit from (obviously) giving up sucrose, white flour and white rice and supplementing with B6 and zinc, over and above the basic supplement program.

---

[212] Dr W Henry Sebrell discusses a doctor in Miami who was treating vitiligo with niacin therapy. Regrettably no further information exists as to dosage or outcome. Neem cream is also a traditional, natural way to treat skin depigmentation.

Take action ♥

Pfeiffer and Holford believe that about 10% of the population may be pyroluric, which symptoms are evident when stress becomes predominant. Pyrolurics may benefit from the following:

- **DIET: COMMENCE THE *FOOD FOR THOUGHT* LIFESTYLE REGIMEN**
- **RESTORE NUTRIENT BALANCE: COMMENCE THE BASIC SUPPLEMENT PROGRAM,** ensuring:
- Vitamin B6, 100 mg, am and pm
- Zinc (derived from zinc gluconate), 35 mg, am and pm
- Manganese, 10 mg, am and pm
- Exercise and rest
- Remove stress!

Schizophrenia

"I have never seen anyone who was able to change his or her self-perception of 'sick' to 'well' while on drugs." Dr Alan Goldstein, professor of psychiatry, Temple University, Philadelphia

Profile

That there are those in our society who can be described as 'disturbed' or 'mentally deranged' is, of course, beyond doubt. Author Bruce Wiseman remarks: *"Since the first eyebrow was raised at the sight of erratic behaviour, society has had to deal with the problem of the madman. And it is a problem. Anyone who thinks otherwise has never lived around insane people nor had his life disrupted by their actions.*

They destroy in the name of some imagined wrong, they refuse to maintain their physical needs and, even if they simply mope, their presence almost inevitably makes life miserable for those around them.

Most families feel considerable relief when they 'put away' the son, daughter or relative who has been screaming obscenities day and night or who believes all are poisoning him. For this reason, mothers, fathers and others at wit's end have welcomed psychiatric services with open arms over the past two centuries. Why wouldn't they? Any offer to remove insanity from one's midst sounds good when one is pressed to the limit of his emotional and financial resources. This has been the foremost function of psychiatry since its inception – to remove the mentally disturbed from streets and shaken homes so the functioning majority can get on with the business of living." [213]

Symptoms

'Schizophrenia' as a diagnosis is aberrant, as the symptoms often attached to it vary considerably. Schizophrenia loosely correlates to society's traditional view of the deranged person. Symptoms variously linked to schizophrenia include dermatitis, inflammations

---

[213] **Wiseman, Bruce**, *Psychiatry – The Ultimate Betrayal*, Freedom Publishing, 2000, p.55

of the mucous membranes, chronic diarrhoea and mental problems, including depression, irritability, anxiety, confusion, migraine headaches, sleep disturbance, delusions and hallucinations. Some have likened serious cases of schizophrenia to a nightmare from which there is no awakening. Certainly, to the sufferer, what they are experiencing seems real and terrifying enough. LSD-induced schizophrenia, which may feature encounters with monsters and demons, as well as gross mental disperceptions and time distortions, at least has the comfort of the clock. After the allotted number of hours, the effect wears off. But for the classic schizophrenic, whose condition has come upon him by degrees, there is a continuing and harrowing nightmare.

Commentary

The problem with the label 'schizophrenia' is that many cannot agree on what constitutes 'the disease'. There are a hundred causations that may underpin the behavioural patterns that can later be diagnosed as 'schizophrenia'. Often, the practitioner needs to wade through histamine, copper, zinc and mercury tests to see if there are abnormal levels of these agents in their patient's system. Psychiatry believes that *"...a return to full pre-morbid functioning in this disorder is not common..."* – in other words, the condition is almost always incurable.

As already seen, there may be a number of reasons why someone will start to behave abnormally. In the previous section on ADD/ADHD, we learned that four factors could come into play in changing behaviour: nutritional deficiency, blood sugar imbalances, toxins in the diet and environment, and food sensitivities. With schizophrenia, things can often be more straightforward. Many nutritionists and orthomolecular psychiatrists hold the view that, in many cases, we might be dealing with nothing more than the continuing reign of a miserable condition known as pellagra, believed for many years to have been banished to the history books.

Nutritional link – the pellagra connection

Pellagra was a fatal disease that threw terror into Europe and the United States during its ravages in the 18th and 19th centuries. Noted originally in the 18th century as a European condition that appeared to be linked to corn diets among the impoverished, pellagra's symptoms were as exotic as they were fatal. Named 'pellagra' (the Italian for 'rough skin'), sufferers of this disease were affected by dermatitis, inflammations of the mucous membranes, chronic diarrhoea, red or inflamed neck (hence: 'Redneck') and mental problems, including depression, irritability, anxiety, confusion, migraine headaches, delusions, hallucinations and dementia.

Dr Abram Hoffer

Dr Abram Hoffer, a leading mental health expert from Canada, claims a 90% cure rate for schizophrenia. Hoffer's definition of a cure for this condition is:

- Free from symptoms
- Able to socialise with family and community
- Paying income tax!

In other words, after *a return to full pre-morbid functioning in his disorder*, the patient is able to retake his place in society and have a life. Hoffer remarks of one such case:

"In October of 1990, a 24-year-old woman arrived at my office. Six months earlier she began to hallucinate and became paranoid. During three weeks in hospital she was started on a tranquilliser. For several months after a premature discharge, she almost starved until a retired physician took her into her home to feed her. When I saw her she still suffered visual hallucinations, but no longer heard voices. I started her on 3 grams of niacin [vitamin B3] and three grams of vitamin C daily. Three days later she was much better. By February 1991 she was well. Today, she is still well and lives with her sister." [214]

Niacin – Vitamin B3

Hoffer pioneered the use of mega-doses of vitamin B3, in the form of niacin or niacinamide. Hoffer and Pfeiffer's therapeutic dosage for B3 is between 2-4 grams a day, a level over 100 times the recommended daily allowance for the nutrient, which, at excessive

---

[214] Pfeiffer, Carl & Patrick Holford, op. cit. p.113

doses over Hoffer's recommendations, can cause liver damage.[215] Having recorded over 4,000 cases and published the results of double-blind trials, Hoffer is convinced vitamin therapy, including high doses of B3, is an effective treatment to schizophrenia. His ten-year follow-up studies on schizophrenics treated with and without vitamin therapy demonstrate that significantly fewer of the vitamin-treated patients were admitted to hospital or suffered suicides.

"The idea that diet could overcome mental problems struck me as preposterous," admitted psychiatrist Frederic Flack, whose 'schizophrenic' daughter Rickie narrowly escaped a recommended lobotomy after undergoing years of institutionalisation, electroshocks, drug treatments and restraints. She was finally cured by Dr Carl Pfeiffer using nutrition. Pfeiffer confided to Flack that other prominent psychiatrists had secretly turned to him for nutritional treatment when it was their child or loved one who needed help.

The actual mechanism by which niacin works for many cases of schizophrenia is still not known. Hoffer postulated that the body, in the absence of sufficient B3, creates adrenochrome from adrenalin. Adrenochrome is a chemical known to cause hallucinations. Niacin also stimulates the production of histamine and helps detoxify excess copper, inappropriate amounts of which are related to mental illness. Niacin also assists in converting essential fatty acids into prostaglandins, which in turn help to regulate neurotransmitter hormones in the brain. Hoffer's schizophrenic treatment included B3 and C.

Take action♥

A full medical examination yields great dividends. Does the patient have seemingly unrelated complaints to his apparent schizophrenia? Rashes on the body? Bad digestion problems? Blood sugar complications? Fungal complaints? Bad breath? These tell a qualified physician a number of valuable things about the patient's overall state of health, which will point to key causative factors.

---

[215] **Hoffer, A**, "Safety, side-effects and relative lack of toxicity of nicotinic acid", *Schizophrenia*, 1969, 1:78-87

- **DIET: COMMENCE THE *FOOD FOR THOUGHT* LIFESTYLE REGIMEN**
- **RESTORE NUTRIENT BALANCE: THE BASIC SUPPLEMENT PROGRAM,** ensuring:
- Vitamin B3 – niacin (no-flush[216]) or niacinamide 1,000 mg (1 gram) twice per day
- Vitamin B1 (thiamine), 100 mg per day
- Vitamin C complex (ascorbates plus bioflavonoids), 1 gram after each meal
- **TIP:** Choose a physician or clinic well acquainted with nutritional and food sensitivity problems
- **TIP:** Allow the physician to test for food sensitivities and mineral aberrations

---

[216] Niacin invariably causes a blushing of the skin, along with prickly sensations, for about 30 minutes. 'No flush' niacin, bound with inositol, is also available. However, when 500-1,000 mg of niacin is taken regularly, flushing stops.

Skin Disorders
Eczema, psoriasis, dermatitis

Profiles and symptoms

Skin conditions are unsightly, uncomfortable and downright embarrassing. Once again, a skin condition tells us the immune system is reacting to an assault and attempting to repel it.

Eczema: Dry, itchy skin, blisters forming with clear fluid in them (serum), a reddening around the affected area. Eczema is characterised by internal causations, i.e. external toxins and agents do not play a primary role (compare with dermatitis). Traditional treatments usually involve systemic or topical corticosteroids and cyclosporin A.

Atopic eczema: Skin rashes associated with asthma and hay fever. Patients (up to 20% of the population!) have a history of allergy or will go on to develop asthma or hay fever.

Seborrhoeic eczema: Caused by *Pityrosporum* yeasts. Affected areas are usually the scalp, nose, eyelids and lips. Mostly associated with those with severe immune deficiencies, such as AIDS.

Dermatitis: Itchy skin, rashes, and blisters caused by external agents, chemicals, detergents, irritants, metals, etc. The primary goal here is to remove the irritant from the patient's environment. This condition is common with nurses, cooks, metal workers, hairdressers, etc. Nickel dermatitis has been found in the European population handling the new nickel euro coins (yet another reason not to join the euro).

Psoriasis: A chronic skin condition manifesting itself as pink scaly skin most commonly affecting the scalp, knees, elbows, buttocks, etc. Skin cells replicate too rapidly, accumulating to form a silvery scale most commonly associated with the condition. Affects approximately 2% of the population and is often associated with bacterial streptococcal infection and also linked with arthritis. Traditional treatments will include steroidal drugs, tar and dithranol. Methotrexate or cyclosporine are sometimes used for the worst cases.

Commentary

I have grouped these skin conditions together as the remedial actions are very similar. The causations are either internal (eczema and psoriasis) or external (dermatitis). Internal causations for eczema and psoriasis will usually involve a classic western profile of stress, poor immunity, fungal/yeast and bacterial problems caused by their ejected toxins, bowel toxaemia, incomplete protein digestion, alcohol consumption, and poor liver function. These internal causations may often result in allergic reactions, e.g. food sensitivities, hay fever, asthma, etc. External causations will usually involve constant exposure to chemical or metallic toxins either in the home or at work.

Take action♥

A complete 40,000-mile service is in order for the skin-rash sufferer. Those suffering from dermatitis need to review carefully the chemicals in their environment with which they come into contact on a regular basis. These can include common household products such as shampoos, skin creams, make-up, perfumes, bath cleaners, washing-up liquid, soap powders, as well as the nightmares you may be using at work... you get the picture (see **Environmental Toxins**).

Action for these skin complaints comes in the form of detoxification, replenishment of nutrients, a bowel cleanse, an anti-fungal program, skin (topical) applications and... a holiday!

- **RESTORE NUTRIENT BALANCE: COMMENCE THE BASIC SUPPLEMENT PROGRAM,** ensuring:
- **ANTI-*CANDIDA*/FUNGAL SUPPLEMENTATION**
- Zinc, 30 mg, twice per day
- Vitamin A emulsion (safe form of A), 50,000 IU per day (do not use if pregnant)
- Selenium, 200 mcg per day
- Silymarin, 70-200 mg, three times per day
- **DETOXIFICATION**: A week's fasting, except for blended vegetable juices taken throughout the day (avoid fruit juices) and plenty of fresh, clean water

- **DETOXIFICATION**: At the same time, commence a two-week magnesium oxide bowel cleanse. Then, after one week....
- **DIET: COMMENCE THE ANTI-*CANDIDA* DIETARY REGIMEN**, ensuring that foods to which you are sensitive are avoided. These might include, but not be limited to eggs, milk, peanuts, soy, gluten products made from wheat, barley, rye and oats (including beer!), citrus and chocolate
- **TIP:** Limit intakes of animal fats, replacing these with oily fish, such as salmon, mackerel, herring, halibut, etc. Ensure these are cold-caught and not farmed
- **TOPICAL TREATMENTS:** applied two to three times a day over the infected area can include preparations containing glycyrrhetinic acid, chamomile or witch hazel. Drs. Murray and Pizzorno recommend preparations of *Glycyrrhiza glabra*, *Arctium lappa* or *Taraxacum officinale* in either their dried/powdered root form or in fluid/tincture extract. An herbalist or naturopathic doctor should be able to help. Avoid steroidals where possible
- Exercise regularly
- Avoid stress and get plenty of rest. In fact....
- Go on holiday, especially the wandering-through-the-bazaar, sleeping-until-noon-and-lazy-days-in-the-surf type. *Moderate* but consistent exposure to the sun is OK (use safe creams only!), unless you burn easily

Sleep Disorders

Profile

Sleep comes upon us when levels of the neurotransmitter serotonin rise while circulating levels of adrenalin decrease. Serotonin is partially made from the protein constituent (amino acid) tryptophan, currently banned for general sale because of a contamination introduced through its production by genetic engineering. Many believe this was done deliberately to save the huge sleeping pill market, as tryptophan is remarkably effective in getting us to snooze. Interesting that now the nutrient has been declared safe, it is still banned!

Take action♥

If you are not getting your share of shut-eye, you may benefit from the following:

- **DIET: COMMENCE THE *FOOD FOR THOUGHT* DIETARY REGIMEN**
- **RESTORE NUTRIENT BALANCE: THE BASIC SUPPLEMENT PROGRAM,** ensuring:
- Vitamin B6, 100 mg, twice per day
- Zinc, up to 50 mg per day
- L-tryptophan, 1,000 mg, twice per day
- Eat calcium and magnesium-rich foods (avoid dairy! Leafy green vegetables are ideal, along with nuts and seeds)
- **TIPS:** Avoid junk and sugary foods
- Avoid food additives
- Remove worries and stress, as far as possible
- Avoid all stimulants after 4pm
- **EXERCISE!** Are you actually 'tired'?

Stroke
Apoplexy, ischaemic, haemorrhagic

Profile
A stroke (formerly: apoplexy) occurs as a consequence of an interruption of blood supply to the brain. What causes the blood flow to become interrupted is the cause of the stroke. This is usually one or several of the problems discussed in the section on heart disease. A stroke is thus the secondary effect of a heart or circulatory condition.

Ischaemic stroke is when the blood supply is prevented by clotting (thrombosis) or by a detached clot that blocks an artery (embolism).

Haemorrhagic stroke results from a ruptured artery wall and consequent loss of supply to the brain.

Symptoms
...can run from a transient mild tingling in a limb, through a sudden weakness or loss of muscle function (temporary), through to fainting, paralysis, coma, leading to death.

Take action♥
Citizens wishing either to exercise prevention or treat an existing stroke condition with nutritional strategies may wish to examine the section on **Heart Disease** and follow the recommendations, under guidance of a physician.

Tardive Diskinesia

Profile

This condition is a side-effect of medication, which can cause the patient's extremities to move spasmodically. Lips, tongue, jaw, fingers, toes and legs twitch or 'dance' as a result of nerve complications. Some doctors, such as world TD expert Dr William Glazier, believe that up to 70% of long-term psychiatric drug users risk getting symptoms of TD. Seymour Rosenblatt, in his *Beyond Valium*, explains how psychiatry first became aware of the condition:

"One day we noticed something peculiar. Some patients developed a strange, wormlike tongue movement. It was hardly noticeable – a twitch of the tongue tip – but you could see it when they held their mouths open. As the days passed, the symptoms grew worse. Their lips began rotating in a chewing movement. Soon the whole mouth was thrusting and rolling, the tongue flicking out like the tongue of an anteater.

What kind of strange behaviour was this? It grew worse. It afflicted their arms and legs. They began to writhe slowly, purposelessly, a few of them developing a to-and-fro rocking motion.

Little did we know it, but we were in the process of observing the first serious drawback of antipsychotics [medication].... It swept through the hospitals like an epidemic. One after another the patients were stricken. Soon we had almost 50% of our mental patients chewing and grimacing in a horrible grotesquerie.

What was the cause? We didn't know. Families of the afflicted patients went running to the doctors. 'What have you done to poor Joe?' they demanded. 'He's writhing so badly we can't stand the sight of him!'"[217]

---

[217] **Rosenblatt, Seymour & Reynolds Dodson**, *Beyond Valium – The Brave New World of Psychochemistry*, Putnam's, New York: 1981, pp.164-165

Rosenblatt later discovered that drugs such as Thorazine were blocking the nerve receptors. The receptors were not getting their usual transmitter messages. They were firing less often and a state of lethargy ensued.

Take action ♥

TD is often thought to be irreversible. Nutritionist Patrick Holford and psychiatrist Carl Pfeiffer, on the other hand, report that TD patients respond well to detoxification, dietary changes, and intakes of zinc, manganese, vitamins C, E, B3 & B6 and Deanol, as well as evening primrose oil. These are required by the body to turn essential fats into prostaglandins, which affect nerve impulse transmissions. A TD patient should be encouraged to follow all the basic steps of diet and nutrition explained in this book for the optimum chance of restoring loss or impaired function to their nervous system.

Varicose Veins

Profile

Varicose veins are dilated, superficial veins which have widened to a degree where the valves within them do not close properly to prevent blood flowing away from the heart. The condition is experienced in some 50% of middle-aged adults and is believed to be due to weaknesses which develop in the vein walls which cause the vein to lose its elasticity and dilate.

People who stand for long periods of time are at risk, since gravity builds pressure within the veins, causing them to dilate. The cusps of the valves within veins now do not close properly, causing the vein to fill with back-flowing blood, leading to the unsightly condition.

Varicose veins do not usually occur in cultures who consume high-fibre, unrefined foods and exercise regularly – they are a peculiarly western phenomenon where diets are fibre-poor and heavily processed and people exercise sporadically. Low-fibre diets produce straining during defecation, increasing pressure in the abdomen, causing a weakening and dilation of the superficial veins in the legs, leading to varicose veins and haemorrhoids. Traditional treatments include removing the offending veins and the wearing of elastic stockings. Varicose veins may also appear in pregnancy, due again to increased pressure in the abdomen, once again dilating veins. However, these usually clear up in the weeks following delivery before any more permanent weakness can develop in the vein walls, so long as an appropriate exercise and diet regimen is maintained.

Symptoms

Blood pooling in superficial veins causes them to bulge and curl tortuously beneath the skin. Sometimes, patients have 'tired' legs, which ache or itch. Sometimes there is no pain at all.

Take action♥

The regimen described below is designed to increase fibre intake, increase exercise and oxygenation and provide key nutrients which assist in repairing, strengthening and providing suitable elasticity to the vein walls.

- **DIET: COMMENCE THE *FOOD FOR THOUGHT* LIFESTYLE REGIMEN**, paying special attention to high-fibre foods that will aid peristalsis. Also, increase intakes of foods such as blackberries, cherries, blueberries ([pro]anthocyanidins), as well as garlic, onions, cayenne pepper and other circulatory stimulants
- **RESTORE NUTRIENT BALANCE: COMMENCE THE BASIC SUPPLEMENT PROGRAM**, especially vitamins C (inc. bioflavonoids) and E. Also:
- A pancreatic enzyme supplement, two capsules taken three times daily away from food
- **EXERCISE**: A regular form of low-impact exercise and weight training will stimulate pooled blood back into circulation. Daily!
- **TIPS:** Avoid standing still for long periods of time
- Avoid overweight or obesity

Other Disorders
(where to go for more information)

Chicken pox, infectious diseases (misc), influenza (flu), malaria, measles, mumps, rubella, severe acute respiratory syndrome (SARS), smallpox, tuberculosis, typhoid
See: *Wake up to Health in the 21ˢᵗ Century*
by Steven Ransom

Cancers: brain, bowel, breast, cervical, liver, lung, osteo, ovarian, pancreatic, prostate, skin, etc.
See: *Cancer: Why We're Still Dying to Know the Truth*
by Phillip Day
Also: *Great News on Cancer in the 21ˢᵗ Century*
by Steven Ransom

Bad breath, constipation, diarrhoea, esophageal reflux, heart diseases, high blood pressure, lactose intolerance, poisonings, putrefaction and misc. digestion problems
See: *Health Wars*
by Phillip Day

ADD/ADHD, agitation, amnesia, anorexia nervosa, antisocial behaviour, autism, bedwetting, bulimia, chemical imbalances, convulsions, criminal behaviour, depression, drug addiction, dyslexia, epilepsy, facial swelling, glucose intolerance, hallucinations, hirsutism, histadelia, histapenia, hyperactivity, hypersexuality, infantile colic, irritability, leaky gut syndrome, nerve pain, nightmares, phobias, schizophrenia, seizures, smoking addiction, stress, suicidal tendencies, twitches
See: *The Mind Game*
by Phillip Day

Environmental Toxins

In many of my titles, I devote a section to potential and actual carcinogens in the personal care and household products marketplace which have seriously affected health for decades. These toxins can also have a direct and cumulative effect on cognitive ability and 'mental health'. The problems stem from governments' inability financially to test and effectively regulate these chemicals with the limited budgets they have available. Compounding this problem are the conflicts of interest that exist between chemical manufacturers and the government regulatory agencies themselves, making independent, objective adjudication of these drugs and chemicals a near impossibility.

Agencies, such as Britain's Environment Agency and America's Environmental Protection Agency exist, so far as the public is concerned, for no other reason than to ensure that we can raise our families and work at our jobs in, as far as possible, a contamination-free environment. All technologically advanced nations have such environmental agencies, and yet every year, people still die by the hundreds of thousands, polluted and poisoned by these substances. So what has gone so wrong?

The major problem is the rate at which new chemicals and chemical products are pouring onto the world's markets. Government agencies, already so tightly controlled financially with annual budget constraints, simply do not have the resources to test more than a dozen or so each year. Therefore they must rely heavily on industry-sponsored reports on product safety *from the manufacturers themselves*, which naturally opens up a wide arena for abuse. Agencies such as the EPA threaten dire fines on pharmaceutical and chemical companies found indulging in any foul play to ram potentially unsafe products through regulation. But prosecution of such cases by government on a realistic scale is rare since litigation consumes prodigious amounts of taxpayers' money.

Worse, the very government regulatory agencies themselves, such as the US Food & Drug Administration and Britain's Medicines Control Agency (MCA), which are supposed to protect the public from potentially dangerous products coming onto the market, are horribly compromised because of personal investments or ties with the chemical/drug industries. A *USA Today* analysis of financial conflicts at 159 US Food and Drug Administration advisory committee meetings from 1st January to 30th June 2000 finds that:

> At 92% of the meetings, at least one member had a financial conflict of interest
> At 55% of meetings, half or more of the FDA advisers had conflicts of interest
> Conflicts were most frequent at the 57 meetings when broader issues were discussed: 92% of members had conflicts
> At the 102 meetings dealing with the fate of a specific drug, 33% of the experts had a financial conflict[218]

"The best experts for the FDA are often the best experts to consult with industry," says FDA senior associate commissioner Linda Suydam, who is in charge of waiving conflict-of-interest restrictions. But Larry Sasich of Public Citizen, an advocacy group, says, *"The industry has more influence on the process than people realise."*

Britain's Medicines Control Agency fares little better with its track record for impartiality when it comes to regulating the drug industry. According to a *Daily Express* investigation, key members of the Committee on Safety of Medicines and the Medicines Commission themselves have heavy personal investments in the drug industry. Yet these committees are the ones which decide which drugs are allowed onto the market and which are rejected!

According to the report, two thirds of the 248 experts sitting on the Medicines Commission have financial ties to the pharmaceutical industry. Drug regulators such as Dr Richard Auty have £110,000 worth of holdings with AstraZeneca. Dr Michael Denham owns £115,000 worth of shares in SmithKline Beecham. Dr Richard Logan has up to £30,000 shares in AstraZeneca, SmithKline Beecham and

---

[218] *USA Today* article by Dennis Cauchon, *FDA Advisers Tied to Industry*, 25th September 2000, http://www.usatoday.com/news/washdc/ncssun06.htm

Glaxo Wellcome. Logan's role with the committee involves examining cases where a drug might have to be withdrawn from the market for safety reasons.

David Ganderton was an advisor for nine years with the CSM panel who used to work for AstraZeneca. His current shareholding with this drug company is worth £91,000. Other members of the committees with substantial holdings for example include Dr Colin Forfar, with £22,000 with Glaxo Wellcome and Dr Brian Evans owning £28,000 worth of shares with Glaxo Wellcome.[219]

The Daily Express report goes on to tell us: *"Tom Moore, a former senior executive with AstraZeneca, told the Sunday Express that the drug companies go out of their way to build strong links. He said, "Their objective is to get as close as possible. They are an extremely powerful lobby group because they have unlimited resources."*

The [drug] *companies provide* [members of CSM and other regulatory committees with] *trips abroad to conferences, large research grants that can keep a university department employed for years, and consultancies that can boost an academic's humble income."*

What remote hope can there be of proper, unbiased, objective research on nutrition? Many of these government regulators will eventually leave their posts to take up positions with the companies they once regulated. This makes excellent strategic sense for the chemical industry, which can use the expertise of such talent to smooth the way through their products' regulation and approval procedures.

Personal care and household products

Poor regulation, self-regulation and a blizzard of confusing and contrary scientific data have resulted in a tragically large number of chemicals making it into our personal lives with little or no warnings attached. Most people have no idea, for example, what the personal care products they use every day are doing to them. As an example,

---

[219] *Daily Express,* micro edition, 6th August 2000

in 1990, 38,000 cosmetic injuries were reported in the US that required medical attention.[220] Health concerns are continuously being raised about ingredients in shampoos, toothpastes, skin creams, talcs, and other personal care products. In fact, researchers in Japan, Germany, Switzerland, and the US say many ingredients in personal care products may be related to premature baldness, cataract formation, environmental cancers, contact dermatitis and possible eye damage in young children. We'll find out what some of these substances actually are in a moment and why these researchers have every reason to be concerned.

The National Institute of Occupational Safety and Health has found that 884 chemicals available for use in cosmetics have been reported to the US Government as toxic substances.[221] So why are these potentially harmful ingredients allowed in personal care products?

In 1938 the US Government created a legal definition for cosmetics by passing The Federal Food, Drug and Cosmetic Act. Cosmetics were defined as products for *"cleansing, beautifying, promoting attractiveness, or altering the appearance."* In this definition, a cosmetic is defined *"in terms of its intended purpose rather than in terms of the ingredients with which it is formulated."*[222] In other words, although the Food and Drug Administration classifies cosmetics, incredibly it does not regulate them. According to a document posted on the agency's Internet homepage, *"...a cosmetic manufacturer may use any ingredient or raw material and market the final products without government approval."*[223]

On 10th September 1997, Senator Edward M. Kennedy of Massachusetts, while discussing an FDA reform bill, stated, *"The*

[220] **Steinman, D & Samuel S Epstein**, *The Safe Shopper's Bible*, pp.182-183, ISBN 0020820852; also Consumer Product Safety Commission (CPSC), Product summary report: Washington DC, 1990

[221] Steinman, D & S Epstein, *The Safe Shopper's Bible*, op. cit.

[222] Consumer Health and Product Hazards/Cosmetic Drugs, Pesticides, Food Additives, Volume 2 of The Legislation of Product Safety, edited by Samuel S Epstein and Richard D Grundy, MIT Press, 1974

[223] http://vm.cfsan.fda.gov/~dms/cos-hdb1.html

cosmetic industry has borrowed a page from the playbook of the tobacco industry, by putting profits ahead of public health." Kennedy further stated, "Cosmetics can be dangerous to your health. Yet this greedy industry wants Congress to prevent the American people from learning that truth. Every woman who uses face cream, or hair spray, or lipstick, or shampoo, or mascara, or powder should demand that this arrogant and irresponsible power-play by the industry be rejected. A study by the respected, non-partisan General Accounting Office reported that more than 125 ingredients available for use in cosmetics are suspected of causing cancer. Other cosmetics may cause adverse effects on the nervous system, including convulsions. Still other ingredients are suspected of causing birth defects. A carefully controlled study found that one in sixty users suffered a cosmetic related injury identified by a physician."[224]

In 1998, Peter Phillips and *Project Censored* listed the year's top 25 censored stories. The number 2 censored story (as detailed in his book) was titled "Personal Care and Cosmetic Products May Be Carcinogenic."[225]

Shocking news indeed. Let's take a brief look at a few of the ingredients that top the list of potentially harmful compounds that are present in products we use every day.

Sodium lauryl sulfate (SLS)
SLS is a very harsh detergent found in almost all shampoos and more than a few toothpastes. Pick up a cross-section of these products next time you visit the supermarket and you will find SLS or SLES in pride of place under the ingredients label. SLS started its career as an industrial degreasant and garage floor cleaner. When applied to human skin it has the effect of stripping off the oil layer and then irritating and eroding the skin, leaving it rough and pitted. Studies[226] have shown that:

---

224 This statement is quoted from Senator Kennedy's office on
http://www.senate.gov/~kennedy/statements /970910fda.html
225 **Phillips, Peter**, *Censored 1998: The News That Didn't Make the News*, Project Censored, 1998 ISBN 1888363649
226 **Vance, Judi**, *Beauty to Die For*, Promotion Publishing, 1998

> Shampoos with SLS could retard healing and keep children's eyes from developing properly. Children under six years old are especially vulnerable to improper eye development (Summary of Report of Research to Prevent Blindness, Inc. conference)
> SLS can cause cataracts in adults and delays the healing of wounds in the surface of the cornea
> SLS has a low molecular weight and so is easily absorbed by the body. It builds up in the heart, liver, lungs and brain and can cause major problems in these areas
> SLS causes skin to flake and to separate and causes substantial roughness on the skin
> SLS causes dysfunction of the biological systems of the skin
> SLS is such a caustic cleanser that it actually corrodes the hair follicle and impairs its ability to grow hair
> SLS is routinely used in clinical studies deliberately to irritate the skin so that the effects of other substances can be tested [227]

Ethoxylation

Ethoxylation is the process that makes degreasing agents such as sodium lauryl sulfate (SLS) less abrasive and gives them enhanced foaming properties. When SLS is ethoxylated, it forms sodium laureth sulfate (SLES), a compound used in many shampoos, toothpastes, bath gels, bubble baths, and industrial degreasants. The problem is, the extremely harmful compound 1,4-dioxane may be created during the ethoxylation process, contaminating the product. 1,4-dioxane was one of the principal components of the chemical defoliant Agent Orange, used to great effect by the Americans during the Vietnam War to strip off the jungle canopy to reveal their enemy. 1,4-dioxane is a hormonal disrupter believed to be the chief agent implicated in the host of cancers suffered by Vietnam military personnel after the war. It is also an estrogen mimic thought to increase the chances of breast and endometrial cancers, stress-related illnesses and lower sperm counts.

---

[227] Study cited by *The Wall Street Journal*, 1st November 1988

Leading toxicologist Dr Samuel Epstein reports: *"The best way to protect yourself is to recognize ingredients most likely to be contaminated with 1,4-dioxane. These include ingredients with the prefix word, or syllable PEG, Polyethylene, Polyethylene Glycol, Polyoxyethylene, eth (as in sodium laureth sulfate), or oxynol. Both polysorbate 60 and polysorbate 80 may also be contaminated with 1,4-dioxane."*[228]

Propylene glycol

Propylene glycol is a common ingredient used extensively in industry as a component of brake fluids, paint, varnishes and anti-freeze compounds. It also appears in many beauty creams, cleansers, makeup and children's personal care products. Judi Vance writes:

"If you were to purchase a drum of this chemical from a manufacturer, he is required to furnish you with a material safety data sheet (MSDS) and it may alarm you to find that this common, widely used humectant has a cautionary warning in its MSDS that reads: "If on skin: thoroughly wash with soap and water."[229]

The American Academy of Dermatologists published a clinical review in January 1991 that showed propylene glycol caused a significant number of reactions and was a primary irritant to the skin even in low levels of concentration (around 5%). However propylene glycol routinely appears in the top three ingredients of a given product, indicating that it is present in high concentration.[230] It has been shown that propylene glycol:

➤ Has severe adverse health effects and has been found to cause kidney damage, and liver abnormalities
➤ Damages cell membranes causing rashes, dry skin, contact dermatitis and surface damage to the skin
➤ Is toxic to human cells in cultures

---

[228] Steinman, D & S Epstein, *Safe Shopper's Bible*, op. cit. pp.190-191

[229] Vance, Judy, *Beauty to Die For*, op cit.

[230] The first two or three ingredients listed on a product label usually constitute over half of a formulation. In some products, the first two or three ingredients can constitute 70-90% of the formulation. Ingredients are listed in descending order, going down to 1% concentration. Below 1%, ingredients may be listed in any order.

Diethanolamine (DEA)
Cocamide DEA
Lauramide DEA

A colourless liquid or crystalline alcohol used as a solvent, emulsifier, and detergent (wetting agent). DEA works as an emollient in skin-softening lotions or as a humectant in other personal care products. When found in products containing nitrates, it reacts chemically with the nitrates to form potentially carcinogenic nitrosamines. Although earlier studies seemed to indicate that DEA itself was not a carcinogen, more recent studies show that DEA has the capacity unequivocally to cause cancer, even in formulations that exclude nitrates.[231] DEA may also irritate the skin and mucous membranes.[232] Other ethanolamines to watch out for are: triethanolamine (TEA) and monethanolamine (MEA).

Fluorides:
Sodium Fluoride,
Hexafluorosilicic Acid, etc.

Fluorides used in the drinking water supplies are a toxic, non-biodegradable, environmental pollutant, officially classified as a contaminant by the US Environmental Protection Agency. Shocking though it may be to contemplate, the reality is, these chemicals are simply hazardous industrial waste - by-products variously from the manufacture of phosphate fertilisers and aluminium smelting - which are disposed of in the public water supply.[233]

Alcohol

A colourless, volatile, flammable liquid produced by the fermentation of yeast and carbohydrates. Alcohol is used frequently as a solvent and is also found in beverages and medicine. As an ingredient in ingestible products, alcohol may cause body tissues to

---

[231] **Epstein, Samuel S**, *The Politics of Cancer Revisited*, East Ridge Press, 1998, p.479

[232] Many nitrosamines have been determined to cause cancer in laboratory animals. Nitrosamine contamination of cosmetics became an issue in early 1977. The Food & Drug Administration expressed its concern about the contamination of cosmetics in a Federal Register notice dated 10th April 1979, which stated that cosmetics containing nitrosamines may be considered adulterated and subject to enforcement action.

[233] For more information on the important subject of water fluoridation, see *Health Wars* – 'Water Under the Bridge'.

be more vulnerable to carcinogens. Mouthwashes with an alcohol content of 25 percent or more have been implicated in mouth, tongue and throat cancers, according to a 1991 study released by the National Cancer Institute. Also a disturbing trend in accidental poisonings has been attributed to alcohol consumption from mouthwashes. After the NCI figures were published, Warner Lambert, manufacturers of the mouthwash Listerine (previously 26.9% alcohol), announced a new version of their product with significantly less alcohol.[234]

Alpha hydroxy acid (AHA)

An organic acid produced by anaerobic respiration. Skin care products containing AHA exfoliate not only destroy skin cells, but the skin's protective barrier as well. Long-term skin damage may result from its use.

Alumin(i)um

A metallic element used extensively in the manufacture of aircraft components, prosthetic devices, and as an ingredient in antiperspirants, antacids, and antiseptics. Aluminium has long been linked to Alzheimer's disease.[235] Use of aluminium pots and pans to cook food and the use of aluminium cans for soda, as well as the unnecessary cultural penchant for spraying aluminium directly into our lymph nodes as underarm antiperspirant all give grave causes for concern.

Animal fat (tallow)

A type of animal tissue made up of oily solids or semisolids that are water-insoluble esters of glycerol and fatty acids. Animal fats and lye are the chief ingredients in bar soap, a cleaning and emulsifying product that may act as a breeding ground for bacteria.

Bentonite

A porous clay that expands to many times its dry volume as it absorbs water. Bentonite is commonly found in many cosmetic foundations and may clog pores and suffocate the skin. Bentonite is

---

234 **Winslow, Ron**, *Wall Street Journal*, 23rd April 1991, p.B1
235 See **Alzheimer's Disease**

used by fire fighters to suffocate forest fires by eliminating the oxygen available.

Butane
Aerosol propellant. Flammable and in high doses may be narcotic or cause asphyxiation.

Animal collagen
An insoluble fibrous protein that is too large to penetrate the skin. The collagen found in most skin care products is derived from animal carcasses and ground up chicken feet. This ingredient forms a layer of film that may suffocate the skin.

Dioxin
(see also Ethoxylation and 1,4-Dioxane)
A potentially carcinogenic by-product that results from the process used to increase foam levels in cleansers such as shampoos, tooth pastes, etc., and to bleach paper at paper mills. Dioxin-treated containers (and some plastic bottles) sometimes transfer dioxins to the products themselves. It has been shown that dioxin's carcinogenicity is up to 500,000 times more potent than that of DDT. [236]

Elastin of High-Molecular Weight
A protein similar to collagen that is the main component of elastic fibres. Elastin is also derived from animal sources. Its effect on the skin is similar to collagen.

Fluorocarbons
A colourless, non-flammable gas or liquid that can produce mild upper respiratory tract irritation. Fluorocarbons are commonly used as a propellant in hairsprays.

Formaldehyde
A toxic, colourless gas that is an irritant and a carcinogen. When combined with water, formaldehyde is used as a disinfectant,

---

[236] Steinman, D & S Epstein, *The Safe Shopper's Bible,* op. cit. p.342

fixative, or preservative. Formaldehyde is found in many cosmetic products and conventional nail care systems.

Glycerin

A syrupy liquid that is chemically produced by combining water and fat. Glycerin is used as a solvent and plasticiser. Unless the humidity of air is over 65%, glycerin draws moisture from the lower layers of the skin and holds it on the surface, which dries the skin from the inside out.

Kaolin

Commonly used in foundations, face powders and dusting powders, kaolin is a fine white clay used in making porcelain. Like bentonite, kaolin smothers and weakens the skin.

Lanolin

A fatty substance extracted from wool, which is frequently found in cosmetics and lotions. Lanolin is a common sensitiser that can cause allergic reactions, such as skin rashes, sometimes due to toxic pesticides present in the sheep's wool. Some sixteen pesticides were identified in lanolin sampled in 1988. [237]

Mineral Oil

A derivative of crude oil (petroleum) that is used industrially as a cutting fluid and lubricating oil. Mineral oil forms an oily film over skin to lock in moisture, toxins, and wastes, but hinders normal skin respiration by keeping oxygen out. Used in baby oils.

Petrolatum

A petroleum-based grease that is used industrially as a grease component. Petrolatum exhibits many of the same potentially harmful properties as mineral oil.

Propane

Aerosol propellant. Is flammable and in high doses may be narcotic.

---

[237] National Academy of Sciences' concern over lanolin contamination: NRC, 1993, p.313

Salt
Very drying, irritating, and corrosive.

Talc
A soft grey-green mineral used in some personal hygiene and cosmetics products. Inhaling talc may be harmful as this substance is recognised as a potential carcinogen. Talc is widely recognised to be one of the leading causes of ovarian cancer.[238] It is used by many around the genital area and can also be found on condoms.

So what do you do? Where can you go to get hold of safe personal care products that are effective and of high quality?

Taking control of the junk
Samuel Epstein MD is a world-renowned authority on the causes and prevention of cancer. He was named the 1998 winner of the Right Livelihood Award (also known as the 'Alternative Nobel Prize'). Dr Epstein has devoted the greater part of his life to studying and fighting the causes of cancer. He is Professor of Occupational and Environmental Medicine at the School of Public Health, University of Illinois Medical Center at Chicago, and the chairman of the Cancer Prevention Coalition. He is arguably one of the world's leading toxicologists.

As the author of *The Politics of Cancer* and *The Breast Cancer Prevention Program*, he advocates the use of cosmetics and other products that are free from suspected carcinogens. Based on Dr Epstein's research and recommendations, he has awarded one company the 'Seal of Safety' from the Cancer Prevention Coalition. This company, Neways International, manufacturers and distributes its own personal care products, which are free of potentially harmful ingredients. Dr Epstein is enthusiastic about the groundbreaking work Neways has done in this area: *"Neways has pioneered and succeeded in providing consumers with cosmetics and toiletries free of cancer-causing and harmful ingredients and contaminants. I warmly congratulate them on their accomplishments."*

---

[238] Steinman, D & S Epstein, *The Safe Shopper's Bible,* op. cit. p.259

During the course of our work on this and other research projects, Credence researchers have had an opportunity to work with Neways technical personnel and examine the Neways product line. I myself flew to Utah to examine their production plant at Salem and talk with their executives at length. As a result of Credence's investigations, like Dr Epstein, we do not hesitate, as an independent, non-affiliated organisation, to recommend Neways' carcinogen-free personal care products and nutritional supplements to all who are looking to make a change for the better.

Tom Mower, President of Neways, lays out the focus of his organisation: *"Neways is in the business of helping people detoxify their bodies. Knowing the chemical constituents of your personal care products and their effects on your body enables you to understand how toxic culprits can contaminate your body. Ingredients like sodium lauryl sulfate (SLS), diethanolamine (DEA), triethanolamine (TEA), propylene glycol, fluoride, and alcohol have been identified by experts as known or potential carcinogens that can be found in ordinary personal care products.*

So Neways provides shampoos without sodium lauryl sulfate. We have lotions without propylene glycol, bubble bath without DEA or TEA, toothpastes without saccharin or fluoride, and mouthwash without alcohol. We use toxin- and carcinogen-free products that give consumers something more than clean skin or fresh breath - they provide peace of mind."

See our *Contacts! Contacts! Contacts!* section for further information on how to obtain non-toxic substitutes for toothpastes, cosmetics, detergents, polishes, sprays and deodorants, or whole bathroom change-out kits. Don't use insecticides. Press for clean, non-fluoridated tap water. Most importantly, as we will find out in an upcoming section, we must 'think clean' with our diet. The new lifestyle we must adopt must be a sensible, easy-to-follow regimen, and we must know why we are following it.

What Shall I Eat?

As we have seen, changes in diet are essential for great health, either if you are sick, or if you don't want to suffer. Don't think you are going to have success unless you respect your body's requirements for proper nutrition. Leading nutritional doctor Max Gerson's approach to changing a cancer patient's diet was uncompromising. We should brook no half measures either.

As mentioned time and again, the main cancer culprit is the good old western diet, heavy in meats, sugars, milks, grains, illegal fats and chemicals, which boost levels of damaging fungi, especially *Candida*, in the body. If you have cancer, removal of all meats, as well as toxic foodstuffs such as additives, caffeine, refined sugars and chocolate, represents a vital start. Beneficial weight loss and a return of energy are almost immediate, and with these benefits comes a regular method of detoxifying the body as part of your future lifestyle.

A properly combined diet, rich in alkali-ash foods (unrefined and uncooked plant dietary) and low in proteins (20-40 g a day) is the way to go. The body takes in amino acids to build human proteins ideally from high quality vegetation, fruits and nuts, so you are not going to run short of protein any time soon. The watchwords are *balance* and *grazing*.

Two diet strategies now follow. The first is ideal for cancer patients and is Gerald Green's **ANTI-*CANDIDA* DIETARY REGIMEN**, formulated by Nikki Zalewksi. The second is **THE *FOOD FOR THOUGHT* LIFESTYLE REGIMEN**, a slightly more liberal diet, ideal for use by recovered cancer patients and the public at large.

The Anti-*Candida* Dietary Regimen
Prepared by Nikki Zalewski

Although appearing to be extremely strict, after following this diet for a few days, you should notice increased energy, easier movement, better sleep, and less digestive problems

Foods to avoid:

All cow's milk products: cheese, yoghurt, whey – all cow's milk derivatives

All yeast products: alcohol, bread, (soda bread is allowed), Marmite, Oxo, Bovril, vinegars, mushrooms, processed and smoked fish and meats

All sugar products: honey, fructose, lactose, glucose, dextrose, Nutrasweet, Canderel, Equal and all aspartame and saccharin products

Nearly all fruit: over-ripe fruits are full of sugar and yeast (hence they go mouldy when over-ripe)

High-sugar root vegetables such as carrots, parsnips, sweet potatoes, beetroots. *NB: If you really can't live without potatoes, wean yourself off them slowly and try to end up with one a day.*

The list below shows you the foods *Candida* loves and thrives on. These need to be eliminated from your diet for between three to six months to start with.

Too much carbohydrate turns to glucose *rapidly*

Avoid:

- Sugar, and sugary foods
- Bread of all kinds and all of its pastry relatives: crackers, pastries, doughnuts, pies, muffins, cookies, etc.
- Cereals, hot or cold, sweetened or unsweetened
- Fast-food snacks, including crisps and pretzels
- White rice, potatoes and corn

- Products made with white flour such as pasta
- Most fruit
- Root vegetables such as carrots, turnips, parsnips and beetroot
- Chick peas, dried beans, lentils and pinto beans
- Coffee and other caffeine containing beverages
- Fizzy, canned drinks
- Alcohol in all forms
- Fruit juices and squash
- All convenience/junk foods, as they contain hidden sugars and other undesirable ingredients
- Cheeses (except non-cow's milk cheeses), milk and yoghurt
- All soy products
- Processed meats such as bacon, sausage, ham, salami, bologna, pastrami and hot dogs
- High salt foods such as processed meats and fish. Smoked fish contains unnecessary levels of sodium that can contribute to water retention
- Mushrooms and fungi, including quorn
- Condiments, such as pickles, toppings and all shop-bought sauces
- Hydrogenated fatty acids and partially hydrogenated fatty acids as contained in stick margarines and man-processed foods
- Saturated fats from tropical oil such as coconut oil
- Saturated fats, primarily from meat, dairy and eggs
- Health supplements containing lactose, gluten, citric acid

The following fruit and vegetables are best avoided until the _Candida_ is under control:

Apricots, artichokes, asparagus, aubergine, avocado, blackberries, courgettes (zucchini), grapefruit, kumquats, okra, passion fruit, peaches, peas, plums, pumpkin, raspberries, sauerkraut, sugarsnap peas, squash, strawberries, tomato, watermelon.

SO what do I eat?!
Good food choices

The foods below have the lowest possible sugar/yeast content and are your best choices. You will notice there are several oils included as certain 'good fats' are vital for health (omegas 3, 6 and 9 essential fatty acids) (See **A Guide to Nutritional Supplements**).

Eat plenty of the following foods:

- Alfalfa sprouts, bean sprouts, bell peppers, (sweet peppers), Bok choy, broccoli, Brussels sprouts, cabbage, cauliflower, celery, cucumber, endive, fennel, garlic, green beans, greens, hot chili peppers, kale, lettuce, onions, parsley, radishes, spring onions, spinach, swiss chard, turnips, yellow beans
- Free range eggs, fresh fish (deep and cold caught) and sea food (**not shellfish**), lamb and veal, poultry, chicken, turkey, (particularly skinless white meat), in **small** amounts. Cancer patients should avoid all animal/fish proteins apart from those discussed in **Cancer**
- Culinary herbs and spices

Fats (in moderation)

Avocado oil, cod liver oil, fish oil, flaxseed oil, grape seed oil, hemp oil, monounsaturated fats, olive oil, primrose oil.

Fluids

Try to drink 8 glasses of water each day: the body is 70% water, so needs fresh supplies daily for optimal hydration and to help flush out toxins. If you can get into the habit of drinking more water, the benefits are many – you'll notice increased energy, better concentration and clearer skin, to name but a few.

Herbal teas, especially Essiac and peppermint, are ideal

Although most fruits are taboo on the anti-*Candida* program, you may have one piece of *firm* fruit a day: apple, pear or kiwi. However, don't take fruit juice as well.

Anti-*Candida*/Fungal Supplementation

The following regimen will be of benefit to those suffering from yeast and fungal infestations. This is a long-term program, and must be adhered to for as long as the condition is in evidence. Many of these supplements need to be taken at least three times per day to ensure the body is washed with their ingredients:

- **COMMENCE THE BASIC SUPPLEMENT PROGRAM**
- **DETOXIFICATION:** Commence a two-week magnesium oxide bowel cleanse (see **A Guide to Nutritional Supplements**)
- **ANTI-PARASITE:** Take fresh sticks of cinnamon (not the processed supermarket dust), and grind them down in a coffee grinder. Take a teaspoon of this ground cinnamon powder, mixed in a glass of warm water and drink two/three times a day
- **ANTI-PARASITE:** Take wormwood (*artemesia*) capsules, one four times a day. A good wormwood and black walnut tincture is also beneficial
- **ANTI-PARASITE:** Enteric-coated capsules of the following oils are all effective antifungals: oregano, thyme, peppermint, rosemary, garlic. These should be taken at least three times a day, spread throughout the day
- **ANTI-PARASITE:** Colloidal silver, as directed
- **ANTI-PARASITE:** Brew Essiac tea properly (see **A Guide to Nutritional Supplements**) and drink at least 2 oz, 4 times per day
- **ANTI-PARASITE:** Take a parasite purge formula (this should contain items such as black walnut, clove, ginger root, anise seed, pau d'arco, peppermint and fennel)
- **ANTI-PARASITE:** Take 3-5 grams of water soluble fibre such as psyllium husks or guar gum to help flush out the bowel as the killing proceeds apace. **THE ANTI-*CANDIDA* DIETARY REGIMEN** will also provide you with haystacks full of bowel-scraping fibre to help broom your innards clean

256

- **ANTI-PARASITE:** L-arginine (as directed) to assist in the removal of ammonia waste products
- **DETOXIFICATION:** Take an enzyme supplement away from food. This should contain, but not be limited to bromelain, papain, thymus, trypsin, chymotrypsin, lipase, amylase, etc.

The *Food For Thought* Lifestyle Regimen

➢ Little or no meat in the diet. Any meat consumed should be hormone and pesticide-free. White meat is better than red. Avoid pork
➢ Avoid sugar, dairy, coffee and alcohol
➢ Eat properly constituted, organic, whole, living foods, a high percentage raw. If you want hot, briefly steam your veggies. Do not murder them. Remember that heat kills enzymes. Excellent recipes are provided in our companion guide, *Food For Thought*.
➢ The ideal balance is: 80% alkali/20% acidic ash foods. Most diets today comprise 90% acid/10% alkali!
➢ Some broiled fish, deep and cold caught, eaten sparingly is OK
➢ Avoid the foods below
➢ Hydrate the body (2 litres (4 pints) of clean, fresh water a day)
➢ Keep high-glycaemic fruit intake down. Eat more fruits that have low sugar-conversion, such as pears and apples
➢ Eat six *small* meals a day, ensuring a) that you don't go hungry, and b) that the body has a constant supply of nutrients
➢ **THE BASIC SUPPLEMENT PROGRAM** will consist of ionised colloidal trace minerals, antioxidant tablets, Vit C and B complexes and essential fats (see **A Guide to Nutritional Supplements**)
➢ Exercise (to get everything moving and assist in detoxing the body in an oxygen-rich environment). A regular walk in the early morning air is also healthy and very invigorating
➢ Rest. Rest. Rest. Rest. Rest
➢ Reduce environmental toxicity (avoid jobs using dangerous chemicals, radiation, etc.)
➢ Use safe personal care products*
➢ Use safe household products*

Foods to avoid

> ➤ Pork products (bacon, sausage, hot-dogs, luncheon meat, ham, etc.) These are high in nitrites and are known homotoxins which can cause high blood urea and dikitopiprazines, which cause brain tumours and leukaemia.[239]

> ➤ Scavenger meats (inc. ALL shellfish and other carrion-eaters – see Leviticus 11 in the Bible). Carrion-eaters, pork and shellfish in particular, concentrate toxins of other animals in their tissues, which we then consume to our detriment. The same goes for the elimination organs of commercially raised animals, such as liver and kidney, which can be high in drug and pesticide residues

> ➤ Aspartame/saccharin, artificial sweeteners. These are known mental impairment problems and cancer risks.

> ➤ Refined sugar/flour/rice. SUCROSE FEEDS CANCER Restricted amounts of wholegrain bread are OK. Use only wholegrain rice. No sugars should be consumed other than those contained naturally in whole foods

> ➤ Hydrogenated & partially hydrogenated fats (margarine)

> ➤ Junk (processed) food, including fizzy sodas and other soft drinks containing sugar, artificial sweeteners or phosphoric acid, which are drunk out of aluminium cans

> ➤ Fat-free foods. Essential fats are *essential*!

> ➤ Olestra, canola, soy, etc. Avoid fake or synthetic fats. Soy, in its unfermented state (meat and milk substitute products), disrupts the hormone (endocrine) system, blocks the absorption of calcium and magnesium, and acts like estrogen in the body. Small usage of unfermented soy and fermented soy products (soy sauce and miso) is OK. For more information on soy, see **The Shadow of Soy**

> ➤ Polluted water (chlorinated or fluoridated – see *Health Wars*, 'Water Under the Bridge')

> ➤ Caffeine products

> ➤ Alcohol products

---

[239] Day, Phillip, *Food for Thought*, op. cit; *Biologic Therapy*, "Adverse influence of pork consumption on human health", Vol. 1, No. 2, 1983

> Excess refined salt. It's better to spice food with ground
> kelp to maintain a healthy iodine intake

**For a full analysis of 'food as it should be', see *Food
For Thought*, the food recipe companion to *Cancer:
Why We're Still Dying to Know the Truth*
(see 'Other Titles by Credence').**

*Implementing Changes – Convert Your Bathroom Pack

As many of the harmful ingredients we examined earlier can be
found in the average bathroom, clear these out in one fell swoop and
replace with safe alternatives. Neways' Convert Your Bathroom pack
contains shampoo, conditioner, bath gel, shaving gel, deodorant,
toothpaste and mouthwash that are not only free from damaging
ingredients, but are of the highest quality. Whether you are
undergoing nutritional therapy for cancer or are simply interested in
cancer prevention, the cumulative toxic onslaught your body
receives at the hands of harmful consumer products has to stop.

Exercise in Moderation

Research shows that those with a sedentary lifestyle are more
prone to cancer and heart problems. A good exercise program will
assist in cleansing the body and getting all the pieces of the body
toned and in proper working order. Simply MOVE! Walking, a non-
threatening hour in the gym twice or three times a week or cycling
are ideal and immensely enjoyable once you get on the pro-active
program. If you sit still all day long, you might as well not breathe!
Life is about healthy action. Celebrate your life by looking, moving
and feeling the way your body was designed to be.

Further resources

Food for Thought, compiled by Phillip Day
Health Wars by Phillip Day

The Basic Supplement Program

Remember that the body likes to take nutrients in collectively. Nutrition works best when the various components are allowed to work synergistically in combination with a natural, whole-food diet, the vast majority eaten raw. A basic, but comprehensive supplement program, such as my ideal one below, can have extremely good results, if carried out *consistently* over a period of time with suitable diet and lifestyle changes.

For the past 17 years, I have been disease-free and have not had a day off work (haven't got the time☺). I put this down to avoiding the minefields, boosting nutrients in the body, staying hydrated, getting exercise and rest, and having a moderately good attitude. The regimen below can hardly be described as a 'basic' supplement program, in view of the complexities of the nutrients involved, but here's the 'basic' version I use anyway!

- **Maximol (ionised mineral and vitamin supplement)**
- **B-complex supplement**
- **Vitamin E, 400 IU per day**
- **Zinc, 15 mg, am and pm**
- **Revenol (antioxidant)**
- **Essential fatty acid complex. Alternatively, 1 tbsp flaxseed oil per day**
- **Apricot kernels, 7 g per day**
- **Vitamin C complex (ascorbates plus bioflavonoids), 1-3 g per day**
-

Once again, this program must be taken IN CONJUNCTION WITH **THE *FOOD FOR THOUGHT* DIETARY REGIMEN** and adequate hydration. It is not a substitute for a good diet!

An advanced supplement program

Can contain any of the above components, plus other items discussed in **A Guide to Nutritional Supplements**. Please consult a health practitioner who is qualified to diagnose and recommend a comprehensive nutritional program for your particular circumstances.

A Guide to Nutritional Supplements

The following section outlines nutritional components that have been studied and used for specific purposes in relation to nutritional support for those who have disorders or those wishing to exercise prevention. The purpose of this section is to inform, not to recommend any particular course of action or product. Health advice from a qualified health practitioner trained in nutrition is always advised. If you would like more details on any of the following, or have a question, please use the Contacts! section of this book to follow up

Smart nutrients and brain food

The human brain is responsible for man's superior mental power. It is the command centre for intellect, memory, awareness, motor control, and sensory perception - the internal regulator of all body processes. The brain's mental energies diminish as chronological age advances. The impact of aging, poor circulation, nutrient-depleted food, polluted air and water, toxic chemicals, and lifestyle stressors can severely impair your body's ability to supply nourishment to the brain. Increase blood flow is very important to the very narrow blood vessels throughout the body increasing the supply of oxygen to vessels that may receive very little oxygen due to their constricting size. The muscles and nerve cells of the brain are composed of phosphatidylserine and phosphatidylcholine. The following ingredients, both of ancient and recent discovery, are known to help enhance circulation and mental/physical energy.

DMAE (dimethylaminoethanol): DMAE is the precursor for choline, which in turn can cross the blood-brain barrier to manufacture the memory neurotransmitter molecule acetylcholine. DMAE has been shown to improve cognitive abilities when taken in doses ranging from 100–300mg. In a 1996 study in Germany, those patients taking the placebo showed no change in their EEG brain patterns, while those on DMAE demonstrated improvements in their brainwave patterns in those parts of the brain which play an important role in memory, attention and flexibility of thinking.[240]

DMAE supports the health of the brain's nerve fibres. Also known as centrophenoxine, it has been shown to decrease lipofuscin in the brain. With age, the number of lipofuscin-containing neurons in the cortex increases. An increase in lipofuscin results in a concomitant decrease in

---

[240] **Dimpfel et al,** "Source density analysis of functional topographical EEG: monitoring of cognitive drug action", *European Journal of Medical Research*, Vol.1, No.6 (19th March 1996): pp.283-290

spontaneous neuronal action potentials and age-related neuropathies. Centrophenoxine is an anti-lipofuscin compound that prevents this age-related increase in lipofuscin. Centrophenoxine also increases acetylcholinesterase activity in the hippocampus thus reversing the age-related decline of the cholinergic system and possibly mediating its effects on cognitive and neuronal synaptic function.

DMAE, marketed as the drug Deaner or Deanol, was shown by Dr Bernard Rimland at the Autism Research Institute in San Diego to be almost twice as effective in treating children with ADD/ADHD than Ritalin, without the side-effects.[241]

5-HTP: 5-HTP (5-hydroxytryptophan) aids in maintaining healthy serotonin levels in the brain to combat feelings of depression, frequent headaches, and muscle aches and pain. 5-hydroxytryptophan is a compound native to the body and use to synthesise serotonin. Decreased levels of serotonin have been associated with depression, frequent headaches, and muscle aches and pain. Supplementation with 5-HTP has the potential to alleviate many of these ailments.

Ginkgo biloba extract: Contains the flavonone glycosides quercetin and kaempferol. It improves blood flow, especially in the microvasculature in the body. In the brain, this improves memory and capacity for learning.[242]

Bacopa monniera extract: Bacopin, the active chemical constituent found in the herb Bacopa monniera, is an excellent antioxidant that helps support mental function and memory. Bacopa monniera extract is used to improve mental performance, memory, and learning. It is useful when stress and nervous exhaustion are decreasing mental function. It acts as an adaptogenic, a tonic for the nervous system, a circulatory stimulant, and a cerebral stimulant. It is also used to promote longevity, and for nervous deficit due to injury and stroke. Other traditional uses include epilepsy, insanity, nervous breakdown and exhaustion.

Phosphatidylserine (PS): Phosphatidylserine contains the amino acid serine and is one of the brain's phospholipids. It plays a vital role in brain nerve cell membrane functions. Phosphatidylserine makes up approximately 105 of the total phospholipids in nerve cell membranes. Phosphatidylserine helps activate and regulate membrane proteins and

---

[241] **Holford, Patrick & Hyla Cass**, *Natural Highs*, Piatkus Books, 2001, p.139
[242] **Blumentahl, et al**, Complete German Commission Monographs, *Therapeutic Guide to Herbal Medicine*, op. cit.

play major roles in nerve cell functions, such as the generation, storage, transmission and reception of nerve impulses. As we age, our cellular membranes begin to change, and become stiffer. Proper functioning of the nerve cell membrane requires that it be more fluid, which phosphatidylserine accomplishes. It also acts as a glutamate blocker, thereby preventing excitotoxic damage to the cell. Those having hypoglycaemia or a strong family history of one of the neurodegenerative diseases should avoid excitotoxins in their food and probably should take these supplements at an early age, beginning in their twenties or thirties. Phosphatidylserine boosts the brain's energy supply, thereby protecting vulnerable brain cells from injury.[243]

When Dr Thomas Crook, from the Memory Assessment Clinic in Bethesda, Maryland, gave 149 people with age-associated memory impairment a daily dose of 300 mg of PS or a placebo, those only taking PS experienced a vast improvement after 12 weeks in their ability to match names to faces – a recognised measure of memory and mental function.[244]

Centella asiatica extract: Centella asiatica, the ancient Ayurvedic herb commonly called gotu kola, maintains healthy blood flow, helps to balance the nervous system, and encourages proper brain function and enhanced mental capacity. It also contains compounds knows as asiaticosides. Asiaticosides are converted to Asiatic acid in vivo and have been researched thoroughly for their ability to elevate antioxidant levels in the blood and decrease the time necessary for wound-healing. The increase in antioxidant levels could be beneficial to those suffering from cerebral insufficiency. Centella asiatica, a source of vitamins A, B, E, and K, and magnesium, is used to support the improvement of memory, and enhance the body's fight against insomnia, fever, headache and inflammatory skin problems. It also promotes bloodflow by strengthening the veins and capillaries.[245] In India, the herb is used to assist against skin disease, syphilis, rheumatism, in the treatment of leprosy, for mental illness, epilepsy, hysteria, and for dehydration. In Southeast Asia, the herb

---

[243] **Crook, T, et al**, "Effects of phosphatidylserine in age-associated memory impairment", *Neurol.*, (1991), 41:664-649; **Cenacchi, B, et al**, "Cognitive decline in the elderly: A double-blind, placebo-controlled multicenter study on efficacy of phosphataidylserine administration", *Aging Clin. Exp. Res.*, (1993), 5:123-133; **Engle, R, et al**, "Double-blind, cross-over study of phosphatidylserine vs. placebo in subjects with early cognitive deterioration of the Alzheimer type", *Eur. Neurophycolpharmacol.*, (1992), 2:149-155; **Kidd, PM**, "A review of nutrients and botanicals in the integrative management of cognitive dysfunction." *Altern. Med. Rev.* Junc, 1999, 4:144-61

[244] **Crook, T, et al**, "Effects of PS in age-associated memory impairment", *Neurology*, Vol.41, No.5, (1991), pp.644-9

[245] Kidd, PM, op. cit.

supports prompt bladder activity, physical and mental exhaustion, diarrhoea, eye disease, inflammations, asthma, and high blood pressure. Additional effects of Centella asiatica (gotu kola) include psychotropic and pharmacological effects. In forced swimming behavioural tests, an extract of Centella asiatica caused a significant reduction in the duration of the immobilisation phase. These tests show the sedative and antidepressive effects of Centella asiatica.

Pregnenalone: Pregnenalone, a steroid naturally produced in the body, supports the brain's natural capacity for recalling facts and events. Pregnenalone is synthesised in the body from cholesterol. The brain has the capacity to use cholesterol to make pregnenalone and other steroids. Pregnenalone can be metabolised into progesterone or converted into DHEA. DHEA in turn can be converted into androgens, estrogens and other steroids (as many as 150 different steroid hormones). Pregnenalone also improves visual perception - colours are brighter. Shapes and forms are more noticeable, increasing one's awareness of the environment. In addition, pregnenalone is a potent anti-depressant and can affect memory capabilities. Pregnenalone can accumulate in the body, especially the brain and nervous system, so effects may take time to manifest.

Phosphatidylcholine: Phosphatidylcholine contains phosphory-lated choline and is one of the brain's phospholipids. It plays a vital role in brain nerve cell membrane functions. Phosphatidylcholine makes up approximately 50% of the total phospholipids in nerve cell membranes. The cell membrane acts as a master switch controlling entry of nutrients, exit of waste products, movements of charged ions through the membrane, membrane shape changes, and cell-to-cell communications. The membrane-based ion pumps, transport molecules, enzymes, and receptors that manage these master-switch activities are the membrane proteins. These membrane protein concentrations and positioning are effected by the phospholipid composition and structure.

Phosphatidylcholine can come from the diet as phosphatidylcholine or choline. In addition, it can be synthesised in the body using free choline. Good dietary sources (in decreasing order of concentration) of phosphatidylcholine and choline are eggs, beef steak, cauliflower, butter, oranges, apples, whole-wheat bread, and lettuce. Dietary phosphatidyl-choline is cleaved by the pancreatic enzyme phospholipase B that leads to small amounts of choline entering the blood system. Phosphatidylcholine is synthesized in the body through two different pathways, the CDO-choline pathway and the PE methylation pathway. In the latter pathway, phosphatidylethanolamine is converted to phosphatidylcholine, freeing ethanolamine and consuming choline.

Phosphatidylethanolamine: One of the brain's phospholipids. It plays a vital role in brain nerve cell membrane functions. Phosphatidylethanolamine makes up approximately 25% of the total phospholipids in nerve cell membranes. Phosphatidylethanolamine is present in foods at approximately equal concentrations as phosphatidylcholine. Phosphatidylethanolamine can be converted to phosphatidylcholine in the liver, generating most ethanolamine in the body. Phosphatidylethanolamine can also be synthesized from free ethanolamine and diacylglycerol by the CDP-ethanolamine pathway. Smaller quantities of phosphatidylethanolamine can be reversibly converted to phosphatidylserine upon demand. Additionally, phosphatidylethanolamine can be converted from phosphatidylserine catalysed by a Vitamin B6-requiring enzyme.

Vinpocetine: Vinpocetine, the active compound in the herb periwinkle, helps the body maintain healthy circulation to the brain in support cerebral capacity. Found in the lesser periwinkle *Vinca minor*, vinpocetine has been shown to be an excellent vasodilator and cerebral metabolic enhancer. It improves glucose transport (uptake and release) through the blood-brain barrier throughout the brain, providing increased nutrients for cellular respiration. Vinpocetine is also a phosphodiesterase-1-inhibitor that in turn suppresses the production of TNF-alpha (responsible for inflammatory cytokines in the nervous system).

Researchers at the University of Surrey in the UK gave 203 people with memory problems either vinpocetine or a placebo. Those taking vinpocetine demonstrated a significant improvement in cognitive performance. Russian research has also shown that vinpocetine is potentially helpful for those with epilepsy.[246]

Phosphatidylinositol: Phosphatidylinositol contains the sugar inositol and is one of the brain's phospholipids. It plays a vital role in brain nerve cell membrane functions. Phosphatidylinositol makes up approximately 5% of the total phospholipids in nerve cell membranes. Phosphatidylinositol plays a vital role in the transmission of some hormonal signals. Phosphatidylinositol is the major source of inositol-1,4,5-triphosphate (IP3). IP3 is a modified sugar that has proven to be a versatile molecule participating in signalling events within many types of body cells (e.g., calcium signalling). Phosphatidylinositol is necessary to convert arachidonic acid to prostaglandins and thromboxanes.

---

[246] **Hindmarch, I et al**, "Efficacy and tolerance of vinpocetine in ambulant patients suffering from mild to moderate organic psychosyndromes", *Int'l. Clin. Psych.*, Vol.6, No.1 (1991): pp.31-43

NADH: NADH (niacinamide adenine dinucleotide) enhances proper neurotransmitter function - the electrochemical transmission of nerve impulses between the brain and body. Niacinamide adenine dinucleotide is required by the brain to synthesize various neurotransmitters. With age, the level of NADH diminishes resulting in a subsequent decrease in energy production and neurotransmitter levels. This in turn alters brain chemistry and can affect mental function. Theoretically, supplementation with NADH should improve one's mental capacities.

Huperzine: Also known as Huperzine A, is a purified alkaloid isolated from the Chinese club moss *huperzia serrata*. It inhibits the breakdown of the neurotransmitter acetylcholine. Acetylcholine is rapidly broken down in the brains of Alzheimer's patients and age-related memory disorders causing dementia. A shortage of acetylcholine appears to contribute to memory loss and other cognitive defects. Huperzine disrupts the enzyme acetylcholinesterase that breaks down acetylcholine. Current research is ongoing to use Huperzine to protect the brain against damage from strokes, epilepsy and chemical weapons. Studies conducted in China on Huperzine A have indicated its efficacy as an acetylcholinesterase inhibitor. Because cholinergic neurons are responsible for memory, theoretically an acetylcholinesterase inhibitor could improve memory.[247]

Ingenious (Neways International)

Enhanced brain nutritional support complex. The specially selected ingredients for Ingenious are well known in ancient Chinese, Ayurvedic, and western medicine for helping provide nutritional support to the brain's system to enhance circulation and revitalize mental energy. Ingenious is effective in supporting the body's natural processes, improving brain function and increasing cerebral and peripheral blood flow, circulation and oxygenation to the brain.

Ingredients: Vitamin B5 (calcium pantothenate), DMAE, 5-HTP, Ginkgo biloba extract, Bacopa monniera extract, Phosphatidylserine, Centella asiatica extract, Pregnenalone, Phosphatidylcholine, Phosphatidylethanolamine, Vinpocetine, Phosphatidylinositol, NADH, Huperzine.

---

[247] **Xu, S, et al**, "Efficacy of Tablet Huperzine-A on Memory, Cognition, and Behaviour in Alzheimer's Disease", *Acta Pharmacologica Sinica*, (1995), 16:391-395

Injectable B17/Laetrile/Amygdalin

Pharmaceutical grade vitamin B17 in metabolic therapy clinics is administered through injection for the first 21 days (Phase 1) and then orally afterwards (Home - Phase 2). 9 grams per day is used for the first 21 days in Del Rio Hospital. Dr Manner used this protocol. Injectable B17 is also invariably administered together with the tissue penetrating agent dimethylsulfoxide (DMSO).

Please note: Clinical tests have repeatedly shown that B17 is only truly effective when used in conjunction with pancreatic enzymes to break down the pericellular coating of the malignant cell.[248] Vitamins A and E in their emulsified form, along with high doses of C complex (ascorbates plus bioflavonoids), are then used in combination with B17 to attack the cancer cell. Clinics administering Metabolic Therapy to their patients always use these or similar supplements.

B17 Laetrile/Amygdalin Tablets

These pharmaceutical grade tablets contain the active B17 ingredient derived from the kernels of apricots. Usually available in 100 mg or 500 mg tablets. These tablets are always taken in conjunction with apricot seeds depending on body weight. For instance, manufacturers recommend:

- 2-4 100 mg tablets per day as a nutritional supplement for prevention (apricot seeds have been recommended by doctors in place of tablets for prevention also).
- 4-6 500 mg tablets per day as a nutritional supplement for clinical cancer sufferers, taken in conjunction with pancreatic enzymes (see below) and vitamins A & E (emulsified). When seeds are added, the B17 tablet dosage is reduced accordingly to avoid patient taking too much B17 at one time. If patient has cancer of the liver, a doctor should be consulted prior to dosing.

Pancreatic Enzyme Supplements

Specific enzymes used in B17 metabolic therapy include trypsin, chymotrypsin (human pancreatic enzyme), pancreatin and calf thymus (animal enzymes), papain (from papayas) and bromelain (from pineapples). Ernst Krebs has an opinion on this: *"The demasking effect of*

---

[248] **Manner, HW, Michaelson, TL, and DiSanti, SJ**, "Enzymatic Analysis of Normal and Malignant Tissues." Presented at the Illinois State Academy of Science, April 1978. Also **Manner, HW, Michaelson, TL, and DiSanti, SJ**, "Amygdalin, vitamin A and Enzymes Induced Regression of Murine Mammary Adenocarcinomas", *Journal of Manipulative and Physiological Therapeutics*, Vol 1, No. 4, December 1978. 200 East Roosevelt Road, Lombard, IL 60148 USA

these enzymes against the pericellular layer of the malignant cell is something very concrete in the immunology of cancer. Now I prefer, rather than advising the use of bromelain or papaya tablets, that the individual seeking these enzymes get them directly from the fresh ripe pineapple and papaya fruit. As much as half a pineapple a day should be ingested."

If taking enzyme supplements as part of nutritional support for cancer and other illnesses, these should be consumed on an empty stomach, otherwise they just digest your food!

Emulsified Vitamin A (www.vitalminerals.org)

In 1963 when Dr Contreras initiated his activities as a clinical oncologist, the use of vitamin A as a useful agent in malignant neoplasm was considered illogical and absurd. Now vitamin A is accepted as an agent of great use for the major epithelial cancers as well as for epidermis carcinomas, chronic leukaemia and transitional cells.

The first formal studies of the possible anti-tumour effects of vitamin A were initiated in Germany, by investigators of Mugos Laboratories in Munich. It was a proven fact that lung cancer in Norwegian sailors was less common than in other groups, even though they smoked since childhood. Logic indicated that it had to be the opposite. After studying this phenomenon, it was discovered that they ate abundant quantities of raw fish liver, high in vitamin A, since childhood. The logical conclusion was that high doses of such a vitamin prevented the growth of lung cancer in heavy smokers. But it was also found that high doses of vitamin A were toxic, and could cause adverse reactions.

The main focus was to find out how to administer enough vitamin A to observe preventive or healing effects, without injuring the liver. The solution was found by one of the investigators, when he discovered that unprocessed milk had the vitamin, and children who were breast-fed never experienced toxic effects. Nature had the solution by including vitamin A in milk in the form of micro-emulsification.

Mugos investigators proceeded to prepare a variety of emulsified concentrations, formulating their famous High Concentration A-Mulsin. One drop contains 15,000 units. They were able to administer over a million units per day in progressive doses, without producing hepatic toxicity. The explanation is that, in emulsified form, vitamin A is absorbed directly into the lymphatic system without going through the liver in high quantities. Having solved the toxicity problem, it was possible to test the product in high doses. It was demonstrated that emulsified vitamin A has the following effects:

- In normal doses, it protects epithelium and vision
- In doses of 100,000 to 300,000 units per day, it works as a potent immune stimulant
- In doses of 500,000 to 1,000,000 units per day, it works as a potent anti-tumour agent, especially in epidermis and transitional carcinomas

Vitamin C Complex (Ascorbic acid/ascorbates plus bioflavonoids, etc.)

Dr Linus Pauling, often known as the 'Father of Vitamin C' and twice awarded the Nobel Prize, declared that large intakes of up to 10g of the vitamin complex each day aids anti-cancer activity within the body and also assists in repairing damaged arteries and removing arterial plaque (atherosclerosis) for heart disease sufferers. Pauling was largely derided for making these declarations (yet he lived to be 94!), but today, large doses of Vitamin C complex are used by many practitioners for cancer patients in nutritional therapy, who believe Pauling was right and that the popular nutrient is indispensable to the body in its fight to regain health from cancer.

Vitamin C is not one nutrient, but a complex of factors common in fruits, vegetables and many other foods. Several studies have suggested that Vitamin C may reduce levels of lead in the blood. Epidemiological studies have shown that people with elevated blood serum levels of Vitamin C had lower levels of blood toxicity. An examination of the data from the Third National Health and Nutrition Examination Survey, enrolling 4,213 youths aged 6 to 16 years and 15,365 adults 17 years and older from 1988 to 1994, found a correlation between low serum ascorbic acid levels and elevated blood lead levels. The authors conclude that high ascorbic acid intake may reduce blood lead levels.[249]

Ascorbic acid or the non-acidic ascorbates (calcium or magnesium ascorbates) should be taken along with bioflavonoids and a healthy, alkalising diet for optimum effects.

---

[249] **Simon JA, Hudes ES**, "Relationship of Ascorbic Acid to Blood Lead Levels." *Journal of the American Medical Association*, 1999;281:2289-2293

An analysis of the Normative Aging Study, which enrolled 747 men aged 49 to 93 years from 1991 to 1995, found that lower dietary intake of Vitamin C may increase lead levels in the blood.[250] A study of 349 African American women enrolled in the project Nutrition, Other Factors, and the Outcome of Pregnancy found that vitamin-mineral supplementation resulted in increased serum levels of ascorbic acid and decreased serum levels of lead. The authors concluded that maternal use of a vitamin supplement with ascorbic acid and Vitamin E might offer protection from lead contamination of the foetus during pregnancy.[251]

Because smoking lowers levels of ascorbic acid in the body, researchers theorised that Vitamin C supplementation may effect blood lead levels in smokers. A clinical study was performed on 75 adult men 20 to 30 years of age who smoked at least one pack of cigarettes per day, but had no clinical signs of ascorbic acid deficiency or lead toxicity. Subjects were randomly assigned to daily supplementation with placebo, 200 mg of ascorbic acid, or 1000 mg of ascorbic acid. After one week of supplementation, there was an 81% decrease in blood-lead levels in the group taking 1000 mg of ascorbic acid daily.[252]

Dosage recommended by Linus Pauling for prevention is between 600mg and 3g a day – or up to 10g/day for those who have been diagnosed with cancer. High levels of Vitamin C however can cause diarrhoea and may be contra-indicated with certain chemotherapy treatments. Vitamin C is especially useful when combined in moderate amounts with Calcium d-glucarate, as formulated in the Neways product D-Toxarate (see D-Toxarate in this section).

VITAMIN P (bioflavonoids): another part of the Vitamin C 'complex'. Dr Albert Szent-Gyorgi, 1937 Nobel Laureate for his isolation of Vitamin C, later found other factors intrinsic to the action of C. Originally believed to be a single nutrient, Vitamin C became the subject of further testing by Szent-Gyorgi, who fought long and hard to have the co-factor (bio)flavonoids included in the C complex. Coining the new bioflavonoids 'Vitamin P', Szent-Gyorgi argued that they were essential for proper functioning of the human organism, derived from plant pigments known as

[250] **Cheng Y, Willett WC, Schwartz J, Sparrow D, Weiss S, Hu H**, "Relation of nutrition to bone lead and blood lead levels in middle-aged to elderly men. The Normative Aging Study." *Am J Epidemiol* 1998 Jun 15;147(12):1162-1174

[251] **West WL, Knight EM, Edwards CH, et al**, "Maternal low level lead and pregnancy outcomes." J Nutr. 1994 Jun;124(6 Suppl):981S-986S

[252] **Dawson EB, Evans DR, Harris WA, Teter MC, McGanity WJ**, "The effect of ascorbic acid supplementation on the blood lead levels of smokers." *J Am Coll Nutr.* 1999 Apr;18(2):166-170

the flavonols and flavones. Bioflavonoids are widely accepted today for their health benefits and are available in hydroxylated and methoxylated forms. They are derived from the pith of fruits (mostly citrus). Quercetin, rutin, catechin, anthocyanidins and proanthocyanidins are examples of flavonoids. The term 'Vitamin P' has been less well received by our medical czars.

B Complex
B, B, B1, B2, B3, B5, B6, B8, B9, B12, B15, B17
One of the most important groups of nutrients for mental health is the B-group. A dip in the intakes of any member of the group will cause problems, and fast. Together however, working in synergy with a sensible, varied diet, the great effects of the 'B's can be startling. B vitamins are water-soluble and rapidly pass out of the body, so a regular intake of a good B-complex is essential. We have variously looked at the B-Vits in my other books as we've made our way through the nutrition maze, so let's sum up.

Vitamin B (choline) is the base ingredient of lecithin. Choline helps in the formation of the 'memory' neurotransmitter molecule, acetylcholine, and has been used to great effect in treating Alzheimer's. It is often used medically in the form phosphatidylcholine (see section entitled 'Phosphatidylcholine').

Vitamin B (inositol) is another B nutrient used to treat mental illness. Bi-polar mental disorders, characterised by interchangeable periods of depression and euphoria, have responded well to high doses of the nutrient. Inositol is mentioned repeatedly in the scientific literature in connection with treating panic attacks and anxieties.[253]

Vitamin B (PABA), also known as paraaminobenzoic acid, is a component of B9 (folic acid) and acts as a co-enzyme in the body. PABA assists other B vitamins in making red blood cells, metabolising proteins, and helping with skin disorders. Nasty red bumps caused by the sun respond well to PABA applied externally or 400 mg internally. Many skin lotions have PABA to help prevent wrinkling of the skin and greying of the hair. A facial mask comprised equal parts of PABA, aloe vera and honey left on the face while sleeping will tighten loose skin and help some wrinkles to vanish. The face mask is removed the following morning with cotton balls saturated in rubbing alcohol followed by warm water. Not for nothing is this nutrient referred to as the 'Cosmetic B'![254]

---

[253] **Heinerman, John**, *Encyclopaedia of Nature's Vitamins and Minerals*, Prentice Hall, 1998, p.15
[254] Ibid, p.18

Vitamin B1 (thiamine) deficiency leads to beriberi. The nutritional pioneer Dr W Henry Sebrell attributed his razor-sharp memory to a daily supplementation of 150 mg of B1 for almost 29 years! Sebrell explains that thiamine is often severely lacking in up to 50% of psychiatric patients. Thiamine binds to lead molecules, thereby assisting in excreting the heavy metal from the body. Sebrell estimated that a daily intake of 100 mg of B1 would afford protection against lead poisoning.[255]

Vitamin B2 (riboflavin) appears under the microscope as a yellow, crystalline substance. This vitamin assists in body growth, repair and cell respiration. It's excellent too in maintaining the health of the nervous system, the assimilation of iron and, along with vitamin A, for great vision. Those suffering from chronic fatigue, oily skin and intestinal gas may test positive for low levels of this nutrient and iron.

Vitamin B3 (niacin) deficiency causes depression and psychosis. Subjects of various ages taking 141 mg of niacin a day demonstrated a measurable improvement in memory of 10-40% in all age groups.[256] Its RDA is only 18 mg in the UK, and yet studies, as we have seen, demonstrate that mega-doses can prove extremely beneficial to 'schizophrenics'. This nutrient is also sometimes prescribed with great effect for rheumatoid arthritis in doses between 150-300 mg to improve joint function and mood. May cause skin flushing. B3 can be purchased bound with inositol, which prevents flushing. Regular use of B3 will cause flushing to cease. B3 is also reported in the scientific literature to be useful in treating and preventing certain forms of cancer.[257]

Vitamin B5 (pantothenic acid), as it is also known, has been hypothesised to increase cholinergic activity in the body, specifically the central nervous system. This increase in cholinergic activity could result in increased memory, learning, and cognitive abilities. B5 (pantothenate) is another potent memory enhancer, assisting in the creation of the essential memory neurotransmitter, acetylcholine. Supplementing 250-500 mg of B5 along with choline may improve memory.

Vitamin B6 (pyridoxine) is essential for making neurotransmitters. It converts amino acids into serotonin, a deficiency of which brings on irritability, violence, poor memory and a dive in overall cognitive and social

---

255 Ibid.
256 **Loriaux, S, et al**, "The effects of niacin and xanthinol nicotinate on human memory in different categories of age – a double-blind study", *Psychopharmacology*, 87, 390-395, 1985; also Heinerman, John, op. cit. p.28
257 Heinerman, John, op. cit. p.29

performance. Folic acid deficiency encourages anxiety and depression. One study showed that about a fifth of depressed people are deficient in pyridoxine.[258] Supplementation is ideally between 30-100 mg a day or more for normal dream recall (B6 can be toxic at high doses. Do not exceed 8000-1,000 mg).

Vitamin B8 (biotin) is known as the energy and beauty nutrient and assists our cells' mitochondria in producing the energy molecule adenosine-triphosphate (ATP). Biotin is used in the transformation of consumed carbohydrates, fats and proteins into energy, which is then stored in the liver and muscle tissue in the form of glycogen. Glycogen, when needed, is released from these stores and readily converted into glucose, which the body then chemically 'burns' as a fuel to produce physical energy. Biotin is very much an enzyme helper and catalyses many enzymatic reactions in the body.

Vitamin B9 (folic acid) was discovered almost simultaneously with B12 and indeed works in conjunction with this essential nutrient. Folic acid is well known in helping to avoid birth defects, such as spina bifida and neural tube defects. Folic acid, like B12, is essential for oxygen delivery to the brain. A deficiency in either causes anaemia. Ideal supplementation for folic acid is around 400 mcg daily.

Vitamin B12 (cyanocobalamin) has been shown to improve the rate at which rats learn. Lack of B12 leads to anaemia, confusion and poor memory.[259] Several of these nutrients can be raised to larger doses as part of a program to eradicate chronic shortages, as we have seen, with spectacular results. B12 supplementation is between 10-100mcg a day. Some people have poor absorption of B12 and can benefit from amounts up to 1,000 mcg a day.

Vitamin B15 (pangamic acid) is another controversial nutrient, traditionally pilloried by the establishment. B15 has been described as 'instant oxygen', and has been used by Russian athletes for years to gain a competitive edge. Almost all research into this nutrient has come from Russia and has been viewed with outright scepticism by the American medical establishment. Pangamic acid has been variously described as the *"hottest substance to hit the ergogenic scene in recent memory,"* and was apparently capable of delivering *"flashy brilliance"* to orgasms and

---

[258] **Stewart, JW, et al**, "Low B6 levels in depressed patients", *Biological Psychiatry*, Vol.141 (1982): pp.271-2
[259] **Pearson, D & S Shaw**, *Life Extension: A Practical, Scientific Approach*, Warner Books, 1982

mopping up free radicals *"like mad"*. It is used in certain clinics today as part of the nutritional support for cancer patients. Some mainstream nutritional references still carry information about pangamic acid; others mention it, but disassociate themselves from its B-vitamin status.

Vitamin B17 (Laetrile, laetrile and amygdalin) is often referred to as the anti-cancer vitamin. Like B15, this nutrient has been clouded with controversy and been the subject of repeated attacks by the medical establishment. Nevertheless, unlike B15, there is an impressive track record of success with B17, which is contained in the seeds of the common fruits, excluding citrus, and a wide variety of grasses, legumes, pulses, vetches and vegetables. I deal with the subject of vitamin B17 in some detail in my books *Health Wars, Cancer: Why We're Still Dying to Know the Truth*, and *B17 Metabolic Therapy: A Technical Manual*. B17 is renowned for its analgesic qualities and its ability selectively to target and kill cancer cells, while nourishing non-cancerous tissue. Broken down in the body, one of its by-products, sodium thiocyanate, reacts with the liver precursor, hydroxycobalamin, to form the other vitamin with a cyanide radical, vitamin B12. (see also 'Apricot Kernels')

Essential fats (inc. Vitamin F)
EFA Recovery Plus &
Omega-3 EPA (Neways International)

EFA Recovery Plus is a daily essential fatty acid mix that contains omega-3 and omega-6 fatty acids. It was designed to help balance one's diet with a 40/30/30 caloric ratio of the three macronutrient sources, carbohydrate, protein and fat, for optimal health and better performance. EFA refers to the 'essential fatty acids' required in our diet, because these fatty acids cannot be synthesised by our body. 'Recovery' refers to EFA's role in restoring and maintaining general health as well as biochemical recovery following physical exercise and work.

The two major energy sources for the production of ATP energy during exercise are carbohydrates in the form of muscle glycogen and fats in the form of fatty acids. Fat is the most misunderstood of the three macronutrient sources. The association between a high-fat diet and serious health problems is widely advertised. This is the reason for today's trend to buy 'fat-free' food products. However, it is important to know that dietary fat consists of three basic types of fatty acids: (1) saturated, (2) monounsaturated, (3) polyunsaturated.

Saturated fat, 'bad fat', found in most animal fat, margarine, shortening, etc. can raise blood cholesterol levels. Partially hydrogenated oils contain trans-fatty acids that are also classified as 'bad fats'. Unsaturated fat, 'good fats', are composed of cis-fatty acids typically found in vegetable oils, cold-water fatty fish (e.g., salmon, herring, etc.), avocado, nuts and some beans. These foods are known for their ability to reduce blood cholesterol levels.[260]

It is just as important to regulate the kinds of fat we ingest as the amount of fat itself. Unsaturated fats play a beneficial role in our body. Fats are the most concentrated source of energy in the diet. Many sources of fat provide important nutrients, carry fat-soluble vitamins, A, D, E, and K through the bloodstream, maintain healthy skin, and are crucial for foetal brain development. The typical western diet does not include a sufficient amount of EFAs, especially those referred to as omega-3 fatty acids. EFA Recovery Plus is a combination of the natural sources of all cis-fatty acids as: alpha-lipoic acid, linoleic acid (omega-6), EPA (omega-3) and DHA (omega-3). These fatty acids are essential. Essential fatty acids are involved in a variety of biochemical processes. EFAs are vital in the role of energy production for muscle cells during exercise and assisting in muscle relaxation.[261]

In addition, EFAs affect the control of blood coagulation.[262] They also affect the release of CCK, a hormone that signals the brain that you're full and to stop eating.[263] EFAs are involved in maintaining conduction velocities for sensory and motor nerves.[264] EFAs are also present in cell membranes and support suppleness of skin[265] and help to lower high blood pressure.[266]

---

[260] **Siguel, E**, "A new relationship between total-high density lipoprotein cholesterol and polyunsaturated fatty acids", *Lipids*, 1996 Mar;31 Suppl:S51-6

[261] **Barbiroli, B, Medori R, Tritschler HJ, Klopstock T, Seibel P, Reichmann H, Iotti S, Lodi R & P Zaniol**, "Lipoic (thioctic) acid increases brain energy availability and skeletal muscle performance as shown by in vivo 31P-MRS in a patient with mitochondrial cytopathy", *J. Neurol.* 1995 Jul;242(7):472-7

[262] **Andriamampandry, M, Freund, M, Wiesel, ML, Rhinn, S, Ravanat, C, Cazenave JP, Leray, C, Gochet, C**, "Diets enriched in (n-3) fatty acids affect rat coagulation factors dependent on vitamin K", *C. R. Acad. Sci. III* 1998 May;321(5):415-21

[263] **Matzinger, D, Degen, L, Drewe, J, Meuli, J, Duebendorfer, R, Ruckstuhl, N, D'Amato, M, Rovati, L, Beglinger, C**, "The role of long chain fatty acids in regulating food intake and cholecystokinin release in humans", *Gut* 2000 May;46(5):689-94

[264] **Julup, O, Mutamba, A**, "Comparison of short-term effects of insulin and essential fatty acids on the slowed nerve conduction of streptozotin diabetes in rats", *J. Neurol. Sci.* 1991 Nov;106(1):56-9

[265] **Horrobin, D F**, "Essential fatty acid metabolism and its modification in atopic eczema", *Am. J. Clin. Nutr.* 2000 Jan;71(1 Suppl):367S-72S

[266] **Lee, R M** "Fish oil, essential fatty acids, and hypertension", *Can. J. Physiol. Pharmacol.* 1994 Aug;72(8):945-53

Alpha-lipoic acid is a sulfur-containing essential fatty acid. Alpha-lipoic acid is directly involved in the availability of brain and skeletal energy during exercise.[267] Alpha-lipoic acid has been used in Europe to help the body control diabetic effects.[268]

Alpha-linolenic acid is an omega-3, polyunsaturated, cis-fatty acid found in flax seed oil. Alpha-linolenic acid is converted to EPA and DHA.

Linoleic acid is an omega-6, polyunsaturated, cis-fatty acid found in safflower oil. Linoleic acid in incorporated in phospholipids – phospholipids are key components of healthy cell membranes.[269] Linoleic acid is converted to special prostaglandins[270] – prostaglandins control blood-clotting.

Omega 3 Fats

Food processing has wrought havoc on daily intakes of Omega 3 fats. It is estimated that the population today may be consuming around one sixth of the Omega 3s that our ancestors ingested back in 1850, due mainly to today's food choices and processing.[271] Omega 3 fats are more susceptible to corruption during the cooking process. EPA and DHA are omega-3 polyunsaturated fatty acids – the 'good fats'. Eicosapentaenoic acid (EPA) and docosahexaenoic acid (DHA) are in high concentrations in cold-water fish (e.g. salmon, tuna, mackerel and herring). EPA is used to support against high cholesterol and to form membranes surrounding cells.[272] EPA is required for the production of prostaglandins, which control blood

---

[267] **Barbiroli, B, Medori, R, Tritschler, HJ, Klopstock, T, Seibel, P, Reichmann, H, Iotti, S, Lodi, R, Zaniol, P**, "Lipoic (thioctic) acid increases brain energy availability and skeletal muscle performance as shown by in vivo 31P-MRS in a patient with mitochondrial cytopathy", *J. Neurol.* 1995 Jul;242(7):472-7

[268] **Ziegler, D, Reljanovic, M, Mehnert, H, Gries, FA**, "Alpha-lipoic acid in the treatment of diabetic polyneuropathy in Germany: current evidence from clinical trails", *Exp. Clin. Endrocrinol. Diabetes* 1999;107(7):421-30

[269] **Raederstorff, D, Moser, U**, "Influence of an increased intake of linoleic acid on the incorporation of dietary (n-3) fatty acids in phospholipids and on prostanoid synthesis in rat tissues", *Biochim. Biophys. Acta* 1992 Dec 2;1165(2):194-200

[270] **Mentz, P, Hoffmann, P, Lenken, V, Forster, W**, "Influence of prostaglandins, prostaglandin-precursors and of a linoleic acid rich and free diet on the cardiac effects of isoprenaline and vasodilators", *Acta. Biol. Med. Ger.* 1978;37(5-6)801-5

[271] Ibid.

[272] **Mizota, M, Katsuki, Y, Mizuguchi, K, Endo, S, Miyata, H, Kojima, M, Kanehiro, H, Okada, M, Takase, A, Ishiguro, J, et al.** "Pharmacological studies of eicosapentaenoic acid ethylester (EPA-E) on high cholesterol diet-fed rabbits", *Nippon Yakurigaku Zasshi* 1988 Apr;91(4):255-66

clotting and other arterial functions.[273] DHA is a component of human brain tissue[274] and the retinal tissue.[275] DHA serves in the transmission of nerve impulses in the nervous system.

Omega 3 Deficiency Symptoms: Dry skin, lack of co-ordination or impaired vision, inflammatory health problems, allergic reactions, memory or learning ability impaired, tingling in the arms or legs, hard to lose weight, high blood pressure or triglycerides, prone to infections.

Omega 6 Fats

Gamma-linolenic acid (GLA) is an omega-6 polyunsaturated cis-fatty acid found in evening primrose oil that helps to increase circulation. Research has shown that it aids in the reduction of platelet aggravation, lowers cholesterol and may reduce the risk of cardiovascular disease.[276] Evening primrose oil added to the diet of alcoholics undergoing withdrawal dramatically reduces symptoms and, in the long-term, improves memory.[277] This feature prompted researchers to see whether the oil would improve the memory of Alzheimer's patients. During a controlled trial, significant improvements were seen.[278] Other sources of Omega 6 fats are the seeds of hemp, pumpkin, sunflower, safflower, sesame, corn, walnut and wheatgerm oil. Omega 6 fats must have adequate levels of zinc, magnesium, B6 and biotin accompanying them to drive the enzyme that makes the conversion to GLA.[279]

Omega 6 Deficiency Symptoms: High blood pressure, eczema or dry skin, PMS or breast pain, dry eyes, blood sugar imbalance or diabetes, chronic fatigue, multiple sclerosis, alcoholism, depression and mood swings, excessive thirst.

---

[273] **Bell, JG, Tocher, DR, MacDonald, FM, Sargent, JR**, "Diets rich in eicosapentaenoic acid and gamma-linolenic acid affect phospholipid fatty acid composition and production of prostaglandins E1, E2 and E3 in turbot (Scophythalmus maximus), a species deficient in delta 5 fatty acid desaturase", *Prostaglandins Leukot Essent. Fatty Acids* 1995 Oct;53(4):279-86

[274] **Ward, GR, Huang, YS, Xing, HC, Bobik, E, Wauben, I, Auestad, N, Montalto, M, Wainwright, PE**, "Effects of gamma-linolenic acid and docosahexaenoic acid in formulae on brain fatty acid composition in artificially reared rats", *Lipids* 1999 Oct;34(10):1057-63

[275] **Neuringer, M**, "Infant vision and retinal function in studies of dietary long-chain polyunsaturated fatty acids; methods, results, and implications", *Am. J. Clin. Nutr.* 2000 Jan;71(1Suppl):256S-67S

[276] **Scheer, James F**, "Evening primrose oil – It's essential", *Better Nutrition*, 1998 Jun;60(6)60-64

[277] **Pfeiffer, Carl & Patrick Holford** *Mental Illness – The Nutrition Connection*, ION Press, London: 1996, p.31

[278] Ibid.

[279] Ibid.

Prostaglandins

Essential fats are, as their name suggests, essential for creating prostaglandins. These are extremely active, hormone-like substances which variously keep blood thin, relax blood vessels, thereby assisting in lowering blood pressure, boost immunity, assist in maintaining the water balance in the body, decrease inflammation, and assist the operation of insulin for correct blood sugar balance. Prostaglandins (series 1 & 3) themselves cannot be supplemented, due to their short-lived and volatile nature. However, an adequate intake of essential fats will equip the body with the raw materials it needs to create them. These two supplements from Neways assist in doing just that. The intake ratio between Omegas 6 and 3 should ideally be around 2:1.

EFA Recovery Plus ingredients: Alpha-lipoic acid, Linoleic acid, Alpha-linolenic acid, Gamma-linolenic acid, Eicosapentaenoic acid (EPA), Docosahexaenoic acid (DHA).

Omega 3 EPA ingredients: Eicosapentaenoic acid (EPA), Docosahexaenoic (DHA), Vitamin E, natural D-alpha tocopherol.

VITAMIN F: The polyunsaturated fatty acids (PUFA's) have been described as 'Vitamin F', a classification that once again hit rough waters with the medical establishment. Saturated fats have no hydrogen atoms missing in their carbon chains, whereas PUFA's may have two, three, four, or more double-bond linkages in the carbon chain with four, six, eight, or more hydrogen atoms missing. PUFA's are long-chain and extra-long-chain fatty acids which naturally occur in nature and are used by the body to prevent hardening of the arteries, normalise blood pressure, enhance glandular activity and assist in physical growth early in life. Despite the American Medical Association loudly denouncing the moniker 'Vitamin F' as quackery, PUFA's have rightly gained prominence in recent years as essential, life-sustaining nutrients. And what are essential, life-sustaining nutrients if not a vitamin?

Essiac

In 1923, a Canadian nurse, Rene Caisse, came upon an ancient Ojibway Indian herbal concoction that appeared to have remarkable powers to offer the sick. In the years since, thousands of patients, many considered beyond hope, have testified that this simple, natural treatment saved their lives where modern medicine had failed. Reported benefits of Essiac include:

1. Preventing the build up of fatty deposits in artery walls, heart, kidney and liver

2. Regulating cholesterol levels by transforming sugar and fat into energy
3. Destroying parasites in the digestive system and throughout the body
4. Counteracting the effects of aluminium, lead and mercury poisoning
5. Nourishing and stimulating the brain and nervous system
6. Promoting the absorption of fluids in the tissues
7. Removing toxic accumulations in the fat, lymph, bone marrow, bladder, and alimentary canals
8. Neutralising acids, absorbing toxins in the bowel and eliminating both
9. Clearing the respiratory channels by dissolving and expelling mucus
10. Relieving the liver of its burden of detoxification by helping to convert fatty toxins into water-soluble substances that can then be eliminated through the kidneys
11. Increasing the body's ability to utilize oxygen by raising oxygen level in the tissue cell
12. Increasing the production of antibodies like lymphocytes and T-cells in the thymus gland, which is the defence of our immune system
13. Inhibiting and possibly destroying benign growths and tumours

For more information on Essiac, please obtain a copy of the Credence title, *The Essiac Handbook*.

Apricot Seeds/Kernels

Apricot kernels are an inexpensive, rich and natural source of vitamin B17. They also deliver the vitamins, minerals and enzymes not found in the pharmaceutical derivative of B17. Consumption should be spread throughout the day, not taken in one sitting.

- 7 g of seeds per day for life are recommended by Ernst Krebs as a nutritional supplement for those exercising cancer prevention. (This equates to 10-12 of the larger kernels or 20-25 of the smaller 'Shalkur' type).
- 20 g of seeds per day are recommended by Ernst Krebs as nutritional support for clinical cancer sufferers.

In a minority of cases, cancer sufferers may experience nausea when taking seeds. In this event, clinics recommend that dosage is reduced and then gradually increased as tolerance is gained. Intake should commence with four apricot seeds a day (spread throughout the day) for the first four days, increasing up to 10-15 a day for a further four days and then to a maximum of 20 - 28 g a day. If of low body weight, then scale down intake accordingly.

Not all apricot seeds are effective. They must have the characteristic bitter taste indicating that the active ingredients are present. Not to be eaten whole. May be pulped, grated or crushed.

Please note: Some cancer sufferers believe that apricot kernels alone are all that is required to fight cancer. Consultation with a qualified health practitioner familiar with Metabolic Therapy is advised for further information. Apricot kernels are usually part of the nutritional support for those exercising cancer prevention *for life* as well as cancer patients undergoing Phase 1 or Phase 2 Metabolic Therapy.

Maximol (Neways International)

The huge rise in incidences of cancer and other degenerative diseases is primarily due to the depleted vitamin/mineral content in today's western diet coupled with environmental/chemical toxin factors. Among many nutrients invariably missing for cancer are B17, vitamin C, vitamin A and the trace mineral selenium. A recent US study showed an overall drop of 50% in cancer deaths and a fall of 37% in new cancer cases, especially lung, bowel and prostate – among 1,300 volunteers taking supplements for four years. [280]

Mineral supplementation is most effective in the ionised 'liquid suspension' form, assisted by fulvic acid, where an unusually high percentage of assimilation by the body can be expected. Our bodies use minerals as raw material. These cannot be manufactured by the body, and so have to be present in the food and liquids we ingest. Sadly, as mentioned previously, our food chain is severely depleted of minerals, resulting in over 150 nutritional deficiency diseases that are now striking our societies with increasing intensity.

To combat this very real threat, mineral and vitamin supplementation, far from being a quaint health fad, is essential for everyone and can literally make the difference between life or death, especially for those with cancer. To combat this threat, Neways has formulated Maximol Solutions, which contains 67 essential and trace minerals, 17 essential vitamins, 21 amino

---

[280] *Daily Mail*, 28th July 1999, p.31

acids, three enzymes, and *lactobacillus acidophilus*.[281] To provide greater absorption of all these ingredients, Maximol contains nature's natural chelator, used by plants and animals for the absorption of minerals and nutrients - organic fulvic acid. It is known that fulvic acid aids in the transport and assimilation of minerals and nutrients into living cells. This may in part be due to its low molecular weight, its electrical potential, and its bio-transporting ability. Fulvic acid aids in the selective trading or supply of minerals and other nutrient stacks inside the cell. Fulvic acid is effective at neutralising a wide range of toxic material - from heavy metals and radioactive waste to petrochemicals.

Before minerals can be utilised, they must first be converted from their particular colloidal state to a micro-colloidal state. Thus, for greater bio-availability, Neways has formulated Maximol Solutions as an organic fulvic acid complexed micro-colloidal solution. In this form, Maximol provides higher percentages of easily assimilated minerals than non-ionised colloidal mineral supplements, whose particles are often too large for easy absorption.

Revenol (Neways International)

Scientists tell us that vitamins A, C, and E, as well as beta-carotene and other antioxidant bioflavonoids, are vitally important to good health. But there are antioxidant formulae around now that have many more times the power of Vitamin C and Vitamin E. Revenol contains antioxidants that are broad-spectrum, including those derived from maritime pine bark and grape seed pycnogenols extracts - up to 95% in concentration and bioavailability. Revenol also contains curcuminoids, nature's most powerful and aggressive antioxidant, which is around 150 times more powerful than Vitamin E, about 60 times more powerful than Vitamin C, and about 3 times more powerful than antioxidants from maritime pine bark and grape seed pycnogenols extract in neutralising harmful oxidation elements in our bodies. [282]

Revenol also contains ginkgo biloba for the brain and circulatory system; alpha and beta carotene to increase potency; esterfied Vitamin C - a bonded form of Vitamin C that increases its power and residual retention in the body (up to 3 days); natural Vitamin E for greater absorption and effectiveness. Micro-spheres are also included which bond to the intestinal wall, allowing up to 400% more of the ingredients to be digested and

---

[281] Contents may vary by country

[282] **Majeed, Muhammed, et al**, *Curcuminoids – Antioxidant Phytonutrients*, Nutriscience Publishers, 121 Ethel Road West, Unit 6, Piscataway, NJ 08854 USA

282

absorbed. Each tablet of Revenol supplies over 60 milligrams of curcuminoids and maritime pine bark and grape seed extract.

Cascading Revenol (Neways International)

Neways has also released an exciting, further version of Revenol, named Cascading Revenol. Oxidation elements, or free radicals as they are sometimes known, are unstable molecules hungry to scavenge additional electrons, thereby damaging healthy cells. These factors are especially dangerous for cancer sufferers. Antioxidants such as Vitamin C can help prevent the damage caused by free radicals by completing their compounds, thus rendering them inert. The problem is, after having entered the body, most antioxidant molecular structures will grab one free radical and then change into an inert state, ceasing to be of further radical-scavenging value. The additional problem is that even when an antioxidant neutralises a free radical, the process creates an off-shoot free radical that is slightly different and less potent in variety, which in turn creates another, and so on. Typical antioxidants have a linear application and thus show no ability to address this free radical cascading effect.

However Cascading Revenol's formulation has been designed to regenerate these scavenging molecules so that they can neutralise multiple free radicals. So, instead of only one free radical being destroyed per antioxidant molecule, each molecule is able to change structure and repeat the process again and again. Thus the value of each individual antioxidant molecule increases exponentially. Cascading Revenol's unique action is devastating to the free radical onslaught that damages cancer sufferers. In my opinion, it is an essential component in any nutritional support program.

Hawaiian Noni Juice (Neways International)

The fruit juice of *Morinda citrifolia* contains a polysaccharide-rich substance with marked anti-tumour activity, according to recent studies into the famous fruit.[283] This research, performed at the University of Hawaii, has resulted in exciting new and scientifically reputable evidence for the potential benefits of Noni fruit juice in the treatment of cancer. Neways Authentic Hawaiian Noni features all the health-enhancing benefits of the noni plant as well as raspberry and blueberry extracts – both powerful antioxidants.

---

[283] **Hirazumi, A & Eiichi Furusawa**, "An Immunomodulatory Polysaccharide-Rich Substance from the Fruit Juice of *Morinda citrifolia* (Noni) with Anti-tumour Activity", Dept of Pharmacology, John A Burns School of Medicine, Hawaii, HI 96822 USA

Purge (Neways International)

Researchers state that the majority of people, especially those with cancer, play host to one form of parasite or another. One of the most troublesome for those with cancer is *Candida albicans*, a normally beneficial yeast found as part of our gut flora that invariably proliferates tremendously in the anaerobic, acidic system of a cancer patient. *Candida's* waste products especially can fuel the fermentation process that drives cancer throughout the body. Fungal infections too can damage tissue which the body then attempts to heal, often with the result of causing cell mutations.

This formula contains: Pumpkin (seed), garlic, black walnut (bark), grapefruit seed extract, clove, citrus seed extract, ginger root wild, slippery elm bark, Sweet Annie (*Artemesia annua*), cranberry concentrate, pomegranate, butternut bark, pau d'arco, red clover, olive leaf, ginseng (American), gentian root, hyssop, cramp bark, peppermint powder, fennel seed.

Magnesium oxide (www.vitalminerals.org)

Colon cleansing, while not a pleasant topic to address, is a subject that cannot be overlooked in the quest for extended youth, weight loss, and total health. Mucoid plaque, parasites and impacted toxic metabolites can be removed with a modified diet as well as with certain purgative agents that can assist in restoring the colon and intestines to full function. It is essential to allow the body to clean itself of detritus that has collected in the digestive system over the years, hampering the body's ability to absorb the nutrients it craves through the intestinal lining. Magnesium oxide, when used as directed, hydrates the colon and assist in flushing the entire length of the digestive tract.

D-Toxarate (Neways International)

As we have already learned, every day we arc exposed to harmful substances in our environment. The air we breathe, the food we eat, and even objects we touch are contaminated by substances that threaten our health in many ways we are only just beginning to understand. D-Toxarate is formulated with two important ingredients to help many of these substances pass through the body without harmful effects. Calcium d-glucarate, the first ingredient, can help eliminate some agents that potentially harm our cells. The second ingredient is ascorbic acid (Vitamin C), an antioxidant with the interesting property we examined earlier - it reduces blood-lead levels.

Chelamin (Neways International)

This calcium, magnesium and Vitamin D supplement is one of my favourites, and is ideal for those seeking to bolster levels of these particular minerals and vitamins in the body for supreme health. Calcium, as we learned earlier, is a vital precursor to so many chemical reactions in the body and should be present abundantly in our diets along with *reasonable* sunlight for optimum effects.

The Shadow of Soy

or

How I stopped loving and learned to worry about the bean

by Sean McNary Carson

You've joined an army of thousands committed to being all you can be. You rise at dawn to pound the pavement, or climb the Stairmaster to heavenly buttocks while listening to Deepak Chopra on your Walkman. Or, maybe you contort yourself into yoga asanas in rooms hotter than a Korean chutney. You drink only purified water as you toss a handful of the latest longevity pills into your mouth. You're hungry, hungry for health, and no doubt about it, you're no stranger to soy.

Faster than you can say *"isoflavone,"* the humble soybean has insinuated itself into a dominant position in the standard diet. And that shouldn't be a surprise. Cheap, versatile, and karma-free, soy in the 1990's went from obscurity as vegan-and-hippie staple to *Time* magazine. With mad cows lurking between whole wheat buns, and a growing distrust of conventionally-produced dairy products, soy seemed like the ideal choice, the perfect protein.

But like all seemingly perfect things, a shadow lurked. By the final years of the last decade, a number of soy researchers began to cry foul. Soy Good? Soy Bad?

As the soy industry lobbied the Food and Drug Administration for a cardiovascular health claim for soy protein, two senior FDA scientists, Daniel Sheehan and Daniel Doerge - both specialists in estrogen research - wrote a letter vigorously opposing such a claim. In fact, they suggested a warning might be more appropriate. Their concern? Two isoflavones found in soy, genistein and daidzen, the same two promoted by the industry for everything from menopause relief to cancer protection, were said to *"demonstrate toxicity in estrogen sensitive tissues and in the thyroid."* Moreover, *"adverse effects in humans occur in several tissues and, apparently, by several distinct mechanisms."* Sheehan also quoted a landmark study (Cassidy, et al. 1994), showing that as little as 45 mg of isoflavones could alter the length of a pre-menopausal woman's menstrual cycle. The scientists were particularly concerned about the effects of these two plant estrogens on foetuses and young infants, because *"development is recognised as the most sensitive life stage for estrogen toxicity."*

It wasn't the first time scientists found problems with soy, but coupled with a Hawaiian study by Dr. Lon White on men, the controversy ended up on national television. While industry scientists criticized both the White study and the two FDA researchers (who are now disallowed from commenting publicly on the issue), other researchers weighed in on the anti-soy side. The tofu'd fight had begun.

What about Asia?

One of the favourite mantras of soy advocates is that the ubiquitous bean has been used *"safely by Asians for thousands of years."* With many soy *"experts"* (often with ties to the soy industry) recommending more than 250 grams of soy foods - and in some cases, more than 100 mg of isoflavones each day - it's easy to get the impression that soy plays a major role in the Asian diet. If you saw it on TV or read it in a magazine, it must be true, right? Well, not exactly.

Sally Fallon, president of the Weston A. Price Foundation (www.westonaprice.org) and author of *Nourishing Traditions*, responds that the soy industry and media have spun a self-serving version of the traditional use of soy in Asia. *"The tradition with soy is that it was fermented for a long time, from six months to three years and then eaten as a condiment, not as a replacement for animal foods,"* she says.

Fallon states that the so-called Asian diet - far from centring around soy - is based on meat. Approximately 65% of Japanese calorie intake comes from fish in Japan, while in China the same percentage comes from pork. *"They're not using a lot of soy in Asia - an average of 2 teaspoons a day in China and up to a quarter cup in some parts of Japan, but not a huge amount."*

Contrast that with modern America, home of *"if a little is good for you, more must be better."* Walk into any grocery store, especially the health-oriented variety, and you'll find the ever-present bean. My recent, limited survey of Marin, California food stores found soy in dozens and dozens of items: granola, vegetarian chilli, a vast sundry of imitation animal foods, pasta, most protein powders and *"power"* bars, and even something called *"nature's burger,"* which, given the kind of elaborate (and often toxic) processing that goes into making soy isolate and TVP, would make Mother Nature wince. There's even a bread - directly marketed to women - containing more than 80 mg of soy isoflavones per serving, which is more than the daily dose in purified isoflavone supplements. All of this, in addition to the traditional soy fare of tempeh, tofu, miso, and soy sauce. It's no wonder that Californians are edamame dreaming.

So, while Asians were using limited to moderate amounts of painstakingly prepared soy foods - the alleged benefits of which are still controversial - Americans, especially vegetarians, are consuming more soy products and isoflavones than any culture in human history, and as one researcher put it, *"entering a great unknown."*

Oddly, nowhere in industry promotion does anyone differentiate between traditional, painstakingly prepared "Asian" soy foods and the modern, processed items that Fallon calls *"imitation food."* And therein lies the rub. Modern soy protein foods in no way resemble the traditional Asian soy foods, and may contain carcinogens like nitrates, lysinoalanine, as well as a number of anti-nutrients which are only significantly degraded by fermentation or other traditional processing.

"People need to realise that when they're eating these soy foods - and I'm not talking about miso or tofu - but soy "burgers," soy "cheese," soy "ice cream," and all of this stuff, they are not the real thing. They may look like the real thing and they may taste like the real thing, but they do not have the life-supporting qualities of real foods," Fallon says.

There's no business like soy business
"The reason there's so much soy in America is because they started to plant soy to extract the oil from it and soy oil became a very large industry," says lipid specialist and nutritionist Mary

Enig, PhD. *"Once they had as much oil as they did in the food supply they had a lot of soy protein residue left over, and since they can't feed it to animals, except in small amounts, they had to find another market."*

According to Enig, female pigs can only ingest it in amounts approximating 1% during their gestational phase and a few percent greater during their lactation diet, or else face reproduction damage and developmental problems in the piglets. *"It can be used for chickens, but it really has limitations. So, if you can't feed it to animals, than you find gullible human beings, and you develop a health claim, and you feed it to them."*

In a co-written article, Enig and Fallon state that soybean producers pay a mandatory assessment of ½ to 1 percent of the net market price of soybeans to help fund programs to *"strengthen the position of soybeans in the marketplace and maintain and expand foreign markets for uses for soybeans and soy products."*

They also cite advertising figures - multi-million dollar figures - that soy-oriented companies like Archer Daniels Midland or ADM spend for spots on national television. Money is also used to fund PR campaigns, favourable articles, and lobbying interests. A relaxation of USDA rules has lead to an increase in soy use in school lunches. Far from being the *"humble"* or *"simple"* soybean, soy is now big business - very big business. This is not your father's soybean.

There's been such a rush to market isoflavones that the before-mentioned multinational corporation, ADM, in 1998, petitioned the FDA for GRAS (generally recognized as safe) status for soy isoflavones. For those who don't know GRAS, the designation is used for foods, and in some cases, food additives, that have been used safely for many years by humans. For those who didn't know - like a number of protesting scientists - that soy isoflavones had been widely used by generations of Americans before the late 1950s, it was a revelation indeed. Ahem.

Dr. Sheehan, in his 1998 letter to the FDA referenced earlier, states *"that soy protein foods are GRAS is in conflict with the recent return by CFSAN to Archer Daniels Midland of a petition for GRAS status for soy protein because of deficiencies in reporting the adverse effects in the petition. Thus GRAS status has not been granted.*" And what about those safety issues?

Requiem for a thyroid

One of the biggest concerns about high intake of soy isoflavones is their clearly defined toxic effect on the thyroid gland. You don't have to work too hard to convince Dr. Larrian Gillespie of that. Dr. Gillespic, author of *The Menopause Diet*, in the name of scientific empiricism, decided to run her own soy experiment - on herself. She notes that she fits the demographic soy isoflavones are most marketed to: borderline hypothyroid, menopausal females.

"I did it in two different ways. I tried the (isoflavone) supplements (at 40 mg), where I went into flagrant hypothryoidism within 72 hours, and I did the 'eat lots of tofu category,' and it did the same thing, but it took me five days with that. I knew what I was doing but it still took me another 7-10 days to come out of it."

In the current issue of the *Whole Earth Review*, herbalist Susan Weed tells the story of Michael Moore - no, not that Michael Moore, but the founder of the Southwest School of Herbal Medicine. In an e-mail to Weed, Moore declares that "*soy did me in.*" Weed describes how Moore, in his own experiment, ate a large amount of manufactured soy products - protein powders, "power" bars, and soy drinks, over a period of three weeks. Weed writes that Moore ended up in a cardiac care unit because the action on his thyroid had been so pronounced.

Harvard-trained medical doctor Richard Shames, MD, a thyroid specialist who has had a long time practice in Marin, says that "*genistein is the most difficult for the metabolic processes of people with low thyroid, so when you have that present in high enough concentrations, the result is an antagonism to the function of thyroid hormone.*"

Far from being an isolated problem, Shames says that recent data tags twenty million Americans being treated for thyroid problems, another thirteen million who ought to be treated if they would get a

TSH (thyroid stimulating hormone) test, and another thirteen million who would show up normal on a TSH test but would test positive on another, more specific test. All in all, Shames believes that low thyroid conditions - many due to exposure to estrogen-mimicking chemicals like PCBs and DDT in environment - are the mother of most modern health epidemics.

That's a lot of thyroid problems. Some estimate the number to be as high as one in ten. Shames says that 8 of 10 thyroid sufferers are women - often older women - like Dr. Gillespie. The same demographic the soy industry has set its targets on.

"If you're a normal person, and one in ten are not normal, the effect [of 50 mg of soy isoflavones] *may be fairly insignificant, but even a normal person can have problems at levels greater than that,"* says Shames.

Dr. Gillespie says the daily amount to cause thyroid problems may be as low as 30 mg, or less than a serving of soymilk.

A number of soy proponents say the thyroid concerns are exaggerated and that if dietary iodine is sufficient, problems won't likely happen. Not so, says Shames: *"Iodine is a double-edged sword for people with thyroid problems, and for those people, more is going to increase their chance for an autoimmune reaction... throwing iodine at it is not going to be the protective solution."* Shames recommends limiting soy foods to a few times a week, preferably fermented or well cooked.

Birth control pills for babies?

Environmental toxicologist Mike Fitzpatrick, PhD says he doesn't have it out for soy. His original concern was for babies: *"They were getting more soy isoflavones, at least on a bodyweight basis, than anybody else,"* he notes. *"It wasn't so much that I knew what that would do, but that I didn't know what that would do."* Fitzpatrick, who is also webmaster of ... Soy Online Services (www.soyonline-service.co.nz), a website devoted to informing people about the potential problems with soy, stresses the potential dangers for the developing human body: *"Any person with any kind of understanding of environmental endocrine disruptors, compounds* [like isoflavones] *that are not in the body normally and can modify hormones and the way they work in the body, any expert will say that infants need to avoid these things like the plague."*

Fitzpatrick was quoted - and misquoted - worldwide a few years ago when he suggested that the isoflavones in soy formula were the equivalent of birth control pills: *"When I first did my review, I did compare the estrogenic equivalents of the contraceptive pill with how much soy infants and adults would be consuming,"* he says. *"It's at least the equivalent of one or two estrogen pills a day, on an estrogenic basis. I've been criticised that it's not the same form of estrogen, but in terms of estrogenicity, it's a crude but valid and alarming statistic."*

The typical response by industry experts has been to downplay the uniqueness of soy isoflavones, stating - accurately - that isoflavones of various kinds are prevalent in most fruits, vegetables, and legumes.

Is it time to toss out the apple sauce?

"No, you're not going to do that because you get exposure from all kinds of things, but the exposure you get from soy is way, way higher," Fitzpatrick says. *"Soy formula is going to give babies a real whack, far in excess of what you might find in apples. Soy is a very rich source of isoflavones - that's how the industry markets its product. You don't see an apple extract to help women deal with menopause."*

You've got to wonder how the industry can market soy isoflavones as a form of estrogen replacement therapy for menopausal women (and a host of other health claims) and still claim that soy formula is safe for infants. And while the mechanism for biological activity is clearly defined, the industry keeps repeating the same tune: *"no credible evidence exists."*

But credible for whom? Says Fitzpatrick: *"We're not talking about little studies here but long-term effects on infants and adults, and that's what concerns me. It's very trite. They (the industry) give half-baked answers. What you really need is long-term studies."* Likewise, *"no credible evidence"* is not good enough for Dr. Naomi

Baumslag, professor of paediatrics at Georgetown University Medical School. She joined a host of others in criticising a recent article in the *Journal of the American Medical Association (JAMA)*, purported to be the definitive study on soy formula safety.

"It was not an acceptable epidemiological study - you can take it to any decent epidemiologist and hear what they think about it, and they use it to say that soy is safe," says Baumslag. *"It's totally unsubstantiated."*

Manganese madness

Besides the dangers of prematurity and other reproductive problems posed by isoflavones, Baumslag mentions the high levels of the mineral manganese (no, not magnesium) often found in soy formula. The problem of manganese is so serious that even one soy manufacturer put warning labels on its soymilk. The company's president, in a press release, states that *"there is mounting evidence of a correlation between manganese in soy milk (including soy-based infant formula) and neurotoxicity in small infants."* With manganese toxicity known for producing behavioural disorders, the press release even goes further, stating, *"If research continues, showing that the current epidemic levels of ADHD in children, as well as impulsivity and violence among adolescents, are connected with the increase in soy-based infant formula use, our industry could suffer a serious setback by not dealing with the issue upfront."*

With all the potential problems with soy formula, Baumslag notes that formula is also missing key immunological factors only found in mother's milk, the lack of which could give a child a life sentence of chronic health problems. She links soy-pushing to corporate profits and the PR campaigns that they fund.

"There's been so much PR in regards to soy formula and I think you also have to ask yourself why it's so much cheaper for them to make, which means there's more profit. How come only 1% in the UK are on formula, where it's closer to 30% in the United States? I don't know why it's so important for them to push soy, they should push breast-feeding." Perhaps it's because breast milk for babies isn't as lucrative as milking the soybean for profits.

Caveat emptor

As a former vegan - and big soy-eater - I'm disturbed by the vast array of modern, processed soy products that have come on the market in the last few years, without any recognition of potential pitfalls. Safe bet: If it hasn't been eaten safely for thousands of years, you probably shouldn't put it at the centre of your diet. We've been sold a bill of goods that says *"soy is good for you"*, but it doesn't tell you what kind of soy or how much, or even definitively if soy really is what makes Asians so supposedly healthy.

It's well known that the Japanese also eat a very large amount of omega 3 fatty acids from fish each day - substances which have been clearly shown to have anti-cancer and anti-heart disease effects. So, is it the soy or is it the fish? As the industry spends millions and millions of dollars to find something isoflavones are good for - some health claim to justify their unprecedented presence in the American diet - I have to ask: why are they trying so hard? Why is there such a push to push soy?

Soy isoflavones are clearly biologically active - they affect change in your body. It's no longer acceptable for the industry to see no bad, hear no bad, and speak no bad. Legitimate concerns need to be studied - and not studies funded by the industry, conducted by soy scientists.

In the meantime, I've located a wonderful, old miso company on the north coast. They age their miso for three years in wood barrels and sell it in glass jars. It's rich, earthy, and real. I enjoy a teaspoon in a glass of hot water a few times a week after dinner. It tastes lively and feels good. I no longer get the *"urge"* to eat soy *"dogs"* or soy *"burgers,"* though I now suspect that urge didn't come from my own instinct, but from the lofty dictates of the soy experts.

But why wait years, while ignorant armies clash over this and that isoflavone and studies that say one thing or another? Perhaps the safest way to use soy, if you choose to use soy, is the way it's been used by Asians for thousands of years: fermented, in moderation, as a condiment. In short, colour me cautious.

Contacts! Contacts! Contacts!

If you wish to purchase more copies of this book or find out where you may obtain any of Credence's other book and tape products, please use the contact details below. Credence has local sales offices in a number of countries. Please see our website at **www.credence.org** for further details on how to contact them:

> **UK Orders:** (01622) 832386
> **UK Fax:** (01622) 833314
> **www.credence.org**
> **e-mail:** sales@credence.org

Obtaining health products

If you need more information or help on any of the materials discussed in this book, such as where to find them, please use the above contact details. Alternatively, you may contact us at:

Credence Publications
PO Box 3
TONBRIDGE
Kent TN12 9ZY
England
infopack@credence.org

Other Titles by Credence

CANCER: WHY WE'RE STILL DYING TO KNOW THE TRUTH

by Phillip Day

The book that has become a classic. This is Phillip Day's simple but stunning overview exposing the ongoing medical, political and economic scandal surrounding cancer and what you can do about the disease YOURSELF.

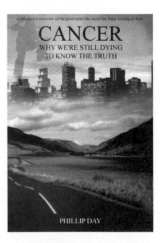

Science has known for 100 years that cancer is a healing process that has not terminated upon completion of its task. This book details the amazing track record of nutrition and its role within the simple protocol of Vitamin B17 metabolic therapy, a science which has been researched to the highest levels of biochemistry, used by leading doctors around the world today to control and eliminate cancers of all kinds.

- Hear the simple facts of the natural treatments from the medical experts themselves.
- Can cancer be treated at home today for just dollars/pounds a day?
- If nutritional therapy works so well with cancer, why doesn't everybody know about it?
- Why aren't chemo and radiotherapy cancer treatments working?
- Why is diet so important?
- Uncover why more people are making a living from cancer than are dying from it.
- Read the amazing testimonies of those like you who have decided to take control over their illness and are now cancer-free.

Whether you have cancer, or are exercising prevention for you and your family, PLEASE get educated on this vital issue today.

B17 METABOLIC THERAPY
IN THE PREVENTION AND
CONTROL OF CANCER
- a technical manual -
compiled by Phillip Day

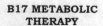

B17 METABOLIC THERAPY

in the prevention and
control of CANCER

a technical manual

compiled by
PHILLIP DAY

From the desks of some of the world's leading cancer scientists comes the empirical proof of vitamin B17 and its associated protocols in the treatment and prevention of cancer. These explosive findings have been the cause of the real cancer war, where vested interests have moved to vilify and denigrate nutrition in order to protect their highly lucrative cancer incomes.

- Find out why 18 'primitive' cultures do not get cancer in their isolated state
- What nutritional components have been found vital in the prevention and the treatment of cancer?
- What can you do to change your diet in ways which will give you maximum protection from cancer and other associated ailments?
- Why do animals not get cancer in the wild, yet succumb to it when 'domesticated' by humans?
- Discover the amazing research of Professor John Beard of Edinburgh University and American biochemist Ernst T Krebs Jr. which shows what cancer actually is. Remove your fear of this disease forever
- Examine the actual technical theses and trials carried out by doctors and scientists that validate this amazingly simple anti-cancer system
- Read the fabulous case histories of those who recovered using these simple methods

GREAT NEWS
on cancer in the 21st century
by Steven Ransom

THERE IS TIME!

A cancer diagnosis calls for decisions – decisions that, because of circumstances, are so often made in haste. *Great News on Cancer in the 21st Century* is the first book that tells us there is time to consider the options! Within these pages is everything you need to know about taking the next step.

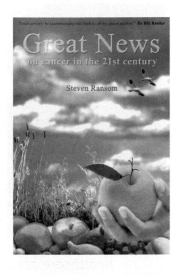

Did you know, for instance, that vested interests in the cancer industry have a direct impact on the advice you are receiving from your doctor? Why aren't we being told about the validated, non-conventional treatments that are saving and enhancing lives daily?

Instead, we are offered profitable chemotherapy and radiation treatments that damage the immune system – sometimes irreparably. Get informed on the dangers associated with these treatments, including the facts and figures they don't tell you. Learn how to interpret misleading information for yourself.

Take mammography, for example. How dangerous is it? Find out about the simple breast self-examination procedures that are just as effective and pose no danger to women's health, and discover the great news that will lift the current fear associated with breast cancer. Read the powerful testimonies of people who are being helped tremendously with various non-conventional treatments - stories of doctors unable to believe the disappearance of supposedly incurable cancers! This summary represents just a fraction of the wealth of information you will uncover in *Great News on Cancer in the 21st Century*.

HEALTH WARS
by Phillip Day

WHY IS OUR HEALTHCARE SERVICE KILLING US?

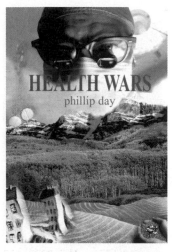

One of the most significant health books to come out in the new millennium, *Health Wars*, compiled by UK health researcher Phillip Day, tears the lid off the shameful medical and corporate scandals that are killing our nations. The author also reports the exciting and straightforward results of research into cancer, heart disease, osteoporosis and a host of other diseases, which we can simply and cheaply prevent or treat with nutrition and lifestyle changes.

- *The proof that western healthcare has become the third leading cause of death in western nations*
- *What simple measures can you take to avoid heart disease and cancer, the two leading killers?*
- *Find out why diets fail and how best to lose weight effortlessly and permanently*
- *Why is WHEN you eat almost as important as WHAT you eat?*
- *What is the truth about vaccinations?*
- *Why are at least 18 cultures living effortlessly to 100 and beyond when we die in the industrialised nations from diseases that do not afflict these long-lived peoples*
- *And much, much more*

Phillip Day: "This entirely pointless and unnecessary global medical catastrophe is growing worse with each passing year, but people are finally beginning to wake up and take action. By necessity, this new century must be the age of the Health Wars."

THE ESSIAC HANDBOOK

by James Percival

In 1923, a Canadian nurse, Rene Caisse, came upon an ancient Ojibway Indian herbal concoction that appeared to have remarkable powers to offer the sick. In the years since, thousands of patients, many considered beyond hope, have testified that this simple, natural treatment saved their lives where modern medicine had failed. Essiac has been studied in detail, research reporting that the benefits of this herbal tea include:

The story of a remedy that defied disease

THE
ESSIAC
HANDBOOK

James Percival

1. Preventing the build-up of fatty deposits in artery walls, heart, kidney and liver
2. Regulating cholesterol levels by transforming sugar and fat into energy
3. Destroying fungi and parasites in the digestive system and throughout the body
4. Counteracting the effects of aluminium, lead and mercury poisoning
5. Neutralising acids, absorbing toxins in the bowel and eliminating both
6. Clearing the respiratory channels by dissolving and expelling mucus
7. Relieving the liver of its burden of detoxification by helping to convert fatty toxins into water-soluble substances that can then be eliminated through the kidneys
8. Increasing the body's ability to utilize oxygen by raising oxygen level in the tissue cell
9. Increasing the production of antibodies like lymphocytes and T-cells in the thymus gland, which make up the defence of our immune system
10. Inhibiting and possibly destroying benign growths and tumours

This book also cites great testimonies of recovered patients, even from Dr Charles Brusch, physician to President J F Kennedy!

FOOD FOR THOUGHT

Compiled by Phillip Day

Much of what we buy from the supermarkets today is actually not food at all, but highly processed commercial material palmed off on the public as 'food'.

Foodstuffs today are often repositories for a daunting host of harmful additives, artificial sweeteners that cause cancer, high levels of hidden sugars, fungi, hormones, pesticides, and other chemicals. The untold health damage that has been wrought on our societies in the name of shelf-life and convenience has been staggering.

The Credence crusade to better health and a disease-free life begins with what we put in our shopping carts each week. *Food for Thought*, our official recipe book, is the ideal companion to our other titles and offers practical and fun advice on healthy eating and disease prevention. This delightful guide takes you through the main concepts of

- acid/alkali
- Vitamin B17 dishes
- the proper combining of foods
- the problems with meat and dairy in excessive amounts
- fruit consumption techniques
- a host of detox menus
- 5-10% meat and dairy recipes
- healthy snacks
- pro-active sickness foods
- children's dishes
- proper supplementation, and much, much more!

Whether you are suffering, or just want to make a change for your extended future, sensible nutrition comes to life in *Food For Thought*, bringing you the most delicious foods that WON'T KILL YOU!

WAKE UP TO HEALTH
in the 21st Century
by Steven Ransom

Despite our increasingly toxic world and the various threats to our health, we CAN live healthily. Spending only a little time educating ourselves in these matters is all that is needed to reap a very healthy return. Discover for yourself:

· **The full and fascinating history of vaccination:** read information never before in the public domain. Discover the dangers and the sensible way forward

· **The truth about antibiotics:** how they are supposed to work and what alternatives there are to this 'magic bullet'

· **Painkillers:** those little pills in your cupboard. Are they doing more than just killing pain?

· **New insight into the 'fast food' industry:** just what *are* those burgers and fries? Educate your friends towards enjoying healthier alternatives

· **The truth about many so-called 'infectious' diseases:** In so many instances, despite the media say-so, the true cause of most serious illness is not viral, but environmental. Much illness can be easily avoided

· **The 'germ theory' of disease:** Was Louis Pasteur correct in his assumptions about illness and disease? Did you know that on his death-bed, Pasteur recanted much of his work? Has money-making germ theory had its day? Discover a fascinating, yet simple approach to the cause, treatment **and prevention** of much illness and disease today

· **Can we be too clean?** Discover how our unquestioning acceptance of germ theory has led us into carrying out some quite extraordinary and unhealthy actions as part of our daily 'health' routine

· **Allergies and allergy testing:** What we're not told about this new diagnostic tool and what we need to know

· **The health of our pets:** Our furry friends are just as much part of the family as we are. Discover some simple facts about commercial pet food and pet care that will improve the health and wellbeing of our animals tremendously

And much, much more!

THE MIND GAME
by Phillip Day

Every new year brings incredible new inventions, advances in technologies, new medicines, further discoveries in physics, chemistry and the other sciences. There are also new political challenges and military threats. News channels such as ABC, CNN, the BBC and Sky report 24 hours a day on the problems besetting this complicated, restless and fretting planet.

But today, ordinary, decent citizens feel imprisoned – witnesses to unprecedented levels of terrorism, street violence, illiteracy, crime and disastrous school standards. We also have the exploding drug culture, the tide of sleaze in our media, corruption in our governments and the misery of what is termed 'mental illness'. Is there a common thread?

- Find out why there is no such thing as a 'mental disease'
- Uncover natural treatments, dietary and lifestyle changes that have a proven track record in reversing so-called 'mental illness'
- Read how psychiatry has killed some of our best loved film and pop stars with its brutalising treatments
- What is the truth behind the rash of schoolyard shootings we have seen in America?
- Why are millions of children being given mind-altering drugs after being diagnosed with the bogus disorders ADD/ADHD?
- How can you improve your attitude and general peace of mind with a few simple but telling techniques?

Phillip Day shines a critical light on the problems besetting 21st century society and leads us to the tremendous answers available for those who seek them. Absolutely do not miss this fascinating, penetrating political and medical insight into our times.

WORLD WITHOUT AIDS

by Steven Ransom and Phillip Day

THE DOOMSDAY VIRUS—THE 10 YEAR INCUBATION PERIOD—THE CHILLING DIAGNOSIS—AFRICA RAVAGED— THE MILLIONS WE MUST RAISE—THE FRANTIC RACE AGAINST TIME. AND THE WORLD BOUGHT IT ALL...

World Without AIDS dismantles one of the world's greatest fears and exposes the deceit, fraudulent science and needless fear-mongering lying at the heart of this supposed global epidemic.

Over ten years in the making, this impeccably researched book gives an eye-opening account of what vested interests can get away with, given a trusting public, an almost limitless supply of money, and scant scruples.

- Read about the hoax of HIV from the experts themselves
- Find out about the fraudulence of the HIV test and how it can trigger a false positive with over 60 different causal factors
- Uncover the real causes of immune suppression
- Expose the AIDS-devastating-Africa myth
- Discover the appalling dangers of the establishment-approved medications prescribed to those who have been written off as 'HIV positive'
- Read the amazing stories of those who had 'AIDS' and are now completely healthy.
- Find out the simple, natural regimens they used.

"Ransom and Day are the Woodward and Bernstein of AIDSgate, exposing the corruption, fraud and lies on which the multibillion-dollar HIV industry is based." Alex Russell, Continuum Magazine

TOXIC BITE
by Bill Kellner-Read

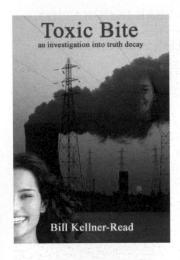

Most people go to the dentist at some point in their lives, and many go regularly. But who really questions what happens when we are in the dentist's chair? Can we be sure that we are receiving the best, long-term treatment for such an important and necessary part of our body? And what are the long-term implications of poor dental hygiene and health?

Finally there's a new book that demystifies dentistry and lets you take control of your own dental health. *Toxic Bite*, by British dentist Bill Kellner-Read, gets to the bottom of some startling questions:

- Could your gum disease be responsible for heart disease or stroke?
- What products are we using every day that contribute to wider toxic illnesses?
- And what about extractions? Do we really need that tooth pulled?
- Should we really be extracting children's teeth for orthodontic correction?
- What are the longer-term consequences of having less teeth in our mouth?
- What about the other correctional work being carried out today?
- Is there a link between nutrition and gum disease?

For the best in toxin-free tooth, mouth and body care, read *Toxic Bite* - the latest addition to the Credence roster of top-selling healthcare titles.

TEN MINUTES TO MIDNIGHT
by Phillip Day

During the coming months, Britain as a nation may cease to exist. If the British people can be talked into joining the euro and the new EU constitution, they will discover that they have been fooled into giving up a lot more than the pound.

Increasingly, Great Britain has been governed from Brussels by an unelected cabal of foreign committees dictating what British citizens can and can't do down to the last detail. Yet the extent of the EU's incompetence, fraud and criminal activity is hardly reported to the citizens soon to be governed completely by this autocratic, unaccountable new superstate. Did you know that:

- Britain is the EU's biggest customer? We don't need to be in the EU to trade with Europe. Other nations not in the EU, such as Switzerland, trade freely and are doing well
- 10% of the EU's total budget disappears on fraud every year?
- The EU Court of Auditors has been unable to sign off the EU's accounts for eight years running because of gross irregularities?
- All agents and officers of the EU's new quasi-FBI police force, Europol, have been granted a blanket immunity from prosecution?
- Joining the euro will be irreversible, even if it proves is a disaster?
- Joining the euro will entail Britain handing over her gold and currency reserves to the EU apart from a small working balance?
- The EU is in the process of restricting a huge cross-section of nutritional products and herbs once widely available?

Yet, in spite of all the problems, *Ten Minutes to Midnight* also explores the heartening character of the British, and why we must, at all costs, face up and fight this second Battle of Britain in order to regain our independence and avoid a new European war.

VIGILANCE

by Ashley Mote

Some people think the United Kingdom has effectively been abolished already. It will certainly cease to exist as a free and sovereign nation unless we reverse the erosion of our ancient rights, freedoms and customs by endless interference in British affairs by the European Union.

In 1975, as new members of the EEC, we thought we were voting for a free trade area. What we have today is an undemocratic, unaccountable police state that makes laws behind closed doors and seeks by stealth to destroy the UK as an independent nation. The European Union is being increasingly rammed down British throats in pursuit of a dream we never voted for. That dream has become a living nightmare. Silent discontent is no longer an option.

If you are concerned about the activities of the EU and its impact on the British way of life, then this book is for you.

Vigilance is not a book about politics in the usual sense. Nor is it academic. It is a simple, clear and horrifying account of what is being done to our country by the EU, why it matters, and why it must be stopped.

Vigilance also paints a vivid picture of the thriving, wealthy, confident and outward looking Britain that will quickly emerge from the ruins of the EU disaster.

The EU issue is of monumental proportions.

Ultimately, it is about British liberty.

Videos

Healthy at 100! - The video
The absolutely NOT TO BE MISSED documentary from Down Under, featuring Phillip Day's tour of Australia, some great slices of his talk in Melbourne before a capacity crowd, and interviews with doctors, practitioners and those who have recovered from serious illness. Funny, poignant, thoughtful and the most highly informative 65 minutes you will spend all year. (PAL format, 65 minutes)

Health Wars - The video
We are told we have the brightest and the best-trained doctors in the world looking after us. So why is western healthcare now the third leading cause of death in our nations today? In this fascinating, independently produced documentary, Phillip Day brings us great news on successful, non-toxic treatments for cancer and other degenerative illnesses, along with expert medical and political opinion which supports his heart-warming, exciting information. Find out how you and your family can triumph over the major disease killers and help others to do the same. (PAL format, 75 minutes)

Audio Cassettes

Cancer, The Winnable War, cassette
(90 minutes) The best highlights of Phillip Day's US tour on cancer, recorded in Seattle, WA, on the prevention of, and nutritional treatments for cancer. This tape also deals with why this information is continuing to be suppressed. A must-have for all the family – even the stubborn ones! Great for distributors and health practitioners. The "Dead Doctors Don't Lie" of the cancer industry.

Health Wars, the truth behind cancer and AIDS, cassette
A 60-minute studio-quality tape featuring two 30-minute overviews on cancer and AIDS by UK author and researcher Phillip Day. This tape is an ideal tool for educating your distributorship and members of the public on the important issues of cancer, AIDS and the toxins wilfully used in our environment, that lead to misery, sickness and death.

Cancer / Politics The Real War, cassette
Total time 63 minutes. In this live US radio interview with Phillip Day, host Tom Mischke asks the tough questions about cancer, the medical industry and the political / financial forces driving it. This is a no-holds-barred expose of the current state of the medical industry and the historical background that puts it all into perspective. Although cancer is the main subject, it is ultimately western healthcare that is on trial. The verdict is a tough pill to swallow.

The Campaign for Truth in Medicine

WHAT IS CTM?

The Campaign for Truth in Medicine is a worldwide organisation dedicated to educating the public on health issues and pressing for change in areas of science and medicine where entrenched scientific error, ignorance or vested interests are costing lives. Our ranks comprise doctors, scientists, researchers, biochemists, politicians, industry executives and countless members of the world public, all of whom have made at least one observation in common. They have recognised that, in certain key areas of global disease, drug treatments and overall healthcare philosophy, the medical, chemical and political establishments are pursuing the wrong course with the maximum of precision, even when their own legitimate scientific research has illustrated the dangers of pursuing these courses.

CTM STANDS FOR CHOICE IN HEALTHCARE

Millions today use nutritional supplements and alternative health strategies for themselves and their families, and yet, increasingly, the public's freedom to choose is being eroded by government legislation and attempts by the pharmaceutical conglomerates to 'buy out' the massive alternative health market. CTM stands for the people's right to choose the healthcare system they feel is right for them, free of big business interference, pointless government regulation, and coercion by the medical establishment which often attempts to compel its own dubious remedies upon an unwilling public.

CTM STANDS FOR SPREADING THE GOOD NEWS

Every month, CTM sends out EClub, its global online magazine, which is forwarded free to CTM subscribers around the world to keep them informed of the latest news, developments, scandals and great news in healthcare and other relevant issues. Within EClub, doctors, researchers, journalists, scientists, leading healthcare advocates, researchers and members of the public share their tips, views and strategies with hundreds of thousands around the world. EClub represents the news you are not being told; information that can literally change or save lives. Don't miss out on this vital resource, forwarded FREE to you every month, containing the very latest in news and views on vital health issues for you and your family.

WHAT YOU CAN DO NOW

Why not add your voice immediately to the hundreds of thousands around the world who are getting united, mobilised and making a difference through CTM in so many lives. Join for FREE today by completing the form in this brochure and sending it in. Alternatively, you may wish to join via our web-site at www.campaignfortruth.com.

Let's be part of a different future. One that celebrates life!

HOW TO ORDER CREDENCE PRODUCTS

Credence has offices and distributors in many countries around the world. If you would like more information, or wish to purchase any of the Credence titles described, please use the details in the **Contacts!** section of this book. Alternatively, why not visit Credence's comprehensive web-site at **www.credence.org**, which contains secure on-line global stores, our famous testimonies section, and many other great features.

Please note: Items not available in your regional shop may be obtained through the Rest of World store.

Index

Chemical additives, 26, 29
Chemotherapy, 271
Chicago, Illinois, 250
China, 267
Chitin, 84, 85
Chlorpromazine, 44, 54
Chocolate, 26, 28, 30, 43, 68, 120, 164, 193, 203, 231, 252
Cholera, 14
Cholesterol, 49, 150, 151, 154, 155, 156
Choline, 51, 53, 213, 262, 265, 272, 273
Chromium, 124, 170
Chromium picolinate, 124, 170
Chronic disorders, 5, 26, 193
Chronic fatigue syndrome, 26, 97, 101
Chymotrypsin, 168
Cigarette smoking, 34, 35, 36, 37, 55
Cocaine, 32
Cocamide DEA, 246
Coeliac (Celiac) disease, 26, 43, 177
Coffee, 26, 164, 166
Colds, 43, 74, 75, 220
Colitis, 169, 175
Collagen, 48, 49, 144, 149, 150, 151, 153, 218, 248
Colloidal minerals, 282
Committee on Safety of Medicines, 240
Coney, Sandra, 182
Confusion, 16, 50, 113, 164, 225, 226, 274
Congestive heart failure, 147
Constipation, 16, 74, 96, 166, 172, 177, 220
Convulsions, 73, 74, 140, 243
Copper, 23, 217, 218, 222, 225, 227
Corpus luteum, 181, 182, 186
Corticosteroids, 67, 175, 229
Cosmetics, 242, 243, 246, 249, 250, 251
Cott, Allan, 74
Cough mixtures, 4
Cramps, 33, 74, 113
Credence Publications, 18, 297, 306
Cretinism, 171, 172
Criminal behaviour, 26, 110

Crohn's disease, 169
Curcuminoids, 282, 283
Current of injury, 80, 81, 84
Cushing's disease, 97
Cyanide, 87
Cysts, 10, 180, 209
Cytomegalovirus, 101

D

Daidzen, 286
Deanol, 51, 53, 213, 235, 263
Delirium, 39
Delusions, 225, 226
Dementia, 50, 51, 64, 267
Demons, 225
Dentistry, 50, 53, 217, 222, 306
Deodorants, 251
Depression, 11, 16, 22, 31, 39, 43, 44, 48, 54, 64, 73, 74, 97, 101, 112, 113, 114, 116, 133, 164, 168, 172, 217, 218, 221, 225, 226, 263, 272, 273, 274, 278
Dermatitis, 73, 74, 176, 224, 226, 229, 230, 242, 245
Dextrose, 166
Diabetes, 21, 43, 76, 112, 118, 120, 121, 122, 165, 167, 168, 169, 170, 173, 197, 276, 277, 278
Diabetic neuropathy, 119
Diagnostic and Statistical Manual for Mental Disorders (DSM), 20
Diarrhoea, 13, 16, 51, 73, 74, 96, 98, 104, 105, 161, 175, 176, 177, 202, 225, 226, 265, 271
Diethanolamine (DEA), 246
Dikitopiprazines, 259
Dimethylaminoethanol (DMAE), 51, 53, 213, 262, 263, 267
Diosgenin, 189
Discipline, 30
Discolouration around the eyes, 21, 30
Diuretics, 56
Diverticulitis, 175, 176
Diverticulosis, 175
Dizziness, 51, 74, 168

Docosahexaenoic acid (DHA), 23, 276, 277, 278, 279
Dogs, 34, 259
Dopamine, 211
DPT, 72
Dream recall, 220, 221, 222
Dry skin, 278
D-Toxarate, 271, 284
Dyes, 26
Dysbiosis, 175, 176
Dysentery, 14

E

Ear infections, 21, 30, 75, 76
Echinacea, 69, 99, 105
Ectopic pregnancy, 189
Eczema, 21, 25, 30, 43, 74, 229, 276, 278
Edema, 16, 147, 204
Egg whites, 44
Eggs, 26, 28, 30, 43, 44, 265
Eicosapentaenoic acid (EPA), 277
Elastin, 150, 248
Electroshock, 114, 227
ELISA test, 14, 15
Embolism, 148
Endometriosis, 96, 180, 189, 190, 191, 209
England, 156, 157, 295
Enstrom, James, 153, 154
Environment Agency, 239
Environmental Protection Agency (EPA), 239, 246
Envoid, 218
Enzymes, 10, 23, 32, 61, 62, 65, 81, 82, 84, 86, 87, 94, 95, 97, 168, 197, 215, 222, 258, 265, 268, 269, 280, 282
Epilepsy, 21, 140, 263, 264, 266, 267
Epstein, Samuel S, 79, 242, 245, 246, 248, 250, 251
Epstein-Barr virus, 101
Equal, 63
Erythrocytes, 23
Essential fatty acids (EFA's), 22, 38, 48, 55, 227, 261, 275, 276
Estradiol, 181, 184, 185

Estriol, 181
Estrogen, 181, 182, 183, 184, 185, 186, 187, 188, 189, 209, 210, 218, 244, 259
Estrogen dominance, 58, 59
Estrone, 181, 185
Ethoxylation, 244, 248
Europe, 154, 225, 277
Evening primrose oil, 22, 235, 278
Exercise, 33, 56, 116, 120, 158, 159, 170, 261, 275, 276, 277
Exorphins, 76

F

Facial swelling, 21, 30, 75
Faroe Islands, 196
Federal Food, Drug and Cosmetic Act, 242
Federal Register, 246
Feelin' Good, 284
Feflux, 97, 175, 177, 201
Feingold, Ben, 26
Fennel, 90, 255, 284
Fevers, 13
Fibre, 48, 150
Fibroblasts, 81
Fibrocystic breast disease, 180
Fibrocysts, 183
Fibroids, 180, 183, 190, 191, 209
Fibromyalgia, 101, 189
Fish, 29, 51, 56, 72, 212, 276, 277
Flack, Frederic, 227
Flax, 53, 56, 69, 277
Florida, USA, 188
Flu, 15
Fluoride, 246
Fluorocarbons, 248
Food & Drug Administration (FDA), 63, 64, 65, 66, 71, 240, 242
Food colourings/additives, 28, 68, 193, 195
Food Science and Nutritional Laboratory, 65
Formaldehyde, 64, 65, 70, 73, 248, 249
Formic acid, 64, 65
Fraud, 22

Free radicals, 283
Fructose, 166
Fulvic acid, 281, 282
Fungal infections, 10, 19, 33, 38, 40, 41, 47, 52, 56, 68, 79, 86, 91, 94, 96, 100, 101, 122, 124, 173, 179, 200, 201, 202, 212, 213, 215, 230, 256
Fungi, 83

G

Gamma-linolenic acid (GLA), 38, 278
Gangrene, 119
Garland, Judy, 113
Gdanski, Ron, 80, 82, 84, 85
Genetics, 211
Genistein, 286, 290
Germany, 242, 262, 277
Gerson, Max, 200, 252
Gesch, Bernard, 107, 108, 110
Gey, Professor, 154
Gingivitis, 73, 214
Gingko biloba, 69, 145, 202, 263, 267, 282
Glaucoma, 142, 144
Gliaden, 26, 43
Glucose, 166
Glucose intolerance. See Hypoglycaemia
Glutamate, 63, 64
Glutamic acid, 168
Glutamine, 38, 51, 53, 213
Gluten, 26, 28, 43, 44, 59, 68, 76, 104, 178, 193, 231, 254
Glycerin, 249
Glycogen, 164, 166, 274, 275
God, 116
Goitre, 171, 172
Goldstein, Alan, 224
Gout, 57, 97
Grave's disease, 171, 172
Green, Gerald, 200
Greenpeace, 188
Guildford, England, 24, 25

H

Haemophilus influenza type b (Hib), 72
Haemorrhoids, 175, 236
Hair, 23, 140, 217, 222, 243, 244, 272
Halcion, 21
Hall, Richard, 108, 272
Hallucinations, 31, 39, 73, 218, 225, 226, 227
Hanging, 220
Harlem, Gro, 112
Hashimoto's disease, 171, 172, 173
Hawaii, 283
Hawaiian noni, 283
Hay fever, 68, 229, 230
Hayes, Jr., Arthur Hull, 65
Headaches, 4, 50, 58, 74, 113, 143, 161, 170, 193, 194, 217, 225, 226, 263
Healing, 49, 150, 151, 168, 185, 244
Health Wars, 43, 48, 50, 51, 211, 246, 259, 275
Heart disease, 48, 49, 127, 146, 149, 150, 151, 152, 153, 154, 155, 156, 157, 159, 183, 218, 306
Hemp, 278
Hepatitis, 18, 161
Heroin, 32, 114, 165
Herpes, 15, 19, 97, 101
Herxheimer's Reaction, 91, 99, 179
High blood pressure, 153, 156, 159, 189
High-glycaemic foods, 52, 82, 88, 89, 120, 166, 258
Hirsutism, 217
Histadelia, 44, 113
Histamine, 44, 45, 67, 113, 114, 117, 177, 194, 217, 218, 225, 227
Histapenia, 217
HIV (Human immunodeficiency virus), 13, 14, 15, 17
Hoffer, Abram, 23, 45, 226, 227
Holford, Patrick, 24, 27, 29, 31, 32, 44, 45, 49, 50, 52, 108, 113, 221, 223, 226, 235, 263, 278
Homocysteine, 212
Hooten, Ernest, 110
Hot dogs, 27

Hot flushes, 218
HRT (hormone replacement therapy), 183, 184, 185
Huber, Fritz, 200
Hunzas, 110
Huperzine, 267
Hydration, 33
Hydrogenated fats, 259
Hyperactive Children's Support Group (HCSG), 22
Hyperactivity, 22, 23, 24, 26, 28, 43, 50, 74, 110, 167
Hyperglycaemia, 119, 164, 165
Hypoglycaemia, 31, 40, 56, 107, 108, 164, 170, 264
Hypothalamus, 182
Hypothyroidism, 59, 102, 171, 172, 173
Hysterectomy, 183, 184

I

Iatrogenic death, 112
Iceland disease, 101
Illinois, 250
Immune system, 23, 43, 71, 72, 74, 76
Immunoglobulin (IgA), 75
Impotency, 54
Incontinence, 196
Infantile colic, 43
Inflammation, 74, 98, 143, 161, 279
Inflammatory bowel disease, 169, 175
Insecticides, 251
Insomnia, 31, 73, 114, 220, 264
Institute of Optimum Nutrition (ION), 27, 77
Insulin, 107, 108, 113, 118, 119, 120, 121, 122, 125, 164, 169, 276, 279
Intestines, 94, 168, 284
Ionised calcium, 281, 282
Iron, 23, 48, 211, 273
Irritability, 225, 226
Irritable bowel syndrome, 97, 176
Isoflavones, 286, 287, 288, 289, 290, 291, 292, 293, 294

J

JAMA (Journal of the American Medical Association), 18
Japan, 137, 196, 197, 200, 242
Jaundice, 74, 161
Jillani, Lisa, 71
Jock itch, 33, 96, 124, 201
Joint crepitus, 57

K

Kaolin, 249
Karposi's sarcoma, 13, 19
Kennedy, Edward M, 242
Kent, England, 323
Kessler, David, 71
Kidneys, 167
Klaper, Michael, 129
Kniker, Ted, 77

L

Lactobacillus acidophilus, 98, 282
Lactose, 166
Lauramide DEA, 246
Laxatives, 56
L-Carnitine, 160
LDL cholesterol, 49, 150, 151
Lead, 23, 30, 50, 107, 109
Leaky gut syndrome, 26, 76, 176
Learning disorder, 20
Leukaemia, 130, 259
Linoleic acid, 277, 279
Lipoprotein(a), 49, 150
Lithium, 114
Liver, 18, 73, 94, 151, 164, 166, 220, 222, 227, 244, 245, 259, 266, 274, 275
Lobotomy, 54, 227
London, 24, 27, 77, 278
Los Angeles, 153
LSD, 225
Lungs, 94, 244
Lupus, 60, 97

Lymph, 13, 84, 95, 101, 167, 176, 247, 280
Lymphatic system, 94
Lysine, 48, 144, 149, 151

M

Maggiore, Christine, 15, 18
Magnesium, 23, 30, 33, 50, 75, 140, 157, 232, 259, 264, 278
Magnesium oxide, 46, 53, 62, 69, 78, 284
Malabsorption syndrome, 175
Malaria, 14, 15, 18
Malnutrition, 14, 153
Maltose, 166
Manganese, 46, 117, 140, 141, 170, 223, 235
Martin, William Coda, 165
Massachusetts, 242
Material safety data sheet (MSDS), 245
Maximol, 281
Meat Board, The, 28
Medicines Control Agency (MCA), 239, 240
Menopause, 218
Menstruation, 181, 182, 183
Merck Manual, 143, 203, 204
Mercola, Joseph, 66, 70, 76, 121
Mercury, 70, 71, 72, 73, 78, 213, 217, 225
Metabolic therapy, 268, 281
Metabolism, 149, 155, 156, 187, 210
Metabolites, 65, 168, 284
Methadone, 32, 114
Methanol, 64
Methionine, 46, 113, 114, 117
Methylation, 114, 265
Mexican wild yam, 189
Mexico, 200
Migraine headaches, 193, 225, 226
Milk, 26, 28, 41, 43, 44, 68, 76, 77, 88, 90, 104, 110, 122, 161, 166, 173, 193, 208, 209, 231, 253, 254, 259, 269
Mineral oil, 249
Minocycline, 211

Mitral valve prolapse, 148
MMR, 72
Molecular mimicry, 198
Monethanolamine (MEA), 246
Monroe, Marilyn, 113
Monsanto, 24, 63
Monte, Woodrow C, 65
Morinda citrifolia, 283
Morphine, 76
Mouthwash, 52, 247, 251
Mower, Tom, 251
Multiple chemical sensitivity, 68, 101
Multiple sclerosis, 64, 76, 95, 97, 123, 124, 169, 196, 201, 278
Mycotoxins, 6, 25, 33, 84, 91, 122, 123
Myelin, 196, 197, 198, 199, 200, 201
Myocardial infarction, 147
Myxedema, 171

N

Nader, Ralph, 138
Nail-biting, 222
Narconon, 32
National Academy of Sciences, 249
National Cancer Institute (NCI), 247
National Institute of Occupational Safety and Health, 242
National Vaccine Injury Compensation Program (NVICP), 71
Natural progesterone cream, 192
Nausea, 54, 73, 74, 119, 143, 161, 193, 194, 220, 221, 280
Neoblasts, 81
Nerve pain, 33
Neurons, 63
Neurotoxins, 107
Neurotransmitters, 21, 23, 51, 63, 113, 114, 211, 217, 227, 232, 262, 267, 272, 273
New England Journal of Medicine, 130
New Jersey, 220
New South Wales, 109
New York, 74, 111, 130, 132, 169, 221, 234
New Zealand, 200, 217

Neways International, 250, 251
Newspapers, 116
NHS (National Health Service), 17
Nicotinamide adenosine dinucleotide (NAD), 51
Nicotinic acid (B3), 155, 156
Nietzsche, Friedrich, 116
Nightmares, 31, 220, 225
Nitrosamines, 246
Nobel Prize, 270
Nutrasweet, 24, 63
Nuts, 26, 232, 276

O

O'Shea, Tim, 72
Obesity, 203, 204
Ochratoxin, 123
Olive oil, 155
Olney, John W, 63, 64
Oranges, 28, 30, 43, 265
Organochlorines, 187, 188
Orthomolecular psychiatry, 30, 225
Osteoarthritis, 57, 58, 59
Osteoblasts, 186, 209
Osteoclasts, 186, 209
Osteoporosis, 183, 186, 187, 189, 206, 208, 209, 210
Ovulation, 181, 182

P

Painkillers, 4
Palmer, Dr K, 136
Palpitations, 74, 164
Pancreas, 118, 121, 164, 165
Pancreatic enzymes, 168, 185
Pantothenate, 155
Paralysis, 71
Parasites, 82, 83, 84, 85, 88, 93, 280, 284
Parasitic infections, 14, 83, 96, 98
Parkinson's disease, 64, 169, 211, 212
Patterns (breaking and establishing), 33
Pauling, Linus, 149, 150, 270, 271
Pavlov, Ivan, 34

Paxil, 112
Peanuts, 28
Pellagra, 51, 218, 225, 226
People Advocating Vaccine Education (PAVE), 71
Periodontal disease, 214
Periodontitis, 214
Pesticides, 50, 212, 249
Petrolatum, 249
Pfeiffer, Carl, 24, 27, 29, 31, 32, 44, 45, 50, 52, 113, 140, 217, 220, 221, 223, 226, 227, 235, 278
pH balance, 187, 210
Phenylalanine, 64, 66
Philadelphia, 109, 224
Philippines, The, 200
Phillips, Peter, 243
Phobias, 217
Phosphatidylcholine, 265, 267, 272
Phosphatidylethanolamine, 266, 267
Phosphatidylinositol, 266, 267
Phosphatidylserine, 263, 267
Phospholipids, 263, 265, 266, 277
Phosphoric acid, 24, 259
Photophobia, 16, 193
Pill, The, 49, 185
Pituitary gland, 171, 182
Placebo, 4, 136, 271
Pneumonia, 13, 74, 94
Polio, 72
Polysorbate, 70, 245
Poppers, 19
Pork, 259
Potassium, 32, 45
Potassium bicarbonate, 32
Prednisone, 96, 143
Pregnancy, 15, 181, 182, 184, 188, 271
Pregnenalone, 265, 267
Premarin, 191
Premenstrual Syndrome (PMS), 168, 278
Proanthocyanidins, 216
Prodromes, 193
Progesterone, 181, 182, 183, 185, 186, 187, 189, 190, 209
Proline, 144, 149, 151
Propane, 249
Propylene glycol, 245
Prostacyclin, 157, 183

Prostaglandins, 21, 23, 227, 235, 266, 277, 278, 279
Protease inhibitors, 18
Prozac, 20, 21, 27, 133, 167
Psoriasis, 97, 176, 229, 230
Psychology, 20
Puberty, 10, 11, 214
Pumpkin seeds, 53, 56, 158, 254, 278
Purdue University, 22
Purge, 284
Pyorrhoea, 222
Pyroglutamate, 51
Pyroluria, 45, 75, 220, 221
Pyrroles, 220

Q

Quackery, 279
Quercetin, 216, 263, 272

R

Ransom, Steven, 4, 5, 18, 19, 78, 97, 98, 105, 126, 127, 129, 134, 299, 303, 305
Rapid eye movements, 196
Rashes, 13, 25, 33, 43, 83, 96, 104, 124, 177, 212, 229, 245
Rat poison, 156
Rath, Matthias, 49, 149, 150, 152, 153, 155, 157
Religion, 115
Retinopathy, 119
Revenol, 282, 283
Rheumatoid arthritis, 60
Rhinitis, 16, 67
Rimland, Bernard, 75, 76, 263
Ritalin, 20, 21, 133, 167, 263
Road rage, 164
Robbins, Anthony, 37
Robbins, John, 128, 129
Root fillings, 214
Rouleau, 59
Russia, 274
Rye, 26, 43, 44

S

Saccharin, 29, 165, 166, 251, 259
Safflower oil, 277
Salem, UT, 251
Salicylates, 26, 43
Saliva, 113, 217, 218
Salt, 250
San Antonio, TX, 77
San Diego, CA, 212, 263
Satanism, 116
Satcher, David, 21
Saul, Andrew, 130
Sauna, 33
Schizophrenia, 43, 44, 76, 77, 217, 221, 224, 225, 226, 227
Schoenthaler, Stephen, 26, 28, 29, 108, 109
Scleroderma, 60, 97
Scurvy, 48, 49, 149, 151, 153, 218
Sebaceous glands, 10
Sedatives, 54, 114
Seizures, 71
Selenium, 50, 62, 69, 90, 202, 216, 230
Sellman, Sherrill, 150, 184, 188, 190
Senility, 47, 50, 52
Serle, G D Company, 63, 66
Serotonin, 23, 40, 64, 194, 195, 232, 263, 273
Sesame seeds, 53, 56, 158, 278
Shalala, Donna, 71
Shampoos, 52, 244
Shellfish, 68, 193, 255, 259
Silymarin, 41, 163, 230
Singer, Adam, 130
Sinusitis, 16
Skin rashes, 21, 30, 249
Sleep disturbance, 225
SLES. *See* Sodium laureth sulfate
SLS. See Sodium lauryl sulfate
Smoking, 152, 158, 159, 271
Soda beverages, 24, 25, 247
Sodium, 32, 244, 245, 251, 275
Sodium laureth sulfate, 244
Sodium lauryl sulfate, 243
Sorbitol, 70

T

U

V

About the Author

Phillip Day was born in England in 1960. He was educated at the British education establishments Selwyn and Charterhouse, and throughout his twenties had a successful entrepreneurial career founding businesses in sales and marketing. With a firm grounding in business and the ways of the media, Phillip's research career began after he became interested in wars going on in the realms of health and politics over issues that were being deliberately withheld or misreported to the public.

Phillip Day heads up the publishing and research organisation Credence, now located in many countries around the world, which collates the work provided by researchers in many fields. Credence's intention is to work with the establishments and organisations concerned to resolve issues that are harmful to the public, and to provide the necessary information for citizens to make their own informed choices in these vital matters. Phillip's speaking schedule is exhaustive and takes him to audiences all over the world.

Phillip Day is married to Samantha and lives in Kent, England.